Japanese Business Operations in an Uncertain World

This book looks at Japanese companies in manufacturing and services sectors and how they are trying to emerge from the prolonged uncertainty of the pandemic. The chapters are written by those dealing with Japanese business under the shadow of the pandemic and being influenced by the continuous and rapid adoption of digital technologies in business and our daily lives.

This book brings together the experiences of big and small corporations while looking at how digital transformation and the pandemic combined have led to a transformation in the product, production processes and services. It highlights the role played by robots, 3-D printing and renewable energy in manufacturing while the impact can be seen in the changes coming to future offices, how we work and interact and how we relax through tourism and travel on the service side. The services sector is as much impacted by digital transformation and the pandemic as any other field in business.

Aimed at academics, researchers and practitioners, *Japanese Business Operations in an Uncertain World* will provide valuable insights into how Japanese organizations are adapting to the dual impact of the pandemic and advancements in digital technologies.

Anshuman Khare is Professor for Operations Management at Athabasca University, Canada.

Nobutaka Odake is Executive Director of the Humanware Network Initiative. He is former Professor, Department of Techno-business Administration (2003–2017).

Hiroki Ishikura is a Professor at the Department of Commerce in Osaka Gakuin University, Japan.

Routledge Advances in Management and Business Studies

Management Control Systems, Decision-Making, and Innovation Development
The CDI Model
Dawid Szutowski

Competition, Strategy, and Innovation
The Impact of Trends in Business and the Consumer World
Edited by Rafał Śliwiński and Łukasz Puślecki

Critical Perspectives on Innovation Management
The Bright and Dark Sides of Innovative Firms
Edited by Patryk Dziurski

Operations Management in Japan
The Efficiency of Japanese Manufacturing
Hiromichi Shibata

Stakeholder Management and Social Responsibility
Concepts, Approaches and Tools in the Covid Context
Ovidiu Nicolescu and Ciprian Nicolescu

Japanese Business Operations in an Uncertain World
Edited by Anshuman Khare, Nobutaka Odake and Hiroki Ishiruka

Entrepreneurship and Culture
The New Social Paradigm
Alf H. Walle

For more information about this series, please visit: www.routledge.com/Routledge-Advances-in-Management-and-Business-Studies/book-series/SE0305

Japanese Business Operations in an Uncertain World

Edited by
Anshuman Khare,
Nobutaka Odake,
and Hiroki Ishikura

Routledge
Taylor & Francis Group
LONDON AND NEW YORK

First published 2022
by Routledge
2 Park Square, Milton Park, Abingdon, Oxon OX14 4RN

and by Routledge
605 Third Avenue, New York, NY 10158

Routledge is an imprint of the Taylor & Francis Group, an informa business

British Library Cataloguing-in-Publication Data
A catalogue record for this book is available from the British Library

Library of Congress Cataloging-in-Publication Data
Names: Khare, Anshuman, editor. | Odake, Nobutaka, editor. | Ishikura, Hiroki, editor.
Title: Japanese business operations in an uncertain world / edited by Anshuman Khare, Nobutaka Odake, and Hiroki Ishikura.
Description: Abingdon, Oxon ; New York, NY : Routledge, 2022. | Series: Routledge advances in management and business studies | Includes bibliographical references and index.
Identifiers: LCCN 2021032303 (print) | LCCN 2021032304 (ebook) | ISBN 9781032105765 (hardback) | ISBN 9781032105796 (paperback) | ISBN 9781003216049 (ebook)
Subjects: LCSH: Manufacturing industries—Japan. | Service industries—Japan. | Technological innovations—Economic aspects—Japan. | Japan—Economic conditions—21st century. | COVID-19 (Disease)—Economic aspects.
Classification: LCC HD9736.J32 J374 2022 (print) | LCC HD9736.J32 (ebook) | DDC 338.4/7670952—dc23
LC record available at https://lccn.loc.gov/2021032303
LC ebook record available at https://lccn.loc.gov/2021032304

ISBN: 9781032105765 (hbk)
ISBN: 9781032105796 (pbk)
ISBN: 9781003216049 (ebk)

DOI: 10.4324/9781003216049

Typeset in Galliard
by codeMantra

This edited book is dedicated to the fond memory of Professor Katsundo Hitomi – a profound scholar and a prolific mentor whose influence was as far-reaching as it was impactful.

Contents

Figures

Tables

Editorial and review board

Contributors

David "Chet" Chetwynd, BSME, MBA, Consultant & Executive Coach, is the Founder and CEO of JMNC Solutions, LLC and is based in the USA.

Kieran Gane is an independent consultant based in Japan.

Yukako Harata works for an energy company in charge of new business development and is a PhD student at Nagoya Institute of Technology in Japan.

Faith Hatani is an Associate Professor at Copenhagen School of Business in Denmark.

Kana Hayase is a project leader for a logistics company in Japan.

Hiroki Ishikura is a Professor at the Department of Commerce in Osaka Gakuin University, Japan.

Anshuman Khare is a Professor for Operations Management at Athabasca University in Canada.

Kanji Kitamura is currently an Assistant Professor at Illinois College and an adjunct faculty member at Hawaii Pacific University in the USA.

Jaeho Lee is a Professor in the Faculty of International Studies at Hiroshima City University in Japan.

Akihiko Nagai is a Professor of Industrial Collaboration Promotion Center in Japan Advanced Institute of Science and Technology.

Nobutaka Odake is a former Professor of technology management at Nagoya Institute of Technology.

Tetsuro Saisho is a Part-time Lecturer of Faculty of Commerce at Waseda University, Japan.

Ayaka Saito is a student at the International Christian University in Japan.

Midori Takao is a Researcher of Institute for Future Initiatives at the University of Tokyo in Japan.

Emi Teshima is an Associate Professor of Marketing at Nakamura Gakuen University in Japan.

Shigetsune Yamoto is a Professor of Innovation Management at NUCB Business School in Japan.

Foreword

About five years ago the world was facing a situation where digital technologies were disrupting traditional ways of doing business. Some welcomed the change while others adopted a wait and watch approach. As a result, some organizations found themselves falling behind. In late 2019, an unknown pneumonia cluster was detected in Wuhan, China. Little did the world know that these were the first signs of a pandemic. In a few weeks, global business went into chaos. Soon thereafter, it was clear that the existing business practices and supply chains were going to be tested as the pandemic took a firm grip on the global economy. Change was forced on businesses, big and small, and they had to find ways to circumvent the impact of the pandemic just to survive.

Organizations were forced to reinvent their business practices and supply chains or face the threat of going out of business. During these times, there was a sudden realization that perhaps the digital technologies have to be adopted faster to continue to be in business. Many companies were successful in reinventing and innovating their processes for products and services. The adoption of digital technologies to survive gained pace, and within a year organizations started settling into a new business paradigm. When we look at the global economy today, it is not a surprise to observe that we may not be going back to the old ways of doing business. There is a "new normal" and "business as usual" was dead.

Just like global businesses, the Japanese businesses also felt the impact of the pandemic and started looking at the digitization aspect more closely. Even though some would believe that Japanese businesses have been leaders in digital technologies in provision of services and manufacturing of products, they too were under pressure to move away from traditional business practices and adopt a creative way to survive. For the global economy to recover, the pandemic must be suppressed all around the world. This would only be possible with collaborative and focused efforts.

This book is an excellent effort to raise the awareness of how organizations in Japan have been impacted by the pandemic and emerging digital technologies. Some chapters in this book deal with the pandemic, some deal with digital transformation and some other chapters deal with both. No doubt that the two factors – digital technologies and a pandemic – will have a lasting impact on how we continue to do business in the coming years.

This is just the beginning of a new way of doing business. This book touches on a small aspect of global business and focuses on Japanese organizations whose efforts are often not well known or understood in the western world.

Anshuman Khare, St. Albert, Canada
July 2021

Preface

COVID-19 has had a global impact. The conventional way of doing business is no more applicable for sustainability of businesses. A radical change is needed to cope with the changed works post-COVID-19. Japanese business understands that to be successful in domestic and international markets, it must change its approach. Among other things, the importance of digitization and digital business has not been lost. It brings agility, resilience and robustness to business. How quickly is Japanese business community able to fundamentally change its approach? Does the answer lie in further digitization?

The new era of globalization and digitization will evolve with new constraints, but it will also bring new opportunities. This book presents to readers what has been the impact of COVID-19 on Japanese business and how it has changed them. It includes new emerging business models and changing practices. Case studies are also included.

Authors of chapters are drawn from academia, industry and consultancy firms closely involved with business and digital transformation of business in Japan. It shares experiences of academics, practitioners and consultants on the challenges and new opportunities for Japanese business.

This book is targeted at business educators and administrators who have interest in Japanese manufacturing systems and processes. The book would also be of interest to those looking to gain a better understanding of global manufacturing and how one of the world's leaders in manufacturing is reacting to digital revolution and the pandemic engulfing all parts of the world.

The review process

We reviewed proposals and invited a selection of authors to submit full papers. The full papers submitted were peer-reviewed by a team of academics and practitioners from around the world. The review process was coordinated by the Editors and an Editorial & Review Board. The papers were reviewed by one of the Editors and at least two others to ensure quality of the work. In the end, fifty percent of the submissions found a place in this book.

Acknowledgements

The editors are thankful to the contributors to this book (Editorial Board members, reviewers and the authors) who helped to showcase the Japanese industry to an international audience. We also thank Christopher L. Boyd Tressler for providing editorial services.

Anshuman Khare
St. Albert, Canada
Nobutaka Odake
Nagoya, Japan
Hiroki Ishikura
Osaka, Japan
July 2021

Section 1
Manufacturing

Nobutaka Odake and Anshuman Khare

Manufacturing is a key sector in Japan and plays an important role in its economy. In this section we present six chapters that focus on some interesting developments in the sector due to advancements in digital technology or the pandemic or both. It would not be a stretch to say that the pandemic has provided a much-needed impetus to digitize. However, creating an industrial system which promotes digitalization and aims for a sustainable society will take time.

This section begins with an analysis of the robot System Integrator (SIer) industry which proposes, designs, and builds robot systems, the metal 3D printer industry, and the renewable energy industry, focusing on the IT-enabled intermediary firms in Chapter 1.

Hitachi is featured in the next chapter. Hitachi's hybrid management style and portfolio reform approach in anticipation of the shift to digital solutions is discussed in Chapter 2. The process of business reform already underway in some Japanese companies may provide a template for a more rigorous response to challenges such as similar crises in the future.

The focus of Chapter 3 is on the various movements toward the diffusion of renewable energy and analyzes the integrator function of the process from the perspective of ecosystem and integration. The engineering and integrator functions are required, and the formation of renewable energy ecosystems is a key point in aiming for a decentralized society.

In Chapter 4, four strategic issues are extracted from the case study of Hyundai Motor Group to respond to the green shift in the automotive industry: electrification, utilization of existing resources, balance between in-house production and outsourcing, and co-creation for the diffusion of hydrogen fuel cell vehicles. It is hoped that the Japanese automobile industry can draw some lessons from the Korean experience.

Japan's solar and offshore wind power generation is discussed in Chapter 5 using the concept of "environmental upgrading." The author believes that Japan has lagged in terms of adapting to the new business environment and contributing to sustainability.

Finally, Chapter 6 presents a case study of a service bureau (contract manufacturer) for metal 3D printers, including the construction of a library for modeling data and metal powder data, the upgrading of services by utilizing existing businesses, and collaboration with players in different fields.

DOI: 10.4324/9781003216049-1

1 Diffusion of innovation and the role of intermediaries as system integrators

Nobutaka Odake

1 Introduction

In the era of COVID-19, digital transformation (DX) will be the catalyst for the next generation of innovation, and traditional manufacturing structures are about to change dramatically. In addition, the development of online meetings and telecommuting is changing the way companies are organized, and the interactions within the boundaries of companies, or ecosystems, are influencing demand creation and company competitiveness.

In Japan, IoT, AI, CPS, etc. have been attracting attention in response to global trends, and COVID-19 has accelerated this trend, and the government has established a Digital Agency in charge of promoting IT and DX of national and local governments. Digitalization and cloud computing in factories and manufacturing sites will improve the resilience of manufacturing. In other words, digitalization is a major enabler for the diffusion of innovation, and startups are often the engines of this diffusion. Diffusion here refers to the process by which an innovation is communicated through certain channels over time among the members of a social system. Communication is a process in which participants create and share information with one another in order to reach a mutual understanding (Rogers, 1983).

High-tech products are often systems supported by a platform. In this context, a system is either a coherent whole made up of interacting elements, a combination of interacting elements to achieve a predefined objective, or a set of intermediary products and end products utilized to achieve a given objective (EIA STANDARD, 1999). This includes, but is not limited to, hardware, software, firmware, people, information, technology, facilities, services, and other supporting elements. A SIer integrates multiple technologies and multiple components into one system and provides it to the user. According to Prencipe (2003), a SIer company that utilizes external resources to commercialize its products constitutes a supplier network based on a strategic perspective.

This chapter focuses on three industrial cases. The first is the Robot SIer, whose presence in industrial robotics has increased in recent years. SIers are companies that have developed from engineering education firms, have their origins in equipment systems such as welding, transport, and assembly, or originate

DOI: 10.4324/9781003216049-2

from trading companies such as machinery and information equipment. Since a production line is a custom-made product, SIers are responsible for solving users' problems while forming an ecosystem during the design, procurement of materials, and manufacturing.

The second case is the metal 3D printing industry or metal Additive Manufacturing (AM). The two main technologies in metal AM are laser beam powder bed fusion (PBF-LB) and binder jetting (BJT). The metal 3D printing process consists of equipment, materials, and design/software, and it is important to combine them with 3D measurements, heat treatment, and related processes. The role of the service bureau as a SIer is important due to its management of these components.

The third case is the renewable energy industry. With the demise of Feed-in Tariff (FIT), local energy systems (Distributed Energy Resource [DER]) are shifting to self-consumption models. DER is becoming increasingly popular as an approach that contributes to the promotion of energy conservation, the expansion of renewable energy, and the strengthening of energy systems. Remote monitoring and control of energy storage systems is making it possible to charge and discharge batteries efficiently with AI. SIers that develop solar sharing, blockchain, platform businesses, etc. are becoming increasingly important.

This chapter looks at SIers, which are intermediary organizations that create markets, from the perspective of digitalization, and explores the possibility of innovation diffusion.

2 Related work

Working with customers to co-create production solutions is important to acquire new business, and the specialization of capital and labor allows open innovation along with bringing economies of scope and scale (Chesbrough, 2011). It is important to know how to adapt a company's capability to the external environment and whether the company has the management capacity, known as Dynamic Capability (DC), to effectively coordinate internal and external resources. The premise is based on the "open and close strategy" pointed out by Ogawa (2014). Teece (2007) argues that value-added investments made within knowledge-based firms are often co-specialized. Co-specialization refers to the combination of assets that do not generate value on their own but generate value in combination with other assets.

One approach that Chesbrough (2011) incorporates into open service innovation is the concept of Service Dominant Logic (SDL), as introduced by Vargo and Lusch (2004). SDL is a comprehensive approach utilized in the field of behavioral economics that does not distinguish between "goods" (tangible products) and "services" (intangible products). SDL is a concept that considers that both goods and services should be treated as services instead of dividing each into separate categories.

Gawer and Cusumano (2002) state that platforms are industry building blocks which have attracted investment from other firms and provide innovation with add-on products or services, having analyzed the competitive strategies of major enterprises. Gawer (2014) identifies a technological platform into three stages: internal platform, supply chain platform, and industry platform.

Iansiti and Levin (2004) typify the strategies of platform companies in business ecosystems into three patterns: keystone, dominator, and niche players, and then argue that firms in a business ecosystem interact with each other in complex ways and that the health of individual firms depends on the performance of the ecosystem as a whole. The keystone strategy is a strategy that enhances the sustainable performance of the keystone firm itself, by working as a network hub, through improving the soundness of the entire ecosystem. Furthermore, Na (2012) points out that interfirm competitiveness is shifting from competition among individual firms to competition among groups of firms, with strong interdependence formed around specific platforms.

Granovetter (1973) pointed out in "The Strength of Weak Ties" that weak ties are critically important in business because they are the starting point for innovation. The first step for companies that want to create new knowledge is to "explore" outside information and combine it with their own in a new way (Iriyama, 2019). March (1991) noted that this exploration includes things captured by terms such as search, variation, risk-taking, experimentation, play, flexibility, discovery, and innovation. A type of ambidexterity, maintaining an appropriate balance between exploration and exploitation, is a primary factor in a system's survival and prosperity.

3 Development of industrial robots and robot system integrators

3.1 Formation of the robot SIers industry

In the wake of COVID-19, the use of collaborative robots is expected to increase as a way of avoiding the "three Cs" (Closed spaces, Crowded places, and Close Contact). In order to cope with the prolonged nature of COVID-19, industries such as the electronics industry, food, pharmaceuticals, cosmetics, and automotive parts manufacturers are introducing collaborative robots as a way to reduce costs and save manpower. Industrial robots are used in various applications such as material handling, welding, assembly, machining, and electronic component mounting in clean rooms. A robot is a machine, which consists of a robot body, software, conveyor, controller, a safety fence, sensors, vision, grippers, feeders, jigs, etc. In 2018, the Japan Factory Automation & Robot System Integrators Association (hereinafter JARSIA) was established as an industry group, aiming to change the prevailing perception of robot SIers as only being subcontractors attached to robot manufacturers.

Even in the robot SIer industry, where the influence of COVID-19 has been large, automation and remote operation technologies have become more important in order to keep business productive without gathering people in crowded offices and factories. The use of digital twins will multiply and an increased number of tasks will be done remotely. Teaching tasks that used to be done

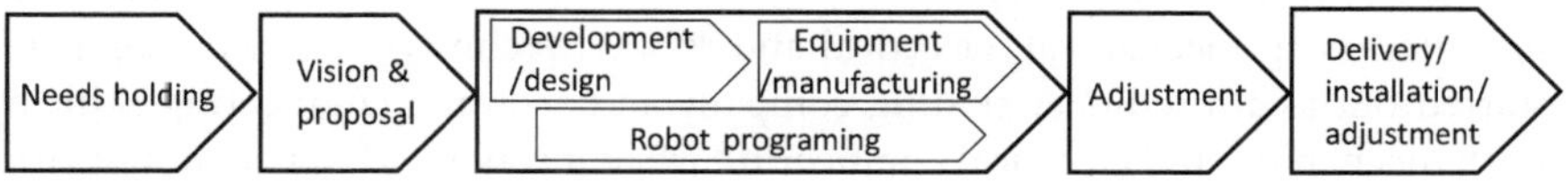

Figure 1.1 Robot SIer's work process.

Table 1.1 Types of robot system integrators (SIers)

Type of SIers	*Outline*
Line builders	A company that can plan, propose and design a production line and build the entire production line simply by receiving specifications from the user that the production line should meet.
Application-specific SIers	A company that has strength in specific applications can develop solutions based on standard system packages and has the ability to propose plans for specific lines.
Industry-specific SIers	Companies that have an understanding of specific industries and tasks, and can design and build robots and systems by receiving specifications from users.
Peripheral equipment SIers	Companies that mainly deliver industrial equipment (jigs, tools, parts feeders, etc.) that form part of the robot system and assist in system construction when the equipment is introduced.

Source: Segawa (2015).

on-site will now be done remotely. The imminent development of the robot SIer is accelerating based on the accumulation of knowledge in the field while using COVID-19 as an opportunity.

Robot SIers are classified into four general categories: line builders, application-specific SIers, industry-specific SIers, and peripheral equipment SIers (Table 1.1). While each category has its use, the boundaries between them are vague and many may fit into more than one category. With the exception of a few line builders, the majority of businesses in this category are small and medium-sized enterprises (SMEs).

These robot SIers consult with customers on manufacturing issues (requirements definition), then plan and design production lines, and then procure, install, deliver, and inspect all necessary machine tools and industrial machinery, transport equipment, and peripheral equipment. Requirement definitions are usually provided free of charge as an industry practice. The accuracy of a requirements definition is vitally important, as an insufficient requirements definition can cause serious problems in subsequent processes. The work process of a robot SIer is shown in Figure 1.1.

3.2 Challenges for SMEs

With the exception of major line builders targeting global manufacturing industries, the introduction of robots into domestic manufacturing is a major challenge for small and medium-sized robot SIers. Sanmei Mechanical Inc., with around 90 employees, operates as the president of JARSIA and describes its strength as its integration capability "to promote the automation of manufacturing lines using mechanical, electrical and robotic technologies." The company started out as a machinery trading company and acquired engineering skills in both mechanical and electrical engineering when it was asked to install, test run, and perform bug fixes while selling production equipment. Furthermore, the company strengthened its factory, FA field, when Yaskawa Electric Corporation expanded its business to industrial robots, and has become a SIer of production lines in specific fields such as casting processes (Enomoto, 2019a).

Table 1.2 shows the background of JARSIA executive companies' entry into the robot SIer market. Most of them are from equipment and parts manufacturers, but some of them are from specialized trading companies.

As a SME, Takamaru Engineers, Ltd. Co., which has about 30 employees, was founded as a machine design corporation. After the current president took over the business, the company entered the robotics and system integration field under contract from a machinery trading company that was looking to escape having to be a subcontractor (Robot Digest, 2020). In the 2000s, the company formed a partnership with the welding machines and materials trading company NI Welding Co. (now SC Welding Corporation) and the welding machine repair

Table 1.2 Background of Japan Factory Automation & Robot System Integrators Association (JARSIA) executive companies' entry into robot SIer

Executive companies	*Background of the entry into robot SIer*
Sanmei Mechanical Inc.	Automation of casting plant material feeders and FA
Bynas Co., Inc.	Computer-related business unit of a major retailer
IDEC Factory Solutions Corp.	Control device, FA system
HCI Co., Ltd.	Manufacturing equipment for cable, wire, and sheet
Office FA.com Co., Ltd.	Control system
Konsei, Co., Ltd.	Automatic lathe, measuring and inspection equipment
Synergy System Co., Ltd.	Conveyors and mechanical systems
Shoei techno service Corp.	Welding service
Startechno, Co., Ltd.	Industrial automation and labor-saving equipment
Takamaru Engineers, Co., Ltd.	Machine design, automatic machines, and robots
Taguchi Machine Works Inc.	Pump parts machining
Togarikogyou, Co., Ltd.	Sheet metal, can making, and assembly
Nihon Sekkei Kogyo, Co., Ltd.	Material handling, coating, logistics systems
HIROTEC Corporation	Body parts, press mold making
VR Techno Center Inc.	VR technology, aerospace personnel training
Mitsuiwa Corporation	Electronics and software-specialized trading company
Yanagihara Mechax Co., Ltd.	Plastic injection molding machine manufacturing
Yutaka Electronics Industry Co., Ltd.	Parts processing, switchboards
LINKWIZ Inc.	Start-up
Robotcom Corporation	Start-up
Tsukuba-Engineering Co., Ltd.	Labor-saving machines and FA equipment
TOYO RIKI Co., Ltd.	Design and manufacture of industrial machinery

Source: JARSIA (2020).

service Temma Wel, but the partnership was dissolved due to the Lehman financial crisis of 2008. In the 2010s, it formed a partnership with the machinery trading company G-Net Corporation (Furusato Group) to complement its trading functions (Enomoto, 2019b).

Takamaru Engineers and G-net Co., Ltd. have established the joint venture company Robot Technical Center (RTC), which operates a robot training business and exhibition hall and provides operation technology, trials, consulting, etc. for robot operators at its facilities located at their offices in Tokyo and Hyogo before introducing robots to factories. The company provides services such as robot introduction, design, manufacturing, installation, operation, maintenance, and operator training. In addition, RTC has established a branch in cooperation with Taguchi Iron Works in the Gifu region, to provide special training courses in industrial robotics, aiming to broaden the base of users and develop their skills, which is driven by the fact that instruction and inspection personnel are required to take special training courses (Newswitch, 2021).

3.3 Summary of the robot SIers industry

Due to COVID-19, the use of collaborative robots is expected to increase as a way of avoiding the "three Cs." The industrial robotics market was started by users with engineering capabilities that could produce components in-house, such as in the automotive, electrical, and electronics industries, but the range of useful applications as well as diverse industrial sector utilization has expanded with the development of related technologies. There is a new shift in emphasis toward software production in the design phase and a renewed interest in industrial robotics. This has been driven by cloud services, CPS, openness, and the development of sensors, network computing, and AI.

System integration is the process of connecting various mechanical and digital systems into a single, larger system by using mechanical and electrical knowledge. In the field of industrial robots, a robot SIer is an intermediate organization which provides a co-creation platform. It is important for them to have a consulting function that dynamically combines related processes according to the established objectives.

4 Metal 3D printer industry

4.1 Trends in the metal 3D printer business

COVID-19 has had a significant impact on the manufacturing industry as problems and issues with existing manufacturing methods and supply chain weaknesses were highlighted. In this context, an increasing number of companies are using 3D printer technology to move away from traditional methods of production and create the next generation of supply chains. In particular, the progress of metal AM technology has been remarkable in recent years, and the range of useful applications have expanded significantly from aerospace to the energy/industrial equipment and automotive fields. This is largely due to the improvement of equipment performance, metal powders, and software (Kyogoku, 2020).

Refinement of metal 3D printing technology is one of the factors driving servitization and innovation in the manufacturing sector, and is expected to significantly change existing business models. In Europe and the US, major manufacturers are acquiring or spinning off service bureaus and moving into full-scale mass production. A service bureau is a company that provides contract manufacturing output services and business services for a fee. The importance of supply chains linking a manufacturer and service bureau is increasing, and the challenge is how to expand into this growing market. In the past, equipment manufacturers used to supply powder as proprietary genuine products; nowadays, there are fewer restrictions, and service bureaus purchase metal powder from specialized manufacturers.

Rayna and Striukova (2016) show the potential for disruptive innovation in the new market of 3D printers, business model transformation, and point out the potential for disruptive innovation and business model transformation in the new market of 3D printers through the introduction of rapid prototyping, rapid tooling, local and cloud manufacturing as well as direct manufacturing for integrated production. Niino (2020) points out that AM technology is a core component for mass customization and that it is not just a processing technology but a "system technology" that employs the adhesion of materials, and that it should be used in conjunction with conventional manufacturing methods rather than replacing them.

According to Takeuchi (2019), in order to solve problems in AM, many hurdles must be overcome, such as business planning, design components, materials, molding, finishing, quality assurance, standards, and data management, as well as equipment innovations. Using EOS, an equipment manufacturer as an example, Takeuchi describes the ecosystem of AM as the relationships created with external partners, group companies, venture capitalists, and others to compensate for problems that cannot be solved solely by the equipment. Taki (2020) sees AM as a service (AMaaS) and service bureaus are the standard bearers.

4.2 Classification of AM technologies

The energy components of metal AM utilizing Powder Bed Fusion (PBF) can be broadly classified into either laser beam (PBF-LB) and electron beam (PBF-EB) technologies. The mainstream use of PBF-LB is mainly in prototyping and small-lot production, while BJT, a method utilizing binders instead of heat, is now becoming popular for mass production. AM technology is roughly divided into three components: (1) equipment, (2) powder material, and (3) process (recipe), but since they are closely related to each other, the entire technology must be integrated. In addition, at the design stage, Design for Additive Manufacturing (DfAM) is required to begin after deciding the printer, material, stacking direction/stacking conditions, separate construction method, combined use of parts, etc. In this section, the development of metal AM technology is discussed, which is becoming more widespread and its usability from the viewpoint of serviceability.

4.3 Domestic initiatives and examples of service bureaus

The service process for metal 3D printers is shown in Figure 1.2a. The service bureau has to not only consider the capability of fabrication during the initial design process but also must consider the entire process including pre- and post-fabrication.

In the field of resin 3D printers, a service has already been created in which 3D data is exchanged via a network, modeling is performed on demand, and the modeled product is delivered to the customer (Niino, 2020). Figure 1.2b shows the process of manufacturing parts. After preparing the modeling file, which is part of the previous process, the file is transferred to the AM manufacturing device. Even if an AM manufacturing device is in a remote location, local cloud manufacturing will be possible based on the same principle.

4.3.1 An example of business ecosystem formation

ExOne Japan Co., Ltd., a Japanese subsidiary of the equipment manufacturer ExOne in the US, sells and maintains Binder Jet type equipment, and also works with a professional engineering office to consider optimization, propose improvements, and evaluate the quality of the formed objects. Pacific Sowa Corporation, a trading company dealing with metal products, equipment, industrial machinery, etc., has entered the 3D printer sector based on its experience with the metal injection molding method, and is developing contract services as the sole agent for marketing metal AM equipment. Nano Seeds Corporation, a company specializing in the evaluation and measurement of physical properties of powders, is conducting joint research with the National Institute of Advanced Industrial Science and Technology (AIST) to evaluate the physical properties of metal powders as raw materials. They have established their own development system with Nimbo HIPER Vacuum Technology Co., Ltd. in China.

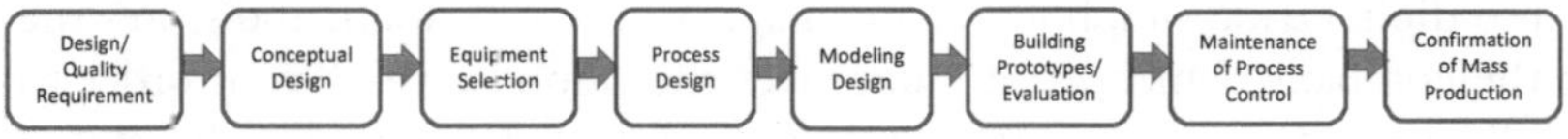

Figure 1.2a Service process (Komatsu, 2018)

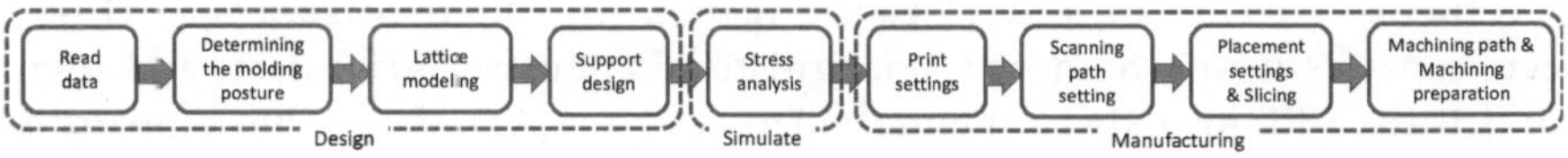

Figure 1 2b Modeling Process: Preparation of molding file (Canon Marketing Inc., n.d.)

Figure 1 2 Parts manufacturing flow using additive manufacturing.

4.3.2 An example of in-house production-related processes

Metal Technology Co. Ltd. is a premier metal casting company founded in 1960 with 553 employees as of June 2020. The company was founded by the metallurgical research group RIKEN for the purpose of magnetic annealing of ferrite and the heat treatment of aluminum die-casting molds. After that, the company introduced the world's largest Hot Isostatic Pressing (HIP) as a new heat treatment technology. Furthermore, starting around 2013, the company has also been involved in 3D printing. Since there are a wide variety of fields that require heat treatment and bonding services, the company has expanded into the fields of precision instruments, aerospace, energy, liquid crystal, and semiconductor manufacturing, as well as accelerators and nuclear fusion. The company constructs its products using a range of manufacturing technologies, including material selection, machining, heat treatment and surface treatment, and joining technologies. The company utilizes its strength in heat treatment technology cultivated through HIP, etc., to carry out all processes in-house, including pre-verification, modeling, heat treatment, finishing, and quality inspection, while also emphasizing partnerships, such as the joint development of implants for cervical vertebroplasty with AMTEK Co., Ltd. in response to market changes. The company responds to customers' needs by setting up bases in the vicinity of the customers' offices in order to identify industrial needs. The basic work of each of the eight domestic factories is almost the same, but since each factory has its own customer-specific processing, each has introduced equipment that can handle it (e.g., NTT data, 2014; ShareLab NEWS, 2020).

4.3.3 Various initiatives based on SMEs

Ifuku Seimitsu Co., Ltd (Kobe, Hyogo) is a small-sized company with 34 employees. After starting out as a lathe machining business, the company has expanded its business to include the design and manufacture of precision parts, jigs, and molds, and is also involved in the development of processing methods for difficult-to-machine and new materials. In order to introduce 3D metal forming services, the company places great importance on sharing the necessary basic knowledge and characteristics of 3D metal printers and information on product design with its customers. In addition, the "Digital Warehouse Service" converts molds into digital data, simplifies data management in the cloud, and stores the files at the company, which greatly improves the response time from order to delivery. The company also creates 3D data of products from used molds stored by subcontractors and manages them for digital repairs (Fukumoto, 2020).

Hara Seisakusho Co., Ltd. (Ueda, Nagano), ten employees, scans a 3D object, converts it into Standard Triangulated Language (STL) data, and then models the STL into 3D Computer-aided design (CAD) data. The company is developing its business based on the concept of reverse engineering, which is the process of creating usable 3D data based on 3D scans of the actual object. Takano Co. Ltd. (Matsumoto, Nagano), around 100 employees, is engaged in precision sheet metal processing which requires a large number of precise (engineering) processes for a relatively small product and has a large catalogue of available items. The company produces items over a wide range of industrial categories. The company introduced 3D CAD design at an early stage to reduce the need for rework and to accumulate data (Takano, 2020). The data measured at Hara Seisakusho is sent to Takano to be formed into an object by a metal 3D printer.

4.4 *Summary of the metal 3D printer industry*

Regarding metal AM, although Japan was late to the development of equipment, the establishment of the service bureau serves as the contact point for those looking to develop metal AM capabilities, and is promoting the diffusion of innovation by entrusting trial runs and small quantity production to various companies. It is important to retain data from trial production runs and the modeling files from customer designs to make a library from the obtained knowledge, which will lead to further technological development. The service bureau is involved in both recipe development and equipment utilization and improvement. In addition, consulting with customers is also an important function of the service bureau. Advanced SMEs use 3D scanners, such as digital repairs, to enable reproduction/repair of an actual product and to create a 3D modeling file for storage without having to create design documents. In the metal 3D printer business, service bureaus, which are intermediary organizations, are SIers and platformers.

The development of the IoT and the servitization of the manufacturing industry are two important wheels driving the cart, but the progress of metal 3D printing technology implies there will soon be a major change not only in the manufacturing field, but also in the business model itself.

5 Renewable energy systems

5.1 *The environment surrounding the spread of renewable energies*

The impact of COVID-19 is having a significant impact on government policy. In the autumn of 2020, the Japanese government declared a goal of reaching zero greenhouse gas emissions by 2050 as a pillar of its growth strategy. In response, major Japanese companies are setting targets for zero emissions. Renewable energy sources such as solar, wind, geothermal, small and medium-sized hydropower, and biomass energy are important low-carbon energy sources because they do not emit greenhouse gases and can be produced domestically.

In contrast to conventional large-scale centralized energy systems, in which huge power plants are built far away from consumers, there is a growing interest in decentralized energy systems where power generation stations are built in multiple locations, close to energy consumers, to meet their needs.

A microgrid is a small-scale power supply network that enables regional self-sufficiency by combining multiple distributed power generation sources and storage systems within an electricity demand area, while controlling the amount of power created according to demand conditions. This microgrid can be far more easily constructed using renewable energy generators compared to traditional fossil and nuclear fuel and is connected to the power system as a single aggregate.

Because of the low hurdle to entry and short development lead time, the FIT system led to a rapid expansion in the use of photovoltaic power generation and a rapid reduction in system costs, including the cost of photovoltaic panels (Lazard, 2019). After the end of the FIT system, self-consumption solar power generation and related solar sharing that balances farming and solar power generation are being developed, and IT-enabled SMES are often responsible for coordinating renewable energy generation companies, landowners, agriculturalists, and other related parties (e.g., MAFF, 2020; MAFF Rural Development Bureau, 2020).

However, as digital technology progresses, various possibilities are expected such as increased sophistication of supply and demand forecasting using AI and IoT, the optimization of power plant operation, demand response (DR) as well as the aggregation and optimum control of distributed power by virtual power plants (VPPs), etc. DR means that the owners of energy resources on the consumer side change the power demand pattern by controlling the energy resources, while VPP means that the owners of energy resources on the consumer side, power generation equipment directly connected to the power system, and power storage equipment control the energy resources to provide the same functions as a power plant. Here, blockchains and Energy Resource Aggregation Businesses (ERABs) related to such energy management systems are taken up and examined below.

5.2 Blockchain and integrator

A blockchain (distributed ledger) is a "block" of data that summarizes transaction records executed within a certain period of time and is linked like a chain for each new transaction, and all transaction information is recorded in multiple locations. It is a general term for electronic databases. Blockchain has a mechanism that can easily detect data tampering by using cryptographic technologies such as "hash" and "electronic signature." It is expected to spread as a way of guaranteeing that renewable energy comes from renewable sources by providing evidence in the blockchain itself.

Chaintope Inc. and Miyama Power HD Co., Ltd. are developing a prototype system to visualize the local circulation of energy and other resources in Saga City using blockchain technology and creating an electronic certificate to confirm the environmental value of locally produced and consumed waste-to-energy generated power. They are examining the possibility of creating a "regional recycling symbiosis zone" (Chaintope, 2021).

With the cooperation of TSUBU Co., Ltd. and Kawachi Shiitake Mushroom Farm Co., Ltd., Denryoku-Sharing Inc. connects farmers who grow fruits and vegetables with green energy through a network to form a business community and uses blockchain technology to create environmental value. They have started a "solar sharing/sharing (SSS) service" (environmental value trading aggregation business) that allows members to exchange information in real time (Denryoku-Sharing, Inc., 2020).

Digital Grid Corporation, which is funded by 54 leading companies (as of October 1, 2020), has created a commercial trading market using blockchain. In their electric power and environmental value trading platform business, the company is promoting the standardization of trading prices through the Digital Grid Platform (DGP). Furthermore, six companies, including FA Products Inc. and MiraiNect Co., Ltd., have jointly created a way to establish the value of the self-consumption status of renewable energy in remote areas so that it can be traded using the platform (DGP) which is also operated by Digital Grid Co., Ltd. (Energy Shift, 2021).

5.3 Diffusion of energy resource aggregation business

ERAB is a business concept to combine DERs, such as EneFarm, EcoFarm, HEMS, owned by demand side parties (consumers) so that they can be utilized as a regulating energy system. The ERAB is expected to be used to coordinate power markets through the use of market and relative transactions as well as a VPP that can be controlled by bundling energy resources on the consumer side that have only been used by the consumer.

Each DER possessed by factories and homes is small, but by bundling them together (aggregation) with advanced energy management technology utilizing IoT and controlling them remotely in an integrated manner, electric power can be effectively managed. It can be used to adjust the balance between supply and demand. This mechanism is called a "VPP" because it functions as if it were a single power plant. Resource aggregators and aggregation coordinators (hereinafter referred to as "aggregators, etc.") are businesses that provide energy services from VPPs and DRs to the wider community by integrating and controlling energy management and DERs on the household side. In 2020, 10 consortia (94 companies in total) are participating in a VPP construction demonstration project (METI, 2021).

Established in 2017 by Grid Solutions, Inc., VPP Japan Inc. has grown to become one of the largest solar power generation companies in Japan and raised JPY 10 billion in funds in 2020. The company has built solar power generation systems in the idle spaces on the roofs of buildings and is developing an "off-the-grid power company supply service" that directly supplies the cleanly generated power to the building it is attached to without going through the power grid. The company aims to build a VPP that optimally controls DERs (photovoltaic power generation, batteries, etc., which are distributed energy sources) in Japan that are resistant to disasters by networking them together (INITIAL, 2021).

5.4 Summary of renewable energy systems

COVID-19 has increased the importance of the renewable energy sector, and the ability to create decentralized energy systems has given us an opportunity to pay attention to each region again. Renewable energy is shifting to self-consumption power generation systems with the end of FIT. In solar sharing systems such as farm-type power generation, relatively small IT-enabled players manage the business. In addition, the structure of local production for local consumption of energy, that is, decentralized systems, has been recombined within existing structures, such as by promoting the interchange of electric power in the local area and the neighborhood, by an integrator, which are often designers/contractors, developers, IT companies, etc. They have been further developed into an autonomous decentralized system networked over a wide area. In businesses such as VPP and ERAB, aggregator businesses and platforms are being developed as an ecosystem to promote the spread of renewable energy.

6 Discussion

The industrial field of this case study is essentially a world of custom-made, low-volume production, where accumulated data can be used to reduce the time from design to manufacture. In the current era of AI and IoT, engineering as a specialized problem-solving discipline is of great importance for innovation and growth. The main actors are often intermediary organizations (integrators), but simultaneously a consulting sector has formed. In the field of robotics, the integrator is a robot SIer, while in the field of metal 3D printers the integrator is a service bureau and in the field of renewable energy the integrator is a designer, builder, developer or platformer.

It is important to consider design data and control data used by robot SIers, design for AM data and powder material recipes, etc. in service bureaus as knowledge assets. In other words, it is important to consider the data as "retention" and "retrieval" phases in the organizational memory process discussed by Walsh and Ungson (1991) and to put them into practice.

According to the classifications by Gawer (2014), robot SIers and service bureaus for metal 3D printers are supply chain platforms, but it is important to note that both are based on internal platforms within the organization. Aggregation businesses such as blockchain and ERAB are industry platforms that have evolved from supply chain platforms. Platforms are not only a place for transactions between companies, but also a place for communication of knowledge.

If the combination of existing knowledge or the reorganization of the framework is innovation, the partnership will expand the business domain of each company and realize collective innovation. In the digitized world, dynamic combinations between corporate organizations are important, and competition is changing from the level of individual companies to the level of competition between highly interdependent groups, that is, the level of an ecosystem. It has a great influence on the corporate competitiveness mechanism. The coupling of prototyping/single-product production and mass production, education and engineering as well as materials and equipment can be realized by functions such as libraries, databases, and platforms, each of which evokes the principle of co-specialization pointed out by Teece (2007). AI and IoT promote the construction of scalable systems through frontloading, by working as enablers.

In each of the industrial fields mentioned, the weight of software and specialized services is high. Effective innovation of services makes it possible to pursue customization and standardization at the same time. By utilizing AI/IoT, the expansion of product ranges such as mass production, single item production, and product integration brings economies of scope and lowers the average cost. In the digital age, openness drives specialization and specialization drives openness.

7 Conclusion

In the post-COVID-19 era, digitalization is accelerating at a rapid pace and changing the way companies are organized. In the context of the increasing importance of software in products and the dominance of services, the three industrial cases discussed are all treated as services. Interactions at the boundaries of firms or ecosystems are influencing demand creation and firm competitiveness.

In the age of digitalization, the amount of software in products is increasing. In addition, services are becoming more and more dominant. At the core of the case studies in these three industries are either IT-enabled SMEs, which play the role of SIers, or intermediaries, which provide a platform to connect users and suppliers. Furthermore, aggregation companies, which integrate distributed resources on the consumer and supply sides, are multisided platforms at the industry level (Evans and Schmalensee, 2016). It can be said that SIers play a keystone role in enhancing their own sustainable performance by improving the health of the entire ecosystem.

As the emphasis shifts from competition at the individual company level to competition as an ecosystem, the role of intermediary organizations or keystones is becoming more important, and the consulting sector is developing as a communication process. As the ecosystem develops, the diffusion of innovation will progress through system integration that effectively combines the processes.

References

Canon Marketing Inc. (n.d.). Modeling process: Preparation of molding file. (In Japanese). https://cweb.canon.jp/3dsystems/3d-metal-print/process/ (accessed May 16, 2021).

Chaintope (2021). News release: Participated in the development and verification work of a system to convert the environmental value of locally produced and locally consumed waste-generated electricity in Saga City into electronic certificates. (January 12) (In Japanese). https://www.chaintope.com/2021/01/12/saga_carbon_neutral (accessed May 25, 2021).

Chesbrough, H. W. (2011). *Open services innovation: rethinking your business to grow and compete in a New Era*, Jossey-Bass, San Francisco, US.

Denryoku-Sharing Inc. (2020). Denryoku-Sharing Inc. Launches blockchain-based "Solar Sharing and Sharing (SSS) Service" and "P2P Service for Renewable Energy and Vegetables" to Realize SDGs. (December 21) (In Japanese). https://www.neweconomy.jp/posts/81486 (accessed May 16, 2021).

EIA STANDARD (1999). Processes for engineering a system. (January 7) http://psconsultech.com/yahoo_site_admin/assets/docs/EIA632.9212432.pdf (accessed May 28, 2021).

Energy Shift (2021). FA products and digital grid P2P trading with non-FIT power supply. (March 30) (In Japanese). https://energy-shift.com/news/743bbd37-4622-44e7-997e-eb5795165e46 (accessed May 16, 2021).

Enomoto, S. (2019a). How does a machine tool trading company turn into a factory system integrator? Capability-building of Sanmei Mechanical. *The Journal of Commerce*. Vol. 61, No. 3–4, pp. 465–505. (In Japanese).

Enomoto, S. (2019b). Takamaru Engineers Co., Ltd.: A small venture's challenge toward an independent contractor in the system integration business. *The Journal of Commerce*. Vol. 60, No. 5–6, pp. 413–471. (In Japanese).

Evans, D. S., & Schmalensee, R. (2016). *Matchmakers: The new economics of multisided platform*, Harvard Business Review Press, Watertown, MA.

Fukumoto, I. (2020). Business model transformation brought about by digitalization, factory management. *The Nikkan Kogyo Shinbun*. Vol. 66, No. 13, pp. 8–13. (In Japanese).

Gawer, A. (2014). Bridging differing perspectives on technological platforms: Toward an integrative framework. *Research Policy*. Vol. 43, No. 7, pp. 1239–1249.

Gawer, A., & Cusumano, M. A. (2002). *Platform leadership: How Intel, Microsoft, and Cisco drive industry innovation*, Harvard Business School Press, Boston.

Granovetter, M. S. (1973). The strength of weak ties. *American Journal of Sociology*. Vol. 78, No. 6, pp. 1360–1380.

Iansiti, M., & Levien, R. (2004). Strategy as ecology. *Harvard Business Review*. Vol. 82, No. 3, pp. 68–78.

INITIAL (2021). Press release. (April 21) (In Japanese). https://initial.inc/companies/A-31743 (accessed May 22, 2021).

Iriyama, A. (2019). *Management theories of the global standard*, Diamond Inc. (In Japanese).

JARSIA (2020). FA / Robot System Integrator Association List of officers in 2020. (In Japanese). https://www.farobotsier.com/about/officer.html (accessed January 11, 2021).

Komatsu (2018). Function of JAMPT, CSTC forum. (Tokai Technology Salon No.114) Lecture materials. (August 31) (In Japanese).

Kyogoku, H. (2020). Metal additive manufacturing. *Chemical Engineering of Japan*. Vol. 84, No. 4, pp. 187–190. (In Japanese).

Lazard (2019). Lazards-levelized-cost-of-energy-version-130-vf. https://www.lazard.com/Perspective/lcoe2019 (accessed April 26, 2021).

MAFF (2020). About farming type solar power generation. *Ministry of Agriculture, Forestry and Fisheries*. (June 10) (In Japanese). https://www.maff.go.jp/j/shokusan/renewable/energy/einou.html (accessed May 22, 2021).

MAFF Rural Development Bureau (2020). Detailed survey on the installation of farm-based solar power generation systems. *Ministry of Agriculture, Forestry and Fisheries*. (March, 2020) (In Japanese). https://www.maff.go.jp/j/nousin/noukei/totiriyo/attach/pdf/einogata-31.pdf (accessed May 22, 2021).

March, J. G. (1991). Exploration and exploitation in organizational learning. *Organization Science*. Vol. 2, No. 1, pp. 71–87.

METI (2021). System of ERAB study group after FY2021. Agency of natural resources and energy. Ministry of economy, trade and industry. (April 16) (In Japanese). https://www.meti.go.jp/shingikai/energy_environment/energy_resource/pdf/015_03_00.pdf (accessed May 21, 2021).

Na, H. K. (2012). Diversity and dynamism of business ecosystem formation. *Journal of Innovation Management*, Spring, No. 9, pp. 143–161 (In Japanese).

Newswitch (2021). The aim is that a parts processing company in Gifu has entered the robot system integrator business. (May 2) (In Japanese). https://newswitch.jp/p/26990 (accessed May 25, 2021).

Niino, T. (2020). Innovation in products and services through additive manufacturing technologies. *Chemical Engineering of Japan*. Vol. 84, No. 4, pp. 171–174. (In Japanese).

NTT data (2014). Proposing higher added value by combining metal lamination molding and HIP processing. *Nippon Telegram and Telephone*. (October 1) (In Japanese). https://www.nttd-es.co.jp/magazine/backnumber/no75/no75-mtc.html (accessed May 28, 2021).

Ogawa, K. (2014). *An open & close strategy: Condition of the Japanese company revival.* Tokyo: Shoeisha Publisher. (In Japanese).

Prencipe, A. (2003). Corporate strategy and systems integration capabilities: Managing networks in complex systems industries in Prencipe, A. Davies, A. and Hobday, M. (eds), *The Business of Systems Integration*, Oxford: Oxford University Press. pp. 114–132.

Rayna, T , & Striukova, L., (2016). From rapid prototyping to home fabrication: How 3D printing is changing business model innovation. *Technological Forecasting and Social Change*. Vol. 102, pp. 214–224.

Robot Digest (2020). [Interview] The system is made by SIer / Takamaru Engineers, Co. Ltd., *President Takamaru*. (In Japanese). https://www.robot-digest.com/contents/?id=1574759237-736891 (accessed May 11, 2021).

Rogers, E. M. (1983). *Diffusion of innovations* (3rd ed.), Free Press of Glencoe, New York. ISBN 9780029266502.

Segawa, Y. (2015). An introduction to industrial trends on robot system integrator in oversea. *Journal of Refractive Surgery*. Vol. 33, No. 5, pp. 305–309. (In Japanese).

ShareLab NEWS (2020). From space to medical care! Efforts of long-established AM service bureau-Metal Giken Co., Ltd. (January 24) (In Japanese). https://news.sharelab.jp/column/mtc-before-tct/ (accessed May 28, 2021).

Takano, Y. (2020). 3D CAD as a common language collaboration between design and manufacturing: The challenge of digital manuals. *Factory Management, The Nikkan Kogyo Shinbun*. Vol. 66, No. 13, pp. 78–81. (In Japanese).

Takeuchi, N. (2019). Metal 3D printer opens the way to manufacturing - advanced technology for additive manufacturing. *Mechanical Engineering*. Vol. 67, No. 12, pp. 38–41. (In Japanese).

Taki, K. (2020). Technology perspective of the additive manufacturing as a service (AMaaS). *Chemical Engineering of Japan*. Vol. 84, No. 4, pp. 175–178. (In Japanese).

Teece, D (2007). Explicating dynamic capabilities: The nature and microfoundations of (sustainable) enterprise performance. *Strategic Management Journal*. Vol. 28, pp. 1319–1350.

Vargo, S. L., & Lusch, R. F. (2004). Evolving to a new dominant logic for marketing. *Journal of Marketing*. Vol. 68, No. 1, pp. 1–17.

Walsh, J. P., & Ungson, P. (1991). Organizational memory. *Academy of Management Review*. Vol. 16, pp. 57–90.

2 How Hitachi's globalization efforts prepared it for COVID-19

David "Chet" Chetwynd

1 Global challenges facing Japan's largest businesses

Japanese companies face challenges when doing business in global markets. They have lower profitability when comparing return on equity (ROE) across primary stock indexes of different countries, although this has been improving (Constable, 2021). Japan's brand of capitalism is unique and deeply rooted in history and culture. Evolution of Japan's capital markets since Japan's peak in the 1980s has been slow and is bounded by constraints related to Japan's system of government, societal norms, and business practices (Keidanren, 2020; Schaede, 2020). With a shrinking and aging population and huge Japanese equity holdings by the Bank of Japan and the Government Pension Investment Fund (GPIF), the Government has a large incentive to see Japan's companies grow globally and become more profitable (Schaede, 2020). This conflicts with what has worked so well in Japan for hundreds of years, which has been to prioritize employees higher than profits because of the historical ties between family and company that have persisted in Japanese corporate culture (Chetwynd & Schaede, 2020). The drive for higher ROE creates pressure on the obligation of lifetime employment. The social contract that large Japanese companies observe explains why, in times of crisis, Japanese unemployment fluctuates less than countries like the US (Saito, 2020). It also is a factor in why large Japanese companies have large cash reserves – to weather potential hard times without layoffs. To shareholders, cash reserves are considered excessive when opportunities for greater return, in many cases fueled by innovation, are forgone in favor of protecting stakeholders. Japan's Ministry of Economy, Trade, and Industry (METI) looked at ways for Japan's global companies to enhance their profitability in their *White Paper on International Economy and Trade* (METI, 2017). METI pointed to the need for greater pricing power in global markets, as well as more human capital investment to improve innovation capabilities. Population growth also plays a role in corporate health. Growth, and in turn the ability to invest, can be lifted or lowered by domestic population growth, and Japan's population peaked at the 2010 census. W.W. Baber et al. (2020 in Khare et al., 2020) ascribe lack of domestic growth in Japan as a factor in investment risk aversion, and thus lower digitalization, which impacts global competitiveness.

DOI: 10.4324/9781003216049-3

1.1 Japanese business priorities

There is no right or wrong definition of how to be successful in business – different cultures have different perspectives, and this impacts how business in conducted. The mechanisms of Japanese business reform are complex, and have been very slow to be adopted when there is not an immediate crisis involved. Former Hitachi Chief Executive Officer (CEO) and Keidanren (Japanese Business Federation) Chairman Hiroaki Nakanishi pointed out that COVID-19 exposed disparities that are growing wider under today's form of capitalism. In Keidanren's Comprehensive Strategy policy proposal, he advocates that Government and businesses must focus on three challenges to create a sustainable form of global capitalism (Keidanren, 2020), as summarized here:

1 Correct disparities by growing the economic pie through the creation of value and distributing it properly
2 Expand investment in the future (inclusive of education, support for families, investing in next generation technologies)
3 Start putting Sustainable Development Goals into practice as a long-term measure of achieving strong growth

Japanese business practices are simply different in many ways than Western business practices. Nonaka and Takeuchi (1995) explained Japanese values in terms of oneness of humanity and nature, oneness of body and mind, and oneness of self and other. These lead to differences in behavior in business and management, as is discussed extensively in their 1995 book, *The Knowledge-Creating Company*. There are also very helpful frameworks for quantifying those differences along multiple dimensions, such as those from Hofstede (2011) and Gelfand et al. (2011). Table 2.1 below provides a simple, very high-level comparison of business priorities and practices in Japan vs the US. Understanding these differences will be important context for the transformation methods described in Sections 3 and 4.

Table 2.1 Historical comparison of business priorities and practices between Japan and the US

Japan	*United States*
Business priorities	
• Concern for employees	• Shareholder rights
• Commitment to customers, suppliers	• Management transparency
• Commitment to society, social harmony	• Financial disclosure
• Long-term sustainability	• Long-term value creation
Business practices	
• Consensus-driven, slow decisions	• Empowered leaders, adaptive
• Employee job security for loyalty	• Employee pay for performance, transient
• Risk-averse, quality sensitive	• Risk-taking, time sensitive

While shareholder rights are gaining traction in Japan through various forms of shareholder activism, a Japanese-style of stakeholder focus is also taking root in global markets through activities such as managing toward a "triple bottom line" (Ho & Taylor, 2007) or focusing on Environmental, Social, and Governance (ESG) objectives. Cremers et al. (2021) assessed North American, European, and Japanese company goal attainment in ESG, and found Japanese companies to be ahead of North America and behind Europe in Environmental goals. In Social goals, Japan and North America both lagged Europe, with one of Japan's biggest deficiencies being in employee engagement (Gallup, 2017). In Governance, Europe and North America were well ahead of Japan, which lagged in transparency, inclusion, disclosure, and accountability.

1.2 The importance of leadership in adapting to change

Unexpected events like the Lehman shock or the Great East Japan Earthquake often highlight weaknesses in a company's structure or even in an entire industry and may result in leadership changes. However, it is the leader at a Japanese company who impacts the scope and permanence of the change that follows any shock. Leaders of Japan's largest companies have indeed made or have announced their intention to make significant changes in response to the latest shock: COVID-19. For example, Christophe Weber of the Takeda Pharmaceutical Company was very clear, perhaps taking advantage of this event to accelerate change:

> We have learned that you can do a lot of work from home and this will change forever the way we work together as colleagues in the company. This is something we are embracing. We are very clear that we will never go back to where we were before the pandemic.
>
> (O'Neill, 2021)

Jean Marc Gilson (2021), who took over as CEO of Mitsubishi Chemical Holdings Corporation (MCHC) Group in April 2021, created guidelines for some clear changes to come in response to the global situation in 2020 in his President's Message:

> The things we thought to be impossible a year ago such as remote work and generalized e-commerce are now a reality. Upon review, the companies that are thriving in this environment all share the same characteristics:
>
> - A simple and clear sense of purpose and strategy understood and embraced by all,
> - A culture of focusing and innovating towards growing markets,
> - A keen sense of quick decision-making, adaptability and calculated risk-taking,
> - A workforce of very engaged and financially responsible employees at every level of the organization.

Adapting to COVID-19 for a variety of manufacturers like MCHC means that non-production functions have been moved to home offices, while office capacity is being reduced. Work hours have become more flexible as the favored practice of a row of desks with a manager at the end of the row breaks down in a virtual world. Face-to-face after work gatherings with colleagues are not a safe option in the pandemic. Change in certain areas is happening fast. When COVID-19 created the imperative for a remote workforce, Hitachi had already spent years pushing forward with initiatives to support mobile and remote work, at least for top executives, as had been a common practice at one of their Silicon Valley-based global subsidiaries from the early 2000s. Early in the pandemic, it was reported in *Japan Chemical Daily* (2020) that Hitachi Ltd. was ahead of schedule deploying remote access and that by March 3, 2020, there were more than 50,000 employees simultaneously using remote access. The following sections use Hitachi Ltd. as a case study to demonstrate how Hitachi's two Presidents, in office from 2010 through 2021, made significant reforms to drive profitability, innovation, and global competitiveness The two methods examined are (1) adoption of hybrid global + Japanese management styles and (2) business portfolio reform.

2 A Hitachi case study

Hitachi is a Japanese multinational conglomerate headquartered in Tokyo, with Fiscal Year 2020 (FY20) revenues of JPY 8,729 billion or about USD 82 billion. The company is managed as five in-house sectors, and also has ownership, but not direct management, of majority stakes in two listed subsidiaries. The five in-house sectors are Information & Telecommunications (IT), Energy, Industry, Mobility (building systems, railway systems), and Smart Life. Hitachi has been divesting their listed subsidiaries, and as of April 2021, only two remain: Hitachi Construction Machinery and Hitachi Metals.

The Lehman shock of 2008 and subsequent deep recession worldwide created a collapse in trade (Saito, 2018), and this put Hitachi in a vulnerable position. From FY07–FY09, losses totaled JPY 952 billion (USD 12.2 billion). In April 2010 Hitachi's board chose 40-year Hitachi veteran Hiroaki Nakanishi as the next President. Turnarounds are sometimes entrusted to foreigners, as was the case with Carlos Ghosn at Nissan Motor Company in 1999, Christophe Weber at Takeda Pharmaceutical Company in 2015, and Jean Marc Gilson at MCHC in 2021. However, Nakanishi had extensive global experience from his time at Hitachi, and was no stranger to Western business culture, Silicon Valley, and the fast-paced world of high-tech. Nakanishi believed that a Japanese President could turn around Hitachi if he had the right background (Harner, 2012), and his performance proves that, using profit as the metric. He saw the greatest challenge, and the greatest threat to Hitachi's survival, as its low profitability. Operating income rose to 6.3% by the end of FY15. Table 2.2 shows income metrics for Hitachi Ltd. over five Mid-Term Management Plan (MTP) periods through FY20.

Table 2.2 Hitachi Ltd. Income metrics at MTP period end and IT segment as % of total

Mid-term plan period (end → value)	*FY07–FY09*	*FY10–FY12*	*FY13–FY15*	*FY16–FY18*	*FY19–FY21 (showing FY20)*
Shocks →	Lehman shock	311 earthquake			COVID-19 pandemic
Hitachi Ltd. Operating income %	2.3%	4.7%	6.3%	8.0%	5.7%
Hitachi Ltd. Net income %	−0.9%	2.6%	2.9%	3.4%	5.7%
IT segment, % of total revenue	19.0%	19.8%	21.0%	22.4%	23.5%
IT segment, % of total Op income	46.8%	24.8%	22.3%	30.5%	54.4%

In the fiscal year ending March 31, 2021 (FY20), Hitachi achieved record high net income at 5.7% and record high cash flow from operations at 9.1%. This is despite the COVID-19 pandemic and makes a case for Hitachi's preparedness through a combination of management reforms and portfolio shifts. In FY20, over 50% of Hitachi's operating income came from the IT business segment, bolstering that sector's influence within Hitachi.

Looking at a longer-term view of Hitachi Ltd. from FY07 through FY20, the company has:

- Reduced the number of in-house consolidated subsidiaries in Japan from 450 to 159.
- Increased global in-house consolidated subsidiaries from 484 to 712.
- Divested dilutive and non-core businesses yielding close to USD 20 billion (based on transaction value, not including minority stake transactions).
- Reduced listed subsidiaries (which are companies owned by Hitachi but also listed on stock exchanges) to two. In April 2021 Hitachi announced that Metals would be divested as well.
- Invested over USD 17 billion in acquisitions (this does not include the announced deal to acquire GlobalLogic for USD 9.6 billion, with a targeted close in 2021).
- Progressed on their diversity goals, starting FY21 with eight non-Japanese and seven female Executive and Corporate officers (Hitachi Ltd., 2021a).

In 2015, Nikkei Business (2015a; 2015b) highlighted Hitachi in a six-part series that demonstrated Nakanishi's globalization progress in rail, IT, and building systems. It featured headlines related to the railroad business such as "Serious delegation of authority, uncharacteristic of Japanese companies," and "Role model to promote international expansion." About the IT business, there were headlines such as "Advanced corporate governance that is not like a Japanese company" and "Resolution time reduced from 1–2 months to 3 days" about engineering and quality assurance issues impacting time to market.

The remainder of this paper will take a closer look at Hitachi's transformation. Section 3 looks at how the activities of one wholly owned subsidiary in Silicon Valley, Hitachi Vantara, were able to influence many other areas of Hitachi, making it a nimbler and digitally transformed entity. Such changes do not spread in a Japanese company without guidance from the top, and this is where the strong leadership of Hiroaki Nakanishi gave momentum to the types of changes that were taking place in areas such as IT and Rail. Section 4 summarizes the transformative portfolio reforms carried out by the next President, Toshiaki Higashihara. Hitachi has recently transformed faster than many other Japanese companies, demonstrating that a large Japanese conglomerate can make bold and significant reforms, even in the absence of a present shock. That phenomenon itself has been referred to by Schaede (2021) as "Hitachi Shock," implying that other large Japanese companies can no longer say that significant reforms cannot be done.

3 Hitachi Vantara's impact on Hitachi Ltd.

The foundation of Hitachi Vantara (Figure 2.1) began in Santa Clara, California, as Hitachi Data Systems (HDS). National Advanced Systems was purchased from National Semiconductor in 1989 by a joint venture between Hitachi Ltd. and General Motor Corp's Electronics Data Systems (EDS) unit (Associated Press, 1989). Hitachi bought-out the EDS share in 1999, making HDS a wholly owned subsidiary of Hitachi within what is today called Hitachi's IT Systems business segment. In 2000, HDS made the difficult decision to withdraw from the mainframe business, giving up about 75% of revenue. This forced a pivot to networked storage in competition with data storage giants EMC and NetApp. Hitachi then secured an agreement with Hewlett Packard to rebrand Hitachi storage, an agreement with Sun Microsystems to resell HDS storage, and developed both direct and channel sales teams at HDS for global markets. In the same timeframe, a software product management team made up of HDS veterans and an influx of new software experts was recruited to HDS after working at start-ups during the dot.com era. This team began to make dramatic improvements to the software that accompanied Hitachi's very high-quality hardware. Sales of both hardware and software climbed. Within a decade, this company had successfully leveraged a combination of global management, sales, and go-to-market capabilities and Western + Japanese product management and engineering to create a highly successful global business. Storage industry expert Chris Mellor (2010) wrote in *The Register* about HDS's lead over EMC and IBM in enterprise storage, bolstered by their first-to-market innovation called controller-based storage virtualization (the USP-V). While the technological innovation in the USP-V was a Japanese engineering victory, it was hard to sell, and the global HDS sales team innovated new business models to make the new product compelling to customers. By 2009, HDS was a strong global business that was pushing new boundaries for Hitachi. Ten acquisitions were made between 2005 and 2017, with an emphasis on software and services.

Software and services went from 23% of revenue to over 50% (Vellante, 2017). Revenue in 2017 was over USD 4 billion across over 100 countries (not including Japan), and Hitachi was now in possession of a large and successful global

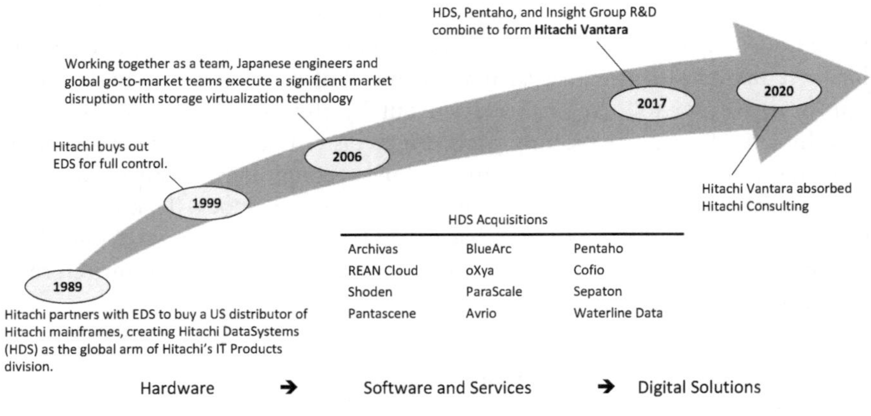

Figure 2.1 Hitachi Vantara history.

salesforce focused on digital solutions and services leveraging software, data, and analytics.

3.1 Agents of change

Hiroaki Nakanishi became the President of Hitachi in 2010, and within a couple of years had taken notice of HDS's CEO Jack Domme, who, along with his executive team, had been key to driving the success of an integrated engineering effort between Western and Japanese teams. Domme became a direct report to Nakanishi in 2013 when he became Hitachi Ltd.'s first non-Japanese Corporate Officer (Kovar, 2013). HDS under Domme's leadership was a great example of cooperation between a Japanese division and their global counterparts, and examples are always helpful for Japanese leaders to point to when driving change in Japan. Nakanishi would hold up HDS as an example of great business results in a globally competitive industry with rapidly evolving markets and competition. He liked the culture and excitement of the HDS team. In 2015, he appointed Domme into the dual role of Chief Executive for the Americas region while continuing to serve as the CEO of HDS.

A Hitachi Ltd. (2015a) press release stated that:

> Mr. Domme's appointment is significant for Hitachi as it is part of a new global management strategy Hitachi is calling "autonomous decentralized global management," which means Hitachi is placing more direct control for key businesses in the hands of talented local leaders to accelerate global growth by enabling faster decision-making based on market and customer needs. Hitachi has elected to deploy this new management strategy globally in order to grow its Social Innovation Business.

This role had never been held by a Westerner before. Nakanishi and Higashihara explained their strategy in the Hitachi Annual Report Shareholder's Letter (Hitachi Ltd., 2015b). The regional Chief Executives would devise and implement their own independent business initiatives at the same time that research and development (R&D) was being reorganized for closer alignment with global customer requirements. Cost structures were being reformed under the Hitachi Smart Transformation Project to enhance cash generation for investing in future growth.

One key function of the Chief Executive for the Americas was to convene a semi-annual meeting of Hitachi's Americas CEOs, a group consisting of over 50 Hitachi Group company and subsidiary CEOs, plus some of their key management team members. Under Domme's leadership, these meetings increased in frequency, and Domme created with the CEOs a sense of excitement around empowered leadership, competitive market-based strategies versus a Japanese product export mentality, business model innovation, and digital transformation across all businesses. Some Hitachi CEOs who were leading successful transformations would speak about how they were able to drive positive change resulting in revenue growth and higher profits. Domme employed the concept of change management through positive reinforcement and peer pressure, in combination with nudging and shaming. This approach is described separately in *The Business Reinvention of Japan* (Schaede, 2020).

Domme had made his impact at HDS and far beyond, and left Hitachi in 2016 after a 13-year tenure with the company (Yoshida, 2016). Domme and the leaders under him at HDS worked with counterparts at Hitachi Japan for over a decade and in some cases multiple decades. Such a long relationship created a level of honesty, mutual understanding, and collaboration across Japanese and non-Japanese managers that only comes with time and trust. It was through these long-term relationships, as well as support from the top of Hitachi, that HDS's functional leaders were able to interface with functional leaders in Hitachi Ltd, from Finance, Human Resources, Marketing and Communications, Information Technology, and other functions to gradually nudge Hitachi's practices and processes in a more globally aligned and digital direction. These foundations, along with similar phenomena at other global groups like Hitachi Rail, contributed significantly to Hitachi's readiness to cope with the challenges of COVID-19. When COVID-19 created the imperative for remote work, Hitachi had already spent years pushing forward with initiatives in Japan to support mobile and remote work, at least for top executives, as had been a common practice at HDS for all employees from the early 2000s. Best practices born out of the influence from global activities would travel far under Nakanishi's leadership, and would permeate but not fully transform the back-office functions of Hitachi in Japan.

3.2 Keys to success in a "hybrid" management approach

HDS was respected by Nakanishi for pushing certain boundaries to demonstrate to Hitachi's mid-level managers a new way of doing global business and innovating in solutions delivery. Part of the challenge faced by Hitachi is grounded in the way that human resources works at a large Japanese company. Employees enter from college and expect lifetime employment, though this is slowly changing. Throughout their careers in the company, they are rotated to different functions, and by the time they are experienced enough to be a senior leader, they have become an expert at Hitachi, but not necessarily an expert in any particular function such as IT, Marketing, or Sales. Even industry knowledge can lag based on being insular to Hitachi or limited to Japanese domestic market dynamics. This contrasts sharply with the US, for example, where an employee may join from a competitor mid-career, bringing with them extensive experience in one function such as Sales, Marketing, or Corporate Development (mergers and acquisitions). Hitachi, like many other Japanese companies, exports products to global markets through global subsidiaries or divisions. This global presence can have business practices spanning from Japanese in nature to local in nature. Anything in-between is a hybrid approach to management. When deep experts in their field and industry, working for a global arm of a Japanese company, are matched with Japanese counterparts at the same level of seniority, the global executive's capabilities are more suitable for success in local markets, whereas the parent executive's company-specific capabilities are more suitable for following processes and procedures of the parent entity in Japan. Both must be done, and doing so in a way that creates lasting change in Japan requires a clear understanding of Japanese business practices and culture, and patience to enable change over multiple mid-term planning period cycles. Given that these cycles are often 3–5 years each, this change is slow by global business standards.

3.3 What type of "hybrid" management is required?

Goals for hybrid management differ depending upon the relationship between the owned global entity and the Japanese parent organization. HDS started the 2000s as a global sales arm for a storage product factory in Japan, with both hardware and software content. To be successful in such a competitive and fast-paced industry, the hybrid approach had to lean heavily toward local business conventions and adoption of more global approaches, even in the Japan-based supply chain. HDS improved software, scrutinized cost of goods, built a global salesforce, and drove software and services acquisitions. This was a hybrid organization that felt more like a Silicon Valley company than a Japanese company, and no other culture would have succeeded.

3.4 Recommended elements of a hybrid approach for a fast-paced global products and services business

Table 2.3 highlights a sampling of recommendations in four key functions. These are most applicable in a situation similar to the one described for HDS and rely entirely on having a leader at the top of the parent company who is motivated to have a globally competitive business and understands with great clarity what it takes to do so.

Table 2.3 Hybrid management approach recommendations – product company supplied by Japan

Global Executive Leadership	• Demonstrate successes first to gain credibility and support from the top. • Define a market leading vision and strategy to help align and focus. • Relentlessly but respectfully share market and competitive data and insights with Japanese counterparts and top leadership. • Annually set ambitious but attainable targets (may diverge from MTP). • Uphold high ethical standards toward employees, customers, partners. • Eliminate Japanese practices at global offices that do not add value (e.g., traditional seating positions in executive meetings). • Rotate leadership meetings through global locations, including Japan. • Communicate regularly with employees via town halls, including expats. • Create accessible, daytime opportunities for socializing and team building.
Global Finance	• Effectively reduce G&A expenses as % of sales, freeing up investment funds. • Emphasize market competitiveness and ultimately require financial transparency (with top-level support) regarding costs from in-house suppliers in Japan; scrutinize what should and should not be a profit center. • Benchmark cost of goods vs competition, understand factory constraints. • Structure shared monetary risks and rewards with Japan counterparts. • Introduce market and competitive data into mid-term management planning process.
Global Human Resources	• Pay globally competitive wages. Attract and retain diverse, top global talent. • Implement performance-based component of pay aligned to key business metrics. • Allow remote work to enable recruitment of best talent in the market.
Global Engineering	• Engage in thorough business planning to increase alignment and understanding. • Introduce agile engineering processes. • Improve Japanese software user experience (UX) for global markets. • Advocate for strategic partnerships where required to compete. • Ensure Quality Assurance (QA) processes match global market needs and timing.

4 Hitachi Ltd.'s portfolio transformation

Transformation at a Japanese company has as much to do with leadership as with any external factors or shocks. COVID-19 had a significant impact on Hitachi's revenues and profit outside of the IT business sector and increased the urgency of change programs, including the use of new software systems, the sale of non-strategic assets, including cross-shareholdings (although they had been very active before COVID-19 as well), and reduction of general and administrative (G&A) expenses. Hitachi is clearly on a longer-term path of reform that takes influence from many areas, from the disastrous financial year of 2009 after the Lehman shock to internal factors like Nakanishi's program of "Smart Transformation." Competitive initiatives, such as Japan's Stewardship Code and the Ito Review in 2014, the Tokyo Stock Exchange's introduction in 2014 of the JPX400 "shame index" (Schaede, 2020), and the Corporate Governance Code in 2015, have set the stage for Japanese corporate leaders and boards (Yanagi, 2018). Higashihara became President after Nakanishi in 2014 and continued his work while also making bold moves to reform the Hitachi portfolio of companies. The following graphic (Figure 2.2) shows Hitachi revenue along with acquisitions and divestitures on a timeline in increments equal to the MTP periods.

In the Hitachi Integrated Report 2020, CEO Toshiaki Higashihara explains the company's often used term "Social Innovation," and that a key element of this is digital technology. He mentions the creation of Hitachi Vantara in January 2020 to "Lead the Development of Digital Solutions on a Global Scale." It is expected to strengthen the digital portfolio of "Lumada," which is what Hitachi calls their advanced digital solutions and services for turning data into insights that drive digital transformation (Hitachi Vantara, 2021). Lumada revenues are quantified in Hitachi's Consolidated Financial Results for the Year Ended March

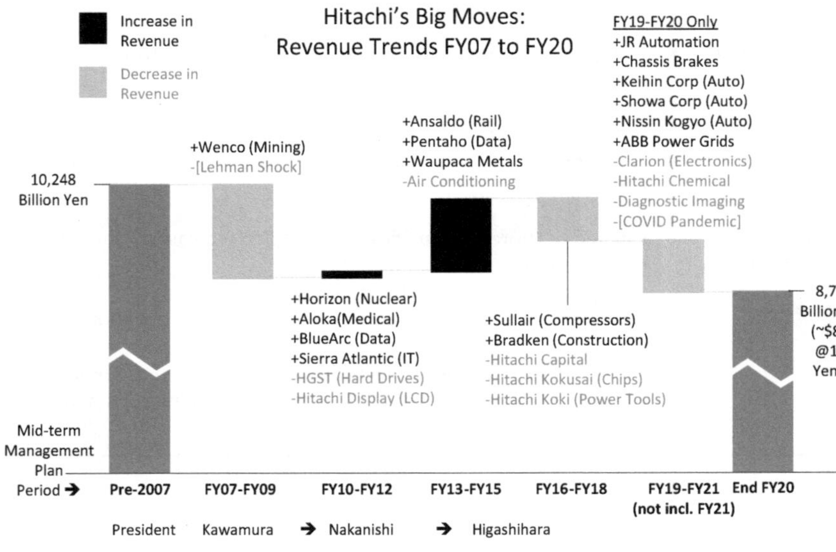

Figure 2.2 Hitachi's major acquisition and divestiture activity, FY07–FY20.

31, 2021 (FY2020). Core digital solutions business accounts for JPY 672 billion (USD 6.2 billion) spanning all five sectors. Another JPY 438 billion (USD4.0 billion) of revenue is classified as "Lumada Related," which are advanced products and systems businesses that are expected to generate synergies with the Lumada core business. This is a similar principal that HDS promoted in the 2010s – that continued customer relevance relied not just on superior hardware, but on compelling software and solutions as well as new business models and global sales capabilities. Hitachi is demonstrating how serious they are about delivering on their promise of Social Innovation in global markets. To further expand on their global digital capabilities in 2021, Hitachi Ltd. (2021b) announced their intent to acquire GlobalLogic for USD 9.6 billion. This is the highest price paid by Hitachi for any acquisition to date. GlobalLogic adds 20,000 employees to Hitachi Vantara's 11,000, and both companies will sit under US-based Hitachi Global Digital Holdings. GlobalLogic is characterized as a digital engineering services company, and a stated value proposition is to add advanced digital engineering capabilities and a solid global client base, including major technology companies.

5 Conclusion

While the COVID-19 crisis has been a catalyst for many companies to undertake drastic reforms, change the structure of their companies, and push a digital agenda internally and externally, Hitachi has been doing this for over a decade. As demonstrated in this chapter, significant reforms occurred under the leadership of Nakanishi and Higashihara in the wake of the Lehman shock, taking lessons, motivation, examples, and best practices from global operations and global business practices. Nakanishi emphasized the need to be globally competitive, and drove reforms by highlighting global success cases, empowering global leaders closer to the markets being served, and reorganizing R&D to be more aligned with market needs. Higashihara boldly reformed Hitachi's portfolio of in-house companies. Since then, Hitachi has become more focused, more digitally capable, and more profitable. Hitachi's leaders have transformed the company persistently and in the absence of shocks since 2011. In the year that many companies suffered large financial setbacks due to COVID-19, Hitachi set a record for net income and operating cash flow.

To what extent has Hitachi changed in Japan and what is required to successfully compete in global markets going forward? Kieran Gane (2020 in Khare et al., 2020) concluded in a case study that non-Japanese business and transformation models will not work in Japan without being tailored to the Japanese people. This indeed has been a challenge when outsiders bring global management approaches into Japan. Nakanishi believed that overseas reforms would bring results to Japan and change Hitachi in Japan by external pressure. Certainly the decades-long relationships between global executives at Hitachi subsidiaries and Hitachi executives in Japan created a lasting impact and some reforms, but inside Japan these remain bounded by interrelated Japanese business practices that are slow to change. Inside Japan, the external business and transformation models cannot be implemented in the same way they would be globally, but Japanese change agents from within Hitachi can make adjustments in Japan, and over time, these have a positive impact on results and remove some of the middle management barriers that can be so prohibitive to change.

Hitachi continues to seek ways to become more global and continues to strive for long-term value creation and shareholder returns, which in turn benefits stakeholders. CEO Higashihara approved the acquisition of ABB Power Grids as another means to create a "driving force behind the transformation of Hitachi's business and corporate culture into something that makes sense in global terms" (Kiba, 2021). Building sustainable, differentiated global offerings with top market shares and industry competitive margins is hard to do, and requires the businesses to operate at the global speeds observed in the applicable industry, as well as adapting to business model shifts brought about by digital advances and sometimes even digital disruption. Hitachi should continue to benchmark themselves against global competitors and work in close collaboration with global management teams that have demonstrated success and a willingness to cooperate, as this seems to be effective at accelerating broader corporate change programs. Further research could look at other Japanese companies with global operations, to see how high-performing global leaders at subsidiaries outside Japan influenced reforms at the parent company in Japan and what role the parent company CEO or President played in creating the conditions for accepting new approaches. It would also be interesting to explore whether a high-performing non-Japanese global subsidiary leader can continue to be as impactful if shifted to a Japan-based leadership role.

6 Acknowledgments

Thank you to family and friends for your support and encouragement. Thank you to my clients, past and present, for the insights we have gained together at the intersection of Japanese and global business practices. Most of all, thank you to colleagues and friends from Hitachi for contributing so much to my understanding of Japanese culture and business practices through your honesty, kindness, and continued support.

References

Associated Press. (1989). Hitachi, EDS Form Joint Venture After Buying National Advance Systems. *apnews.com*. (May 1). https://apnews.com/article/f96a89a409be0457f7713fe731b0d4e2 (accessed April 22, 2021).

Chetwynd, D., & Schaede, U. (2020). *How Japanese Companies Compete Globally* [Video]. Japan Forum for Innovation and Technology, UC San Diego. (September 22). https://jfit.ucsd.edu/zoominar/past-japan-zoominars.html#How-Japanese-Companies-Compete- (accessed April 15, 2021).

Constable, S. (2021). Japanese Stocks Are Back on U.S. Investors' Radar. *The Wall Street Journal*. (April 3). https://www.wsj.com/articles/japanese-stocks-are-back-on-u-s-investors-radar-11617462000#comments_sector (accessed April 30, 2021).

Cremers, V., Goerg, M., Grundin, G., Nuttall, R., & Yamada, Y. (2021). Charting a Path from the Shuchu Kiyaku to ESG for Japanese Companies. McKinsey's Sustainability Practice. *McKinsey & Company*. (March 11). https://www.mckinsey.com/business-functions/sustainability/our-insights/charting-a-path-from-the-shuchu-kiyaku-to-esg-for-japanese-companies (accessed April 25, 2021).

Gallup. (2017). State of the Global Workplace. [online] Gallup.com. http://www.gallup.com/services/178517/state-global-workplace.aspx?ays=n#aspnetForm (accessed May 17, 2021).

Gelfand, M.J., Raver, J.L., Nishii, L., Leslie, L.M., Lun, J., Lim, B.C., Duan, L., Almaliach, A., Ang, S., Arnadottir, J., & Aycan, Z. (2011). Differences between Tight and Loose Cultures: A 33-Nation Study [Electronic version]. *Science*, 332(6033), 1100–1104.

Gilson, J.M. (2021). Mitsubishi Chemical: Message from New President and CEO, Jean Marc Gilson. *Mitsubishi Chemical Holdings Press Release*. (April 1). https://www.mitsubishichem-hd.co.jp/english/news_release/pdf/01043/01194.pdf (accessed April 26, 2021).

Harner, S. (2012). Hitachi Ltd. CEO Nakanishi Writing Template for Restoring Global Competitiveness for Japanese Industry. *Forbes Asia*. (October 29) https://www.forbes.com/sites/stephenharner/2012/10/29/hitachi-ltd-ceo-nakanishi-writing-template-for-restoring-global-competitiveness-for-japanese-industry-1/?sh=7d1ac5de2870 (accessed April 22, 2021).

Hitachi Ltd. (2015a). Hitachi Appoints Jack Domme as Chief Executive for the Americas. *Hitachi Americas Press Release*. (February 5). https://www.businesswire.com/news/home/20150205005790/en/Hitachi-Appoints-Jack-Domme-as-Chief-Executive-for-the-Americas (accessed April 22, 2021).

Hitachi Ltd. (2015b). 2015 Annual Report. (July 15). https://www.hitachi.com/IR-e/library/integrated/2015/ar2015e.pdf (accessed May 17, 2021).

Hitachi, Ltd. (2021a). Hitachi Achieved 10% Ratios for Female and Non-Japanese Executive and Corporate Officers, Setting a New Goal of 30% Ratios. Hitachi Ltd News Release. (April 20). https://www.hitachi.com/New/cnews/month/2021/04/210420.html (accessed April 30, 2021).

Hitachi, Ltd. (2021b). Web Conference on the Acquisition of GlobalLogic, a U.S.-based Digital Engineering Services Company. (April 1). https://www.youtube.com/watch?v=Z6jklkWis-Y (accessed April 27, 2021).

Hitachi Vantara (2021). Hitachi to Acquire GlobalLogic, a Leading U.S.-based Digital Engineering Services Company. *HitachiVantara.com*. (March 31). https://www.hitachivantara.com/en-us/newsroom-hvtv/in-the-press/2021/gl210330.html (accessed April 27, 2021).

Ho, L., & Taylor, M. (2007). An Empirical Analysis of Triple Bottom-Line Reporting and Its Determinants: Evidence from the United States and Japan. *Journal of International Financial Management & Accounting*, 18(2), 123–150.

Hofstede, G. (2011). Dimensionalizing Cultures: The Hofstede Model in Context. *Online Readings in Psychology and Culture*, 2(1). https://doi.org/10.9707/2307-0919.1014 (accessed April 20, 2021).

Japan Chemical Daily (2020). Coronavirus Report – Part 38: Companies Lean Increasingly on Telework Arrangements Following State of Emergency Declaration. *Japan Chemical Daily*. (April 13). https://www.japanchemicaldaily.com/2020/04/13/coronavirus-report-part-38-companies-lean-increasingly-on-telework-arrangements-following-state-of-emergency-declaration/ (accessed April 26, 2021).

Keidanren (2020). Comprehensive Strategy. The NEW Growth Strategy. *Japan Business Federation Policy Proposals.* (November 17). https://www.keidanren.or.jp/en/policy/2020/108_proposal.html#s1 (accessed May 19, 2021).

Khare, A., Ishikura, H., & Baber W.W. (Eds). (2020). *Transforming Japanese Business, Rising to the Digital Challenge.* Springer Nature. https://doi.org/10.1007/978-981-15-0327-6 (accessed April 22, 2021).

Kiba, H. (2021). Origins to be Cherished More than Ever in the New Normal [Interview]. *Hitachi Review*, 70(3). https://www.hitachi.com/rev/archive/2021/r2021_03/message/index.html?WT.mc_id=ksearch (accessed April 27, 2021).

Kovar, J. (2013). HDS CEO Jack Domme Becomes Hitachi Ltd.'s First Non-Japanese Corporate Officer. *CRN.* (April 12). https://www.crn.com/news/storage/240152855/hds-ceo-jack-domme-becomes-hitachi-ltd-s-first-non-japanese-corporate-officer.htm (accessed April 22, 2021).

Mellor, C. (2010). Hitachi Data Systems: A Storage Giant Lost in Translation. *The Register.* (July 26). https://www.theregister.com/Print/2010/07/26/hds_enigma/ (accessed April 25, 2021).

METI (2017). *White Paper on International Economy and Trade* [White Paper]. Ministry of Economy, Trade, and Industry. https://www.meti.go.jp/english/report/data/wp2017/pdf/2-3-1.pdf (accessed May 17, 2021).

Nikkei Business (2015a). 日本企業らしからぬ 本気の権限委譲 [Serious Delegation of Authority that Is Not Like a Japanese Company]. *Nikkei Business.* (July 6).

Nikkei Business (2015b). 日本企業らしからぬ 先進的な企業統治 [Advanced Corporate Governance that Is Not Like a Japanese Company] *Nikkei Business.* (July 6).

Nonaka, I., & Takeuchi, H. (1995). *The Knowledge-Creating Company: How Japanese Companies Create the Dynamics of Innovation.* New York: Oxford University Press.

O'Neill, M. (2021). Takeda CEO Christophe Weber Discusses Challenges of Shire Acquisition. *Business Insider.* (February 18). https://www.businessinsider.com/takeda-ceo-christophe-weber-discusses-challenges-of-shire-acquisition-2021-2?am (accessed April 25, 2021).

Saito, J. (2018). *Why Was Japan Struck So Hard by the 2008 Crisis?* Japan Center for Economic Research. (October 1). https://www.jcer.or.jp/english/why-was-japan-struck-so-hard-by-the-2008-crisis (accessed April 26, 2021).

Saito, J. (2020). *Labor Market Adjustment Under COVID-19.* Japan Center for Economic Research. (June 15). https://www.jcer.or.jp/english/labor-market-adjustment-under-covid-19 (accessed April 25, 2021).

Schaede, U. (2020). *The Business Reinvention of Japan.* Stanford Business Books, Stanford University Press, Stanford, US.

Schaede, U. (2021). なぜ「日立ショック」がKAISHA再興に重要なのか [Why "Hitachi Shock" is Important for KAISHA Revival]. *Nikkei Business.* (March 17). https://business.nikkei.com/atcl/gen/19/00235/031000003/ (accessed April 24, 2021).

Vellante, D. (2017). Hitachi Vantara: The Strategy Behind the Name [theCUBE Interview]. *Wikibon.* (November 7). https://wikibon.com/hitachi-vantara-whats-behind-new-name/ (accessed April 25, 2021).

Yanagi, R. (2018). *Corporate Governance and Value Creation in Japan: Prescriptions for Boosting ROE.* Springer Nature.

Yoshida, H. (2016). With Our Greatest Gratitude and Best Wishes for the Future. *Community.hitachivantara.com.* (July 31). https://community.hitachivantara.com/s/article/with-our-greatest-gratitude-and-best-wishes-for-the-future (accessed April 22, 2021).

3 Efforts to promote renewable energy

Ecosystem and regional perspectives

Nobutaka Odake and Kana Hayase

1 Introduction

The increase in the number of people infected by the new coronavirus pandemic (COVID-19) and the stagnation of economic and social activities due to extended lockdowns has led to increased unemployment and a decline in consumption in many countries around the world. In addition to the recovery from the economic crisis, there is a growing movement, both at home and abroad, for a green recovery to redress the social disparities highlighted by the longstanding climate crisis and COVID-19. Globally, the growth of renewable energy, especially solar and wind power with their remarkable cost reductions (Lazard, 2019), has been phenomenal. According to the REN21 (2020) report on the COVID-19 pandemic and its impact on renewable energy, electricity demand will be reduced by 20% on average and the share of renewable energy supply will be the highest in history in China, Europe, India, and the USA.

The accelerated adoption of new business strategies, such as online sales and digitalization techniques due to the large-scale human toll of Covid-19, has led to the development of digital transformations (DX) in industrial systems which has resulted in lowering the cost of renewable energy production by increasing the speed and efficiency of services and operations. In the residential sector, shelter in place and telework have increased household electricity consumption, and there is growing interest in renewable energy, especially photovoltaic (PV) power generation and storage systems. In this context, distributed energy resources (DERs) systems, which make effective use of "local production for local consumption", can contribute to the promotion of energy conservation, the expansion of renewable energy, and the strengthening of energy systems. DERs are increasingly being used to promote energy conservation, increase the use of renewable energy, and contribute to the resilience of the energy system (METI, 2020).

This trend is not limited to the level of individual companies, but as will be shown later, there are many efforts as an ecosystem that is a flexible network between companies. This chapter will focus on looking toward renewable energy penetration in Japan and analyze them from the perspective of ecosystems and region.

DOI: 10.4324/9781003216049-4

2 Renewable energy policy trends in Japan

The "Energy Supply Enhancement Act" ("Act for Partial Revision of the Electricity Business Act, etc. for the Purpose of Establishing a Robust and Sustainable Electricity Supply System") (METI, 2020), enacted in 2020, is intended to make the electricity supply system strong and sustainable. One of the core revisions of the Act on Special Measures for Renewable Energy dictates that, (1) in addition to the feed-in tariff (FIT), establishes a new feed-in premium (FIP) system that adds a certain premium to the market price in addition to the FIT, (2) establishes a nationwide levy system to support part of the cost of reinforcing the power grid, including interregional interconnection lines, which is necessary for expanding the introduction of renewable energies, and (3) obliges commercial solar power producers to calculate disposal costs externally. (4) In order to correct the situation where the grid is not used effectively, if the system is not put into operation within a certain period of time after certification, the certification will be revoked (Agency for Natural Resource and Energy, 2020).

The government classifies renewable energy power sources into two categories: competitive power sources and community-utilized power sources. Competitive power sources are encouraged to be cost competitive and independent from the FIT system. On the other hand, community power sources, such as residential PV and biomass, will continue to benefit from the FIT system because their generation costs have not yet been sufficiently reduced. The community power sources are classified into two types: self-consumption, such as residential photovoltaic (PV) power generation, and community consumption (community-integrated), which is assumed to be used by local residents.

In order for renewable energy to become a major power source long term, it must be stable and it is important that it can continue to generate power after the end of the FIT acquisition period. When the cost of power generation is equal to or less than the existing cost of traditional power generation known as reaching grid parity, and when the purchase price under FIT is lower than the price of electricity purchased from power companies, the introduction of renewable energy through on-site power generation is expected to expand.

After the total liberalization of electricity retailing, the domestic electricity business system was divided into three categories: generation, transmission and distribution, and retail electricity businesses. Power producers and suppliers (PPSs) are newcomers to the electricity business that started with the partial liberalization of electricity generation and distribution in 2000. In contrast, Independent Power Producers (IPPs) were introduced in 1995 with the revision of the Electricity Business Act, and their purpose is to sell electricity at wholesale-to-large regional utilities.

3 Photovoltaics and the PPA model

PV power generation is the most important renewable energy source (Agency for Natural Resource and Energy, 2021). The power purchase agreement (PPA) model for PV power generation is a model in which a third party rents a site such as a roof of an electricity consumer, installs PV panels, and supplies the generated electricity to the consumer, which is called the third-party ownership (TPO) (e.g., Nikkei, 2021; ORIX, 2021). This PPA model or TPO model is a business scheme in which the initial investment is recovered by providing a service in which equipment that requires a large initial investment, such as solar panels and batteries, are installed on the rented property and the electricity generated by the solar panels is supplied to customers and monthly charges are made. The PPA model has been growing because the cost of PV power generation has decreased and it has become more competitive with fossil fuel-produced power sold by retail electricity companies. This model aims to reduce carbon dioxide (CO_2) emissions through the use of renewable energy and the energy-saving functions of the energy management systems (EMS) during normal times, but in the event of an unplanned power outage, such as those due to a natural disaster, the system will automatically switch to battery back-ups, allowing businesses to continue operating during emergencies and makes it possible to supply the community with daily necessities such as food.

Self-consumption PV power generation, in which electricity generated by PV systems is used directly by the company generating the power, is also making progress. In addition to the reduction of electricity costs, the system is expected to reduce corporate taxes through an immediate depreciation of the asset and by promoting environmental management (reduction of CO_2 emissions). The standard requirements for installation of PV systems for self-consumption are that the roof or rooftop has a total of $500m_2$ or more of sunshine space and that a high-voltage contract is in place.

In 2017, I-Grid Solutions and other businesses established VPP Japan (ITOCHU, 2020), a company specializing in off-grid power supply services, which has become a model for third-party PV ownership. VPP Japan combines energy storage solutions with PV power plants installed on supermarket buildings to maximize the use of clean energy, regardless of the amount of sunlight during daylight hours, and creates "negawatt" power by controlling the facility's equipment in response to fluctuating power generation (a negawatt-hour is a unit of energy saved as a direct result of energy conservation measures) (Nikkei BP, 2020). In addition, the company is constructing an energy platform that can make the best use of the unstable nature of PV power generation and can use electricity even in times of disaster by bundling and controlling DERs, integrating surplus power among consumers, and adjusting supply and demand through market transactions. The energy platform is Virtual Power Plant (VPP), which is the optimal control of scattered small-scale facilities, such as renewable energy power generation and storage batteries, and a network system that manages power demand using Artificial intelligence (AI) etc. It can be said that it is exactly aimed at DX.

Among the major power companies, several companies are building models for PV energy retail. TRENDE (Tokyo, Japan), a retail company in the Tokyo Electric Power Holdings group, is developing a third-party solar ownership model for households, and Kyocera and Kansai Electric Power have established a joint venture for newly built homes. ORIX Corporation, a financial services company, is developing a PPA model with Chubu Electric Power Company Inc. and Barrow Holdings Co., Ltd. that includes a BCP function (ORIX, 2019). ORIX will install and operate a PV power generation system, lithium-ion batteries and an EMS at each Barrow shop and provide electricity to each shop that was generated on site. Chubu Electric Power Co. Inc. will act as a manager for this service and will supply shops with electricity when energy needs are not met by solar power generation alone.

LOOOP Co., Ltd., established in 2011 with a focus on self-consumption/ PPA, is engaged in electricity retailing, the sale of PV power plant systems, and the operation of renewable energy power plants. The company integrates industrial and residential solar as well as power development businesses within its organization. It also incorporates energy storage (battery systems), maintenance and management services (O&M), and remote monitoring services.

Next, Energy & Resources Co., Ltd., which develops and sells related materials such as solar cell modules and constructs and maintains power generation equipment, has partnered with NGK Insulators, Ltd. This partnership provides a system of prepackaged NAS batteries and solar power generation equipment to energy supply companies (electric power retailers) that develop third-party-owned models (NGK, 2021).

Under the influence of deregulation and various governmental policies, a new combination of companies from different fields has formed and is becoming a leader in renewable energy.

4 Solar sharing (agriculture power generation)

Agricultural solar power generation (solar sharing), in which solar panels are installed on farmland, is spreading. This approach has overcome the main difficulty of selecting appropriate crops that will receive diminished sunlight (office of EERE). As the number of suitable sites for large-scale solar power generation (mega-solar) diminishes, more and more companies are entering the solar sharing market as a way to increase renewable energy production. After the introduction of the FIT, mega-solar power plants developed rapidly on locations such as defunct golf courses, but the number of suitable sites for large-scale power generation has become limited. However, abandoned land as of 2015 was 423,000 hectares (AgriweB, 2020) and the Japan Photovoltaic Energy Association (JPEA) predicts that the cumulative amount of PV power generation will be 420 million kW by 2050, of which 106 million kW will be from cultivated or abandoned land.

The Engineering, Procurement and Construction contract, in which the construction of facilities is undertaken as a whole, is progressing, and in some cases O&M is also undertaken as a PV support service. The O&M business is being upgraded by the use of drones and weather forecasting technology in response to DX. O&M consists of basic management and additional management.

Table 3.1 Examples of solar sharing initiatives

ENEOS Holdings, Inc.	ENEOS Innovation Partners, a subsidiary, has invested in Agritree, a farming start-up, and Agrist, an agricultural machinery start-up, to develop a farm-to-fork power generation system combined with an automatic crop harvesting system.
ATOM HOME Co., Ltd.	A farm-based solar power generation system that installs solar power generation equipment on abandoned farmland to grow turmeric and graze goats for meat, while using energy-saving equipment as a business.
Chiba Ecological Energy Inc.	An environmental and energy venture from Chiba University that organizes a value chain for farm-type solar power generation. Electricity generated by agricultural land panels is stored in storage batteries and used for mowers, etc., and also supplied to electric vehicles.
Minna-denryoku, Inc.	A CDP-certified renewable energy provider that provides consulting services to farmers and power producers.

Sources: ENEOS MIRAI HUB (2021), MAFF (2021), PR TIMES (2020a), and Veggie (2020).

Basic management is, such as monitoring, alert management through analysis of remote monitoring data, and additional management covers such as panel washing, slope greening, weed removal. These prevent the loss of efficiency and improve the profitability of PV power generation.

Table 3.1 shows some examples of solar-sharing initiatives in Japan. Companies such as new power companies, integrators, consultancies, and housing services are working in partnership with the agricultural sector and universities. Many of these efforts are mainly SMEs and start-ups or IT companies involved as intermediate organizations.

5 Regional initiatives: the case of Fukushima prefecture

Since the Great East Japan Earthquake in 2011, Fukushima Prefecture has been making efforts to promote renewable electricity, including the construction of dedicated power transmission lines, and various efforts are being made at the regional level with the aim of locally producing and consuming energy that does not rely on fossil fuels or nuclear power.

5.1 Iitate-madeina solar power generation Co. Ltd.

Iitate-mura, Fukushima Prefecture, together with Toko Electrical Construction Co., Ltd., which is developing renewable energy power plants all over the country as an electrical integrator, has installed a solar power plant with a capacity of 11.8 MW (interconnected output of 10 MW) and a wind power plant with a capacity of 6.4 MW on the village-owned pastureland. The utilization rate of the interconnection facility has improved to 30% due to the cross power generation of "solar power – wind power" in one interconnection frame. Profits from the electricity generated have been used for the reconstruction of the village (ITmedia, 2020).

5.2 Genki Up Tsuchiyu

Genki Up Tsuchiyu Co., Ltd. is a community development company established with local capital to promote the reconstruction and development of Tsuchiyu Onsen-machi in Fukushima. The company created a new community development project utilizing renewable energy, focusing on two “pillars of reconstruction”: a small-scale hydroelectric power generation project using an erosion control weir on the Higashi Karasu River that runs through the town, and a geothermal binary power generation project using hot spring heat from the source of Tsuchiyu Onsen. The company sells electricity in accordance with the FIT system for renewable energy electricity, and after amortizing the investment, uses the income generated for the reconstruction of the town, focusing on urban development and the creation of tourist attractions. The company also operates a shrimp farming business, a konjac product manufacturing and sales business, and a public bath management and operation business (KOKOCARA, 2018).

5.3 Aizu electric power plant

Aizu Electric Power Co., Ltd. is an electric power company established in August 2013, based in Kitakata City, Fukushima, with the slogan of “building a safe and sustainable society that does not depend on nuclear power and making the Aizu region energy independent”. The company was established by citizens, mainly business owners, in the Aizu region of Fukushima, which suffered relatively little radiation damage from the accident at the Fukushima Daiichi Nuclear Power Plant following the Great Tohoku Earthquake (Jichiken, 2019).

6 Wind power generation

Wind power generation is a system in which the kinetic energy of the wind is used to turn the blades of a wind turbine, which in turn transmits its power to a generator to produce electricity. There are various types of wind turbines such as propeller, Savonius, gyro-mill, crossflow, Darrieus and tornado type. Most wind power generation facilities are imported products. Japanese manufacturers withdrew from the production of large wind turbines by 2019. Interest is rising again as offshore power generation attracts attention (ITmedia, 2021). The number of components in a large wind turbine for offshore power generation is between 10,000 and 20,000 parts on average per unit, providing the wind power industry with a wide base and making it a sustainable industry (MILT, 2020). The wind power industry is expected to revitalize other industries such as iron- and steelmaking, shipbuilding and steel structures. The foundations of offshore wind turbines use a large amount of steel. Although there are manufacturing bases for generators, gearboxes, bearings, etc., a considerable amount of investment is required for offshore wind turbines, and there is potential for industrial development (Mizuho Information & Research Institute, 2015).

6.1 A tornado-type wind turbine developed independently by a private company

The main obstacles to the widespread use of wind turbines are cut-outs in strong winds, low frequency and mechanical noise, and bird strikes. The tornado-type wind turbine, designed and developed by Eco-Technology Co., Ltd., is almost as efficient as the propeller-type wind turbine in terms of power generation efficiency, and is characterized by high availability. It is low noise and resistant to strong wind gusts and typhoons. It has no need for cut-out protection and has a wide range of use depending on wind speed. This tornado type can be installed on the roof of a building or in a steep mountainous area because of its small footprint. One major problem, lightning strikes, is alleviated by lightning rods on each pole to minimize damage. In anticipation of global demand for wind power, the company has obtained a Patent Cooperation Treaty patent for the tornado-type turbine. As the company is solely a mechanical and architectural design firm, fabrication is carried out by a subcontractor. An Institute has been commissioned to carry out experiments and fluid simulations. For the time being, the maximum output has been limited to 20 kW or less, but the company is aiming to scale up energy production significantly. The company is also developing a micro-hydropower system using its expertise in wind power generation systems, and is promoting a project aiming to extend the range of hybrid electronic vehicles by using regenerative energy from wind power and brakes to generate electricity during vehicle operation as well as by installing a high-capacity battery. As the sole proprietor, the company is developing by building its own ecosystem with sheet metal, can manufacturing, welding companies, blade manufacturing companies, research institutes responsible for simulation, AI and internet of things (IoT)-related start-up companies, electric power companies, and EV-related companies (Odake, 2021).

7 Small hydropower

Small-scale hydropower is a type of hydropower that does not require water storage facilities such as large dams, and is characterized by stable power generation and high-capacity utilization. There is no national standard to define small hydropower in Japan, but in Europe, power output of 10,000 kW or less is considered small-scale hydropower (NEDO, 2013). The Japanese electric power industry has traditionally used the term “small hydropower” to refer to power output of 10,000 kW or less, but hydropower output of 1,000 kW or less is now recognized as a “new energy” form under the April 2008 revision of the enforcement order for the New Energy Act. There is no clear definition of micro-hydropower, but since the Japanese system simplifies various procedures for power generation facilities of less than 200 kW, this size is collectively referred to as “micro-hydropower”. The Japanese Association for Water Energy Recovery (J-WatER), a nationwide industry organization, has been established for small hydropower promotion. Its members include power producers, general developers, consultants, power generator manufacturers and suppliers, related equipment manufacturers and suppliers, and installers. The turbines themselves are custom-made, and it is necessary to select the appropriate type according to the conditions such as flow rate and drop. According to J-WatER, there are about 550 hydropower stations nationwide, which are categorized according to the location type such as rivers, agricultural canals, erosion control weirs, water supplies, and sewage treatment water.

7.1 The Yudani river small hydropower station

A local general construction consultant group company started a feasibility study in 2011, and the following year received approval from the prefectural government for this project as a management innovation plan, after which they explained the project to the local community, and to Nanto city administration, they conducted surveys related to obtaining water rights such as flow observation and fish surveys, conducted exploratory drilling and boring surveys, designed facilities, and applied for new water rights. It has been in operation since 2019 and is engaged in power sales business electricity utilizing FIT (NNE, 2019).

7.2 Tsukubane power plant

In 2013, local volunteers started a project to revive the former Tsukubane Power Station (1913–1963) with the aim of revitalizing the village, and later established the Higashi Yoshino Hydro Power Co. Music Security Co., Ltd. provided about one fourth of the necessary funds through the Tsukubane Small Hydropower Revival Fund (citizen's fund) and the remaining three quarters was raised by borrowing from financial institutions to revive the Tsukubane Power Station. The power station started generating electricity in 2017, and Higashi Yoshino Hydro Power Co., Ltd. manages and operates the power station and sells electricity using FIT (Kuroda, 2016).

7.3 The scheme of the small hydropower plant project

The Yutani River Small Hydropower Station is being promoted by a local construction consulting company, while the Tsukubane Power Station is being promoted by a local entity. They select geological survey and construction companies, and coordinate with the local government and the river office of the Ministry of Land, Infrastructure, Transport and Tourism (MILT) for financing and permits. In all these cases, businesses are centered on SMEs.

8 Expectations for geothermal and tidal power generation as a base load power source

Japan, a volcanic country, is ranked third in the world (equivalent to 23.47 million kW) after the United States and Indonesia (JGA, 2016). However, the total power output of geothermal power plants in Japan is between 540 MW and 2,559 GWh (JOGMEC, 2019), which is only about 0.3% of Japan's electricity demand. The Natural Parks Act, which made it difficult to build geothermal power plants in national and quasi-national parks, has been partially relaxed. Due to this deregulation, it is now possible to build geothermal power plants in national parks and quasi-national parks, but it is necessary to coordinate with hot spring areas because of concerns about the impact on businesses that rely on heated groundwater. However, the development of geothermal power generation is being reevaluated in view of the potential for efficient renewable energy.

There are about 20 geothermal power plants with 1000 kW or more in Japan, but the largest power plant in Japan is the Hatchobaru Power Station in Oita Prefecture, with a capacity of 112,000 kW (JOGMEC, 2021). In a hot spring area where high temperature groundwater gushes out, binary power generation can be used to generate electricity from high temperature water (70–120°C) and then use the lowered temperature, but still hot water, for bathing. At Tsuchiyu Onsen in Fukushima City, a 400 kW-class hot spring binary power generation system is being utilized.

On the other hand, in the field of tidal current power generation, the demonstration project has started from 2016 in Naruseto, Nagasaki prefecture. As a project of the Ministry of the Environment, Kyuden Mirai Energy Company, Inc. and the co-implementer Nagasaki Marine Industry Cluster Promotion Association are working on a demonstration project using a large tidal current generator and power generation has started from February 2021 (Nikkei BP, 2021).

9 Development of demonstration projects

9.1 Energy Resource Aggregation Businesses

Renewable energy has inherent instability, but there is a need for an adjustment function that absorbs power uncertainty by adjusting the balance between supply and demand and controlling the frequency. Energy Resource Aggregation Businesses (ERAB) are expected to be used to coordinate power through market transactions and relative trading. Energy resources on the consumer side, which were only used by an individual consumer, can be controlled as a VPP by bundling (aggregating), and are expected to be used as an operating force through market transactions and bilateral transactions. Aggregation businesses that locally produce and consume energy, such as new regional electric power that bundles electric power from local solar power and wind power, then integrates it as if coming from a single power plant, are being developed in various places under the initiative of local governments.

In the future, aggregators will stand between consumers and grid operators to control supply and demand, contributing to grid stabilization and maximizing the use of renewable energy. It is expected to create a new electricity business sector as various players enter the market.

9.2 Blockchain

The amount of electricity generated by PV power generation and wind power generation is unstable, making it difficult for retail electric utilities to procure a stable electricity supply. In addition, there is a cost to prove that the energy came from a renewable source, which is not required for other energy sources. Blockchain has a mechanism that can easily detect data tampering by using cryptographic technologies such as "hash" and "electronic signature". If proof of renewable energy can be guaranteed by the evidence contained in a blockchain itself and the proof process can be eliminated, then diffusion of renewable energy will be promoted.

Sasakawa (2019) provides an analysis of the situations where blockchain is used, following the classification system of Andoni et al. (2019). According to the report, decentralized energy transactions are the most common, followed by cryptocurrency, tokens, and investment, the IoT, smart device automation and asset management, electric vehicles, and grid management. Table 3.2 shows examples of blockchain-based renewable energy projects in Japan.

Small and medium-sized IT companies are also involved in these projects in collaboration with large companies.

Table 3.2 Examples of blockchain-based renewable energy projects in Japan

Chaintope Inc. and Miyama Power HD Co., Ltd.: prototype a system that visualizes the regional circulation of energy in Saga City and creates an electronic certificate for the environmental value of locally produced and locally consumed waste-generated electricity.
Hitachi, Ltd. has developed a visualization system that utilizes smart meters and blockchain technology to visualize the power usage status of buildings, equipment, and services that operate on electricity derived from renewable energy.
Mitsubishi Electric Corporation, in collaboration with Tokyo Institute of Technology, has developed a unique blockchain technology to optimize P2P power transactions.
Six companies, including FA Products, Inc. and Mirinect, Co., Ltd., jointly developed a blockchain platform (DGP) operated by Digital Grid, Inc. to value the private consumption of renewable energy in remote areas in a tradable form.
Based on the results of electricity transactions tracked by ENARIS Co., Ltd.'s blockchain-based electricity transaction management platform, environmental value tokens will be issued and managed by D-Callet's "blockchain-based digital grid platform".
Ricoh Co., Ltd. has developed an electricity transaction management system that tracks the entire process from generation to consumption of renewable energy in real time, utilizing the functions of blockchain.
Digital Grid Corporation, a joint venture between Hitachi, Sony, Kyushu Electric Power, and others, is commercializing a blockchain-based trading market.
Minna-denryoku, Inc. commercialized a blockchain-based electricity trading and traceability system in 2018, and succeeded in aggregating approximately 400,000 kW of renewable energy power sources (as of July 2020).

Source: TC HUB (2021a, 2021b, 2021c), PR TIMES (2020b), Nikkei (2020a, 2020b), and The Sankei News (2020).

10 Discussion

As mentioned at the beginning, COVID-19 has triggered the renewable energy business, and the decentralized energy system and local production for local consumption of energy has given us an opportunity to pay attention to the region again. As the emphasis shifts from large-scale centralized energy systems to decentralized energy systems, the number of players becomes relatively small and the relationship with local communities becomes more important. But even in such a case, the network connections with the outside and remote areas are also important rather than being isolated within a region. In the field of PV power generation, the combination of solar cells, PCS, battery storage systems, new power generation, O&M, etc. may be carried out by a single company, but usually it is a network among small and medium-sized companies. This also applies to small and medium-sized wind power generation and hydroelectric power generation.

Technology can be thought of as combinations of processes, which makes design a process of combination. Engineering and problem-solving go hand in hand for a more systemic reason. A solution is an appropriate combination that carries out a given task (Arthur, 2009). The players are often small and are a combination of organizations made up of several players. The energy systems themselves are a combination of various elements such as solar cells, custom-made water turbines or wind turbines, generators, PCSs, and batteries, with O&M services as a component, making it important to form partnership. In ERAB, blockchain, etc., it is built on digitalization such as AI, IoT, and IT platform.

According to Iansiti and Levin (2004), an ecosystem is a system of business infrastructure based on a relationship in which the boundaries of multiple industries are fused together and coexist, and keystone companies play a hub function in this ecosystem. They build platforms and services that can be used by participants, promote collaboration among companies, and share the value created there with other members. The integration of distributed energy such as ERAB and blockchain and the engineering process from design and construction to O&M will inevitably embed digitalization services, such as AI, IoT, and platforms. Ecosystems are the starting point of competitiveness, and the keystones are often start-ups and SMEs, including IT firms. The loose integration of decentralized renewable energies, one of the preconditions for a sustainable decentralized society, will be important.

For the mass deployment of electricity from solar and wind power, which are highly variable and unstable, it is essential to provide transmission lines and resolve grid constraints. For this purpose, it is important to promote “non-firm type connections” that link the power generation facilities that have been strengthened and controls the output when the system is congested. At the same time, it is possible to promote the construction of transmission lines as an Environmental, Social, and Governance investment.

11 Conclusion

In the COVID-19 era, there has been a marked change in lifestyle from a metropolitan-centered society to a decentralized one, and in parallel, energy sources are becoming more decentralized. DX in the entire value chain has advanced and brought about changes in the system. Based on the above, this chapter can be summarized as follows. Renewable energies will be led by SMEs and start-ups, often IT firms. The digitalization of the industry has reduced the barriers between industries and has increased the participation of other industries. The organization of ecosystems as a starting point for competitiveness will be important, and the role of start-ups and SMEs as keystones will increase. The engineering and integrator functions are required to integrate the processes from design and construction to maintenance. The formation of regional systems will be a key factor in the development of a decentralized society, and networks not only within the region but also with other regions and remote areas will be important.

References

Agency for Natural Resource and Energy (2020). Electricity resilience from the perspective of the "legal system" electricity resilience from the perspective of the "legal system". (October 8) (in Japanese) https://www.enecho.meti.go.jp/about/special/johoteikyo/denjihokaisei_05.html (accessed May 5, 2021).

Agency for Natural Resource and Energy (2021). To accelerate the introduction of distributed resources. (February 16) (in Japanese) https://www.meti.go.jp/shingikai/enecho/denryoku_gas/saisei_kano/pdf/024_02_00.pdf. (in Japanese) (accessed March 27, 2021).

AgriweB (2020). Current state of agricultural land. (March 6) (in Japanese) https://www.agriweb.jp/knowledge/1229.html (accessed March 27, 2021).

Andoni, M., Robu, V., Flynn, D., Abram, S., Geach, D., Jenkins, D., McCallum, P., and Peacock, A. (2019). Blockchain technology in the energy sector: A systematic review of challenges and opportunities. *Renewable and Sustainable Energy Reviews*, 100, pp. 143–174.

Arthur, B. W. (2009). The nature of technology: What it is and how it evolves, section 3 Phenomena, Penguin Group.

ENEOS MIRAI HUB (2021). Sustainable agriculture, solving global food problems. Sharing the world's problem-solving image with ENEOS from local areas. (March 4, 2021) (in Japanese) https://www.eneos-innovation.co.jp/english/interview/int-agrist (accessed May 5, 2021).

Iansiti, M., & Levin, R. (2004). Strategy as Ecology. *Harvard Business Review*, March, pp. 1–11.

ITmedia (2020). Japan's first "renewable energy cross-power generation" starts, simultaneous operation of solar and wind power on a single grid frame. (September 10) (in Japanese) https://www.itmedia.co.jp/smartjapan/articles/2009/10/news110.html (accessed March 27, 2021).

ITmedia (2021). "New wind" in Japanese wind power generation, new entry into the "offshore market" one after another-What are the aims of each company? (April 15) (in Japanese) https://www.itmedia.co.jp/smartjapan/articles/2104/15/news028.htm (accessed May 5, 2021).

ITOCHU (2020). Strengthening capital and business alliance with VPP Japan Co., Ltd. and promoting next-generation energy business. (March 4) (in Japanese) https://www.itochu.co.jp/ja/news/press/2020/200304.html (accessed May 5, 2021).

JGA (2016). Geothermal power plant in Japan. (in Japanese) https://www.chinetsukyokai.com/information/nihon.html (accessed May 5, 2021).

Jichiken (2019). [Interview] Aizu electric power's efforts to produce energy independent of nuclear power by its own hands. (March 31) https://www.jichiken.jp/article/0110/ (accessed May 5, 2021).

JOGMEC (2021). Geothermal power plant in Japan. (in Japanese) https://geothermal.jogmec.go.jp/information/plant_japan/index.html (accessed May 5, 2021).

KOKOCARA (2018). Power generation from hot springs! Revitalizing Fukushima with Geothermal Energy -- The Challenge of the Men of Tsuchiyu Onsen in Fukushima City. (June 11) (in Japanese) https://kokocara.pal-system.co.jp/2018/06/11/power-generation-in-tsuchiyu-hot-spring/ (accessed March 27, 2021).

Kuroda, T. (2016). The issues and outlook for providing community power through small–scale hydropower generation. *Rikkyo Journal of Social Design Studies*, No. 15. (in Japanese).

Lazard (2019). lazards-levelized-cost-of-energy-version-130-vf. https://www.lazard.com/Perspective/lcoe2019 (accessed April 26, 2021).

METI (2020). Cabinet decision on the bill for the act of partial revision of the electricity business act and other acts for establishing resilient and sustainable electricity supply systems. (February 25) https://www.meti.go.jp/english/press/2020/0225_001.html (accessed May 5, 2021).

MILT (2020). Overview of the vison for offshore wind power industry (1st). (December 15) (in Japanese) https://www.mlit.go.jp/kowan/content/001390488.pdf (accessed May 5, 2021).

Mizuho Information & Research Institute (2015). Wind power generation related industrial agglomeration survey, etc. commissioned business report. (March, 2015) (in Japanese) https://www.pref.fukushima.lg.jp/uploaded/attachment/128684.pdf (accessed March 27, 2021).

NEDO (2013). Renewable energy technology white paper. (in Japanese) https://www.nedo.go.jp/content/100544823.pdf (accessed March 27, 2021).

NGK (2021). Signed an agreement with next energy to study a new service combining NAS batteries and solar power generation. (March 4) (in Japanese) https://www.ngk.co.jp/news/20210304_10941.html (accessed March 27, 2021).

Nikkei (2020a). ENERIS, au financial holdings, au payment, D-Callet; P2P electricity trading platform construction demonstration project started. (December 4) (in Japanese) https://www.nikkei.com/article/DGXLRSP601269_U0A201C2000000/ (accessed March 27, 2021).

Nikkei (2020b). Ricoh starts demonstration experiment of real-time power transaction management system utilizing blockchain technology. (August 21) (in Japanese) https://www.nikkei.com/article/DGXLRSP539245_R20C20A8000000/ (in Japanese) (accessed March 27, 2021).

Nikkei (2021). Hokuriku Electric Power Co., Inc. introduces solar power generation "third-party owned model" to Sumitomo Electric Industries. (April 27) (in Japanese) https://www.nikkei.com/article/DGXZQOJB278470X20C21A4000000/ (accessed May 5, 2021).

Nikkei BP (2020). VPP Japan raises 10 billion JPY to introduce 100 MW of distributed solar power. (March 5) (in Japanese) https://project.nikkeibp.co.jp/ms/atcl/19/news/00001/00664/?ST=msb (accessed May 5, 2021).

Nikkei BP (2021). Current power generation in Goto Islands; Kyuden Mirai Energy demonstrated with 500kW machine. (March 24) (in Japanese) https://project.nikkeibp.co.jp/ms/atcl/19/feature/00007/00030/?ST=msb (in Japanese) (accessed May 5, 2021).

NNE (2019). The Yudani river small hydropower station. (January 7) (in Japanese) https://www.shinnihon-cst.co.jp/nne/works_3.html (accessed May 5, 2021).

Odake, N. (2021). Personal communication. (March 23).

ORIX Corporation (2019). About the introduction of a third-party model of a PV power generation system with BCP function -Promoted by ORIX, Chubu Electric Power, and Barrow Holdings- (December 16) (in Japanese) https://www.orix.co.jp/grp/company/newsroom/newsrelease/191216_ORIXJ.html (accessed May 5, 2021).

ORIX Corporation (2021). Third-party (PPA) model of PV system; Largest in Japan (2.2MW), introduced at a long-established manufacturer factory in Hiroshima. (April 5) (in Japanese) https://www.orix.co.jp/grp/company/newsroom/newsrelease/pdf/210405_ORIXJ.pdf (accessed May 6, 2021).

PR TIMES (2020a). Chiba Eco was adopted as a farming type solar power generation system full utilization project. (June 22) (in Japanese) https://prtimes.jp/main/html/rd/p/000000013.000051786.html (June 22, 2020) (accessed May 5, 2021).

PR TIMES (2020b). P2P power trading demonstration project started. (February 5) (in Japanese) https://prtimes.jp/main/html/rd/p/000000001.000054540.html (February 22, 2020) (in Japanese) (accessed May 5, 2021).

REN21 (2020). Renewables 2020 global status report. (June 2020) (in Japanese) https://www.ren21.net/reports/global-status-report/ (accessed May 5, 2021).

Sasagawa, A. (2019). The use of blockchain technology in the energy sector: Opportunities and challenges in the German and US case studies, IEEJ. (in Japanese) https://eneken.ieej.or.jp/data/8528.pdf (accessed November 5, 2020).

TC HUB (2021a). Chaintope develops a system to record the environmental value of Saga City waste power generation on a blockchain and convert it into an electronic certificate. (January 21) (in Japanese) https://jp.techcrunch.com/2021/01/21/chaintope-miyama-phd-saga-city/ (accessed May 5, 2021).

TC HUB (2021b). Hitachi visualizes renewable energy usage status for each facility and service with smart meters and blockchain. (January 27) https://jp.techcrunch.com/2021/01/27/hitachi-powered-by-renewable-energy/ (accessed May 5, 2021).

TC HUB (2021c). Tokyo Institute of Technology and Mitsubishi Electric develop blockchain technology to optimize P2P power trading according to consumer trading needs. (January 27) https://jp.techcrunch.com/2021/01/27/tokyo-institute-of-technology-mitsubishielectric/ (accessed May 5, 2021).

The Sankei News (2020). [Minna-denryoku Inc.] Aiming to realize traceability in lifestyle areas such as air. (in Japanese) https://www.sankei.com/economy/news/200730/prl2007300264-n1.html (accessed May 5, 2021).

Veggie (2020). Minna-denryoku started "solar sharing business" that supports electric power and organic farming. (August 20) (in Japanese) https://www.kankyo-business.jp/news/025838.php (accessed May 5, 2021).

4 Adaptation strategies of Hyundai motor group to the green shift in automotive industry post Covid-19

Jaeho Lee

1 Purpose and research background

In this chapter, we will take the case of Hyundai Motor Group (HMG) and consider the key elements of adaptation strategy to the green shift in automotive industry. HMG's attempts to upgrade itself from a follower to a first mover through this adaptation strategy will further add to the uncertainty of the business environment for Japanese automakers. We define the green shift of the automotive industry as a process of the power train technology innovations, including electrification and transforming the industrial structure in response to social demands for decarbonization.

Currently, the environmental regulations faced by automakers have become increasingly strict. First, achievement targets for corporate average fuel economy (CAFE) regulations are becoming stricter year by year. According to the official announcements of each region and country, CAFE regulations in the US, EU, China, Japan and South Korea have required major automakers of 25% reduction on carbon dioxide (CO_2) emissions (g/km), over the past five years (E-Daily News, 2018). If automakers fail to achieve these goals, they may be substantially fined in proportion to the overall car sales. At the worst case, they may be banned from selling cars. In the EU, for example, if automakers are unable to clear CAFE's 2021 goal of 95 g/km of CO_2 emissions, they will be fined €95 per gram for excess emissions from each unit. Second, in addition to CAFE, in the US and China, zero emission vehicles, such as battery electric vehicles (BEVs), plug-in hybrid electric vehicles (PHEVs) and fuel cell electric vehicles (FCEVs) are required to be sold at a certain percentage of sales volumes. China has replaced zero emission vehicle with the name "New Energy Vehicle". Third, increasing number of countries have set strict goals to ban all new vehicle sales of conventional passenger cars and light commercial vehicles from some point in the future. Here, conventional vehicles mainly refer to the internal combustion engine vehicles fueled by gasoline or diesel. A hybrid electric vehicle (HEV) is often considered a conventional type of vehicle.

Then, is Covid-19 pandemic easing this trend of strict regulations and obstructing the green shift in automotive industry? The answer seems to be No,

DOI: 10.4324/9781003216049-5

as far as the latest data is seen. Although automakers have been given some grace to enforce strict regulations, there was no significant change in the direction of the green shift. Moreover, the expansion of zero emission vehicle (PHEVs, BEVs and FCEVs) purchase subsidies introduced as an economic measure against the Covid-19 pandemic is accelerating the green shift. For example, in 2020 Germany raised the zero emission vehicle purchase subsidy up to €9,000. As a result, the sales of zero emission vehicles in Germany are 190,000 units (7% of whole sales), 3.1 times larger than in 2019. In 2020, the share of zero emission vehicles in major European countries increased rapidly. The total share of zero emission vehicles in Germany, France and the UK markets were 7%, up five points from 2019 (Nikkei, 2021).

Another issue about the green shift is that the current environmental regulations are based on the "Tank to Wheel" approach, which takes up CO_2 emissions at the vehicle level for discussion. Some researchers argue that current regulations based on the "Tank to Wheel" approach has a loophole (Nakanishi, 2018), from the viewpoint of "Well to Wheel", which states that the amount of CO_2 emission generated in the process of producing fuel for automobiles should be considered, or from the viewpoint of "Life Cycle Assessment" that covers the whole environmental impact from the entire process of supply chain. However, the point of introducing the "Well to Wheel" or "Life Cycle Assessment" perspectives into environmental regulations is not delaying or hindering green shift of automotive industry but expanding the scope of CO_2 emissions regulations to auto parts and energy supply chains.

Although there is no doubt about the direction of the green shift in the automotive industry over CO_2 emissions, the pace of actual movement is somewhat in flux amid COVID-19 pandemic. Therefore, from the viewpoint of existing automakers, the key issue should be how to accurately grasp the pace of the green shift and how flexibly to adapt to this complex industry evolution of automotive industry. In discussing existing automakers' adaptation to the green shift, HMG's attempt is noteworthy, because this group is one of a few automakers leading in the HEVs, PHEVs, BEVs and FCEVs in the global market.

2 Factors contributing to the HMG's growth so far

2.1 Overview of the HMG

Hyundai Motor Corporation (when referring to Hyundai alone, hereinafter Hyundai) started its vehicle assembly business in 1968 from license production of Ford models. Britain's Ford Cortina was the first mass-produced model of Hyundai. However, realizing that the license production contract limits Hyundai's managerial independence, including discretion of exports, the company promptly started developing its own model vehicles. Eventually, it successfully launched an original model called Pony in 1976. Later, Ponies became as popular as national cars in the protected domestic market. However, Pony was equipped with Mitsubishi's Saturn engine. It was in 1991 when the company successfully developed original engines (α engines) with its own technology. Since then, the company has grown through benchmarking advanced automakers in Japan, Europe and the US.

In the late 1990s, the group was at two turning points. The first is the change of management rights from Se-Yung Chung, younger brother of founder Ju-Yung Chung, to Mong-Koo Chung, who is the founder's son. The second is the Hyundai's acquisition of Kia Motor (Kia), which was about to go bankrupt. HMG, led by Mong-Koo Chung, intensified the investment in the quality, design, marketing and long-term research of its vehicles. It was also successful at maximizing the synergies from integration of Hyundai and Kia. Hyundai's non-consolidated sales grew from about ₩11.5 trillion in 1996 to ₩49.2 trillion in 2019. Kia's sole sales totaled ₩7.9 trillion in 1999, but it recorded ₩33.9 trillion in 2019 under the HMG. HMG has expanded its market share in the global market. In 2019, the group grew to fifth in the world in new vehicle sales.

2.2 Prior research on growth factors of the HMG

The factors of HMG's fast growth to a global automaker have been discussed from various perspectives.

Lee (2006) attributes the foundation for HMG's sustainable growth to the managerial autonomy coming from developing original brands and technologies, as seen in Hyundai developing Pony. However, until the early 1990s, Korean automakers' growth remained largely dependent on protected domestic market and low wages (Mizuno, 1997). Regarding the production system of Korean automakers, including Hyundai, Kia, Daewoo, many problems have been pointed out, contrasted with the Japanese lean production system which was successful in accomplishing high quality, low price and flexibility to multi-product and change (Womack et al., 1990). In the wake of the fundamental organizational change, HMG has been focusing on modularization and quality management. It turns out that such efforts have paid off. According to IQS (Initial Quality Survey) and VDS (Vehicle Dependability Study) announced by J.D. Power, the quality and durability of HMG's vehicles sold in North America made a dramatic improvement from 1999 to 2013 to the global top level (Lee, 2013).

Regarding the group's rapid qualitative growth since the late 1990s, the following factors have been clarified so far. First, some previous studies emphasize the CEO's strong commitment and leadership to quality management as a significant factor in the growth of HMG. Since 2005, the group has introduced the GQMS (Global Quality Management System), which comprehensively manages and improves quality issues at development, production, sales, after service, laboratories, suppliers and overseas production; the top management is deeply committed to this activity (Lim, 2010; pp. 104–127; Lee, 2013; pp. 214–217). Second, it is considered that "ultimately front loading" through the pilot production in the Namyang R&D Center driven by engineers has greatly contributed to the improvement of the HMG vehicle's initial quality (Lee, 2013; pp. 217–219; Jo et al., 2016). Pilot building No.1 (established in 2002) and No.2

(established in 2005) have three pilot production lines, where three models can be tested and mass-produced at the same time. One pilot production line can produce about 50 new vehicles within three months (Lee, 2013; pp. 217–219). Third, introduction of modularization and Just in Sequence, which is a component procurement system for synchronous order production, have also contributed to the company's quality improvement (Ku, 2015). HMG has changed the former Hyundai Precision into a modular supplier, Hyundai Mobis, streamlining modular procurement of key components. Fourth, there is a study evaluating the economies of scale and economies of scope from collaboration between Hyundai and Kia through the pooling and the joint use of management resources (Lee & Hirano, 2013). Finally, in terms of international marketing strategy, HMG's efforts to concentrate resources on the volume zone of global emerging markets ahead of other companies (Shioji et al., 2012) and the building a rapid overseas production network have contributed to the group's rapid growth (Su, 2014). Choi (2015) investigated the trajectory of HMG's building styling-driven capabilities as one of its growth factors in the global market.

3 HMG's response to the transition of electrification in the automotive industry

Most prior studies are common in discussing the HMG's fast catch-up strategy, or latecomer advantage in existing internal combustion engine vehicle market (Shioji et al., 2012; Jo et al., 2016). In this section and beyond, we will describe HMG's subsequent counter-measures to the electrification of automotive industry and clarify its distinctive adaptation strategies properties different from findings of previous studies.

HMG is one of the few automakers that built a mass production and sales system for HEVs, PHEVs, BEVs and FCEVs in 2015. Its cumulative sales volume of 17 models of HEVs, PHEVs, BEVs and FCEVs in 2019 was 1,350,000 units, ranking fourth in the global market. Its sales of BEVs and PHEVs ranked fifth in the world. It retained its globally dominant market position in FCEV sales and cumulative sales in 2019 (Inside EVs, 2020; Chosun Biz, 2021). HMG's achievements in electrification are considered commensurate with its position as the fifth largest automaker in the world.

Even Covid-19 pandemic does not seem to slow down HMG's implementation of its aggressive adaptive strategies for the green shift. According to the new "Hyundai 2025 Strategy" announced in December 2020, Hyundai has revised part of its initial long-term investment plans in accordance with the management environment change caused by the Covid-19 pandemic. The final financial target for 2025 was the same as that of "Hyundai 2025 Strategy" announced in 2019, but the intermediate target for 2022 has been revised slightly downward. The ₩61 trillion as a strategic investment was also reduced by about 1.6% (about ₩1 trillion). On the contrary, the investment for the construction of eco-friendly vehicles and hydrogen industry ecosystems expanded by 43% than the first investment plan (Hankyung, 2020; Maeil Business, 2020).

In the next section, we will analyze HMG's case based on interview surveys with the Hyundai Motor Future Research Institute on June 10, 2014, and the president of the Korea Electric Vehicle Association on December 17, 2018, as well as secondary data on related industries and attempt to derive significant factors.

3.1 Emergent strategies

As for the HMG's electrification measures, we can identify that there are both consistency and flexibility in its R&D and launching plan. According to our interview with HMG in 2014, it had the market prospect that:

> HEVs will continue to be mainstream of eco-friendly vehicles for a relatively long period of transition, and the ultimate next-generation vehicles after HEVs should be zero emission vehicles. Among zero emission vehicle types, FCEV will be more promising than BEV.

However, it turned out that the spread of BEVs, supported by substantial infrastructure such as charging stations, was ahead in the market. Acknowledging that its own market forecast was not accurate, the group changed its market launch plan to resume intensive support for BEVs instead of FCEVs. This can be proven from the difference between its planning in the "22.2 Eco Friendly Vehicle Promotion Plan (22.2 Project)" announced in 2014 and actual results in 2020. As you can see in Table 4.1, as of 2014, the group had four HEV models: Grandeur (Hyundai), Sonata (Hyundai), K5 (Kia), K7 (Kia); two BEV models: Soul (Kia), Ray (Kia); and one FCEV model: Tucson (Hyundai). However, as of August 1, 2020, HMG ranks fourth in the world in sales with a total of 20 models: eight HEVs, four PHEVs, seven BEVs and one FCEV.

Inevitably, there should be a slight difference between planning and result. However, BEV has a track record of launching seven models that significantly exceed the original target of two models, while the number of HEV, PHEV and FCEV models launched are slightly short of the original target. This result shows that there was revision to the initial eco-friendly vehicle launch schedule to intensify investments in BEVs.

Table 4.1 The number of HMG's eco-friendly vehicle models in 22.2 Eco Friendly Vehicle Promotion Plan announced in 2014 and recorded in 2020

Eco-friendly vehicle types	*Record in 2014*	*Plan for 2020*	*Record in August 2020*
HEV	4	12	8
PHEV	0	6	4
BEV	2	2	7
FCEV	1	2	1
Sum	7	22 (Global No. 2)	20 (Global No. 4)

Source: HMG (2014, 2020).
Note: Those figures include the number of exclusive models for China.

It seems that the strategic shift from focusing on FCEV to BEV took place around 2015. In 2015, there were three significant events accelerating the electrification of global automotive industry. First, COP21 adopted the Paris Agreement and a global agreement was reached on the need for environmental regulations in this year. As a result, both developed and developing countries were able to share the goal of keeping the rise in global temperatures below two degrees compared to the era of the industrial revolution and peaking out the global greenhouse gas emissions. Second, in 2015 the discovery of the Volkswagen (VW) emissions scandal shook the global automotive industry. Triggered by this incident, many European automakers, once inclined to develop clean diesel engine vehicles as a core of eco-friendly vehicles, changed their minds and decided to pay more attention to BEVs. Third, in 2015 China launched a policy vision called "Made in China 2025" for upgrading domestic industries in a short period of time. In the policy of the automotive industry, the Chinese government strongly supported the electrification, especially the spread of BEVs through measures to foster domestic industries, including abundant subsidies and license plate priority assignment system for "New Energy Vehicles". As a result, New Energy Vehicle sales in China's new vehicle market soared from 330,000 units in 2015 to 770,000 units in 2017 (Nakanishi, 2018). In line with these global trends and fluctuations in the international competitive environment, HMG revised its commitment to FCEV and decided to give priority to BEVs and grow them intensively.

We will continue to discuss about what kind of initiatives HMG has taken to strengthen BEVs. It is said that the competitive advantage of BEV depends on the performance of secondary battery cells. In the case of the HMG, battery cells are procured from LG Chem (LG Energy Solution since February 2020), SK Innovation and CATL, all of which are leading global secondary battery makers. However, HMG's BEVs high performance is not simply due to improved battery cell performance, but also to the upgraded design of the entire vehicle.

The group has greatly improved the power efficiency by integrating drive motors, motor reducers, electric power control units (EPCUs) and on-board battery chargers (OBCs) that make up BEVs power train modules. Until 2017, the group's first-generation BEVs such as Ioniq and Soul EV had the separated component structure connected by power cables. Now, when you investigate the power train modules of the second generation BEVs, including Kona Electric launched in 2018 or New Soul EV launched in 2019, you can see that the weight and volume of an EPCU and an OBC are reduced, and the four components stated above are more tightly combined and became lighter and more compact as a module than before.

Figure 4.1 shows that HMG's second-generation BEV models, Hyundai's Ioniq and Kona Electric, Kia's Niro EV are highly ranked in diving range per secondary battery size in the BEV market in North America.

In addition, the energy density of the second-generation BEV was increased by improving the cooling system. The group used air-cooled type cooling systems for the first-generation BEVs, but the air-cooled system required enough space for air passage to cool down the battery cells. Accordingly, the number of

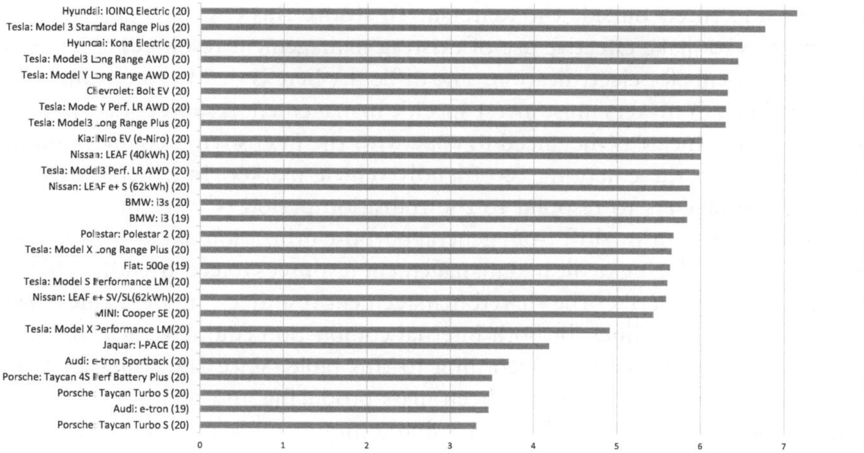

Figure 4.1 Driving range per secondary battery size in BEV models on sale in the North American market (Km/1kWh).

Source: Inside EVs (2020)

Note: The parentheses in the model's name indicate the sales year.

battery cells that could be loaded in the vehicle was limited. By introducing its own water-cooled system, the group was able to significantly raise the loading efficiency of battery cells and improve overall energy density. As a result, the power loss by operating heating system in the car was minimized. According to a January 2020 survey conducted by the Korean Environment Department on the ratio of driving range loss from in-vehicle heating for BEV models sold in domestic market, Hyundai's Kona Electric and Kia's Niro EV recorded –10% and showed a better power efficiency than Renault Samsung SM3Z.E (–43%), BMW 1394AH (–42%), Tesla model 3 Standard (–40%), Jaguar I-Pace (–33%), GM Bolt EV (–31%) and Tesla model S Standard (–18%) by turning on the heating in the car.

As described above, from the findings that HMG shifted its emphasis from FCEV to BEV around 2015 in response to the global eco-friendly vehicle market change, we can see both flexible and emergent aspects in HMG's eco-friendly vehicle market launch strategy.

3.2 Effective use of existing management resources and the economy of scope during the transition period

Due to the diversification and complexity of power train technologies seen in the transition period of electrification of vehicles, it should be enormously costly for existing automakers to cope with electrification. For example, it is estimated that it would cost automakers an extra $7,300 to switch production of a single internal combustion engine vehicle to a BEV with comparable performance (Nikkei, 2020). About one-third of BEV's selling price is said to be used for the purchase of secondary batteries, but much of the added value depends on battery manufacturers outside the Keiretsu. To absorb this cost, it is necessary for automakers to make effective use of existing management resources along with new investments for electrification. The difficulty here is that from certain point on, existing automakers must invest specific management resources dedicated to eco-friendly vehicles as they need to cope with the intensifying competition for performance in the emerging eco-friendly vehicle market. In other words, for existing automakers to respond to the transition period of electrification, it is important to smoothly shift from general purpose utilization of management resources to introducing dedicated management resources to eco-friendly vehicles.

Table 4.2 summarizes the shared management resources: model names, platforms and assembly lines for both internal combustion engine vehicle and eco-friendly vehicle production. According to this table, since launching an LNG HEV model in 2009, HMG has been mass-producing and selling HEV, BEV, PHEV and FCEV models until 2015, using common model names and platforms with internal combustion engine vehicles. In 2016, the company introduced a platform dedicated to eco-friendly vehicles along with the model name Ioniq, which can be shared with HEV, BEV and PHEV versions.

In 2018, the group brought compatibility between conventional and eco-friendly vehicles in the process of enhancing the entire types of sport utility vehicle (SUV) segment performance. For example, Hyundai's Kona has internal combustion engine vehicle, HEV and BEV versions, all of which share one platform. The platform was also used for Kia model Niro's HEV, PHEV and BEV versions. Since a SUV is taller than a sedan, it has more space for in-vehicle battery pack than a sedan. This structural feature of a SUV provides design flexibility even when making it a BEV. Accordingly, it should be easier to share management resources such as platforms between conventional vehicles and various eco-friendly vehicles within the SUV segment.

However, in the same year, the group launched a dedicated FCEV model. In the late 2010s, with the advancement of BEV equipped with dedicated platforms such as Tesla, competition for performance in the eco-friendly vehicle market became more intensified. At the same time, as the market for eco-friendly vehicles has steadily grown to a certain extent, it became easier to enjoy economy of scale through mass production of each type of eco-friendly vehicles. Therefore, the group seems to be specializing in the eco-friendly vehicle field for each type from 2021. In 2021, the company launched Ioniq 5 using its own BEV-specific common platform called Electric-Global Modular Platform (E-GMP). The Ioniq 5 inherits the model name "Ioniq" from the previous Ioniq electric launched in March 2016, but Ioniq 5 uses a completely different platform from Ioniq electric.

Next in the assembly lines where the launched eco-friendly vehicles are produced, the group has maintained the flexible system that allows mixed-flow production of conventional cars and eco-friendly vehicles until 2020. However, since 2021, the group has started producing most BEV models with E-GMP on some dedicated assembly lines.

Table 4.2 HMG's share states of existing management resources, model names, production platforms and assembly lines for concurrent production of internal combustion engine (ICE) vehicles and eco-friendly vehicles

Launch year/model	*Names of models (within a company)*	*Platforms (within a group, common in Hyundai and Kia)*	*Assembly lines (within a company)*
2009/Avante LPG HEV, Porte LPi HEV	Shared with an ICE vehicle model	Shared with a common platform group of ICE vehicle models	Shared with ICE vehicle models
2011/YF Sonata HEV, K5 HEV	Shared with an ICE vehicle model	Shared with a common platform group of ICE vehicle models	Shared with ICE vehicle models
2011/Ray BEV	Shared with an ICE vehicle model	Shared with a common platform group of ICE vehicle models	Outsourcing
2013/ix35 FCEV	Shared with an ICE vehicle model	Shared with a common platform group of ICE vehicle models	Shared with ICE vehicle models
2014/LF Sonata HEV, K5 HEV	Shared with an ICE vehicle model	Shared with a common platform group of ICE vehicle models	Shared with ICE vehicle models
2015_16/LF Sonata PHEV, K5 PHEV	Shared with an ICE vehicle model	Shared with a common platform group of ICE vehicle models	Shared with ICE vehicle models
2016/Ioniq HEV&BEV, Niro HEV	Dedicated, shared between HEV, PHEV and BEV	Dedicated but revised from ICE vehicles, shared between HEV, PHEV and BEV	Shared with ICE vehicle models
2017/Ioniq PHEV, Niro PHEV	Dedicated, shared between HEV, PHEV and BEV	Dedicated but revised from ICE vehicles, shared between HEV, PHEV and BEV	Shared with ICE vehicle models
2018_19/Kona BEVand HEV, Niro BEV	Shared with an ICE vehicle model	Shared with a common platform group of ICE vehicle models	Shared with ICE vehicle models
2018/Nexo FCEV	Dedicated	Dedicated	Shared with ICE vehicle models
2021/Ioniq5 BEV, EV6	Dedicated	Dedicated to plural BEV models (E-GMP)	Dedicated assembly line to plural BEV models

In this way, HMG has changed the degree of compatibility and specialization of management resources such as model names, platforms and assembly systems in line with the pace of green shift in automotive industry, step by step.

3.3 Independence of core technologies and outsourcing of complementary resources

It is difficult for automakers to cover all the technologies and resources required for the development and mass production of HEVs, PHEVs, BEVs and FCEVs. In other words, it is important to decide adequately whether to develop technologies internally or outsource them. This section discusses how HMG obtained the core technology of FCEV.

The group decided to develop FCEV in 1998 before Hyundai acquired Kia. At that time, Hyundai's attempted to develop FCEV was a secret project in-house and started with a small team composed of two to three members. However, it is thought that the company's technology at that time was at the stage of collecting the basic information.

The turning point in HMG's FCEV development was signing the "FCEV Joint Development Agreement" between Hyundai and International Fuel Cells Co. (IFC) in the US in 2000. The parent company of IFC is United Technologies Company Power (UTC Power). Pratt & Whitney, the mother of UTC Power, had been supplying fuel cells to Apollo spacecraft and NASA space shuttles since 1964. IFC had been conducting joint development of FCEV with Ford, BMW and VW around 2000 when HMG and IFC reached this agreement. According to this joint development agreement, IFC was given a role of developing fuel cell systems, while HMG was assigned the role of developing control equipment for vehicles and fuel cells. It is said that HMG had invested about $40 million between 2000 and 2003.

The first target of this agreement was to develop a 75 kW-class prototype of FCEV by the end of 2000 and the second target was to start mass production of FCEV in 2005. As a result, the group completed a prototype of FCEV based on an existing SUV model Santa Fe in 2000, achieving the first goal. One of the factors that enabled the rapid development of prototypes of the FCEV in this way is that the space for power train of an existing SUV can be easily utilized because the size of the fuel cell is small. The Santa Fe FCEV prototype has 160 km range or more, and the fuel cell output is 75 kW class. In addition, it has a maximum speed of 124 km per hour. It took 13.4 seconds to reach 100 km per hour, realizing performance close to conventional vehicles.

However, they failed to achieve the second target. In 2004, the company started test sales and continued to improve, but it was not successful at mass production and sales. It should be noted that in 2003, HMG launched another project to develop FCEV equipped with its own fuel cell system (including a core component, stack) separately from the joint development project with IFC. In 2006, the group succeeded in developing the world's highest level FCEV independently by achieving domestic production of major parts.

Subsequently, HMG continued to improve its power performance, modularization of core components, development of low-cost materials and development of mass production methods. Finally, it started production of the world's first mass-produced FCEV model, ix35 Tucson, in 2013.

This model was developed and equipped with its own fuel cell system. Its mass production and sales became available, supported by cooperation with 133 domestic suppliers.

In this way, through joint development with external specialized companies, the group realized vehicle-level development of FCEV, and through this process, it also learned how a stack works in the drive system. Ultimately, it was successful at developing its own stack.

On the other hand, secondary batteries that affect the performance of eco-friendly vehicles are outsourced from several global specialized companies. The group has outsourced battery cells primarily from LG Chem, SK Innovation and CATL. When these battery makers supply battery cells to HL Green Power, the joint venture company between Hyundai Mobis (51%) and LG Chem (49%), HL Green Power assembles those battery cells into battery pack, added with Battery Management System (BMS) and cooling system. It supplies these battery packs into Hyundai and Kia. Some said it was necessary to produce secondary batteries in-house, but the group ultimately chose a strategic alliance with LG Chem, SK Innovation and CATL, which are leading global automotive secondary battery makers.

In this way, by selecting and concentrating on the core technology development, HMG was able to respond flexibly to the green shift, despite its eco-friendly vehicles cover HEV, PHEV, BEV and FCEV.

3.4 Pioneering the future market and saving on upfront investment by making strategic partnership

While acknowledging the social significance of the green shift in the automotive industry, the reason why eco-friendly vehicles cannot be expected to dramatically replace conventional vehicles in the short run is that the inconveniences suffered by users have not yet been resolved. In other words, in the green shift, both social value and customer value should be increased at the same time. Especially a FCEV still has many issues to be solved to continuously create customer value.

Spreading FCEVs in an eco-friendly vehicle market requires to smoothly rotate the entire value chain composed of a demand cycle and a couple of related supply chains (Figure 4.2). A demand cycle is a process by which customers use the product. A supply chain refers to a step-by-step resource supply process, necessary at all stages of demand cycle.

Despite that currently HMG, Toyota and Honda launched high-performance FCEVs, the absolute shortage of hydrogen (H2) stations for refueling is a bottleneck in the demand cycle. Korea has 47 H2 stations for FCEVs. Even Japan, which is a leading county in hydrogen industry, has only 135 H2 stations as of 2020 (Kukmin Daily, 2021). In addition, there are not enough supply chains for repair, inspection and insurance for FCEVs.

Therefore, further investment in the demand cycle and supply chains is required for widespread use. Such upfront investments can be expected to be made by national and local governments. However, when such investments from public sectors are insufficient, FCEV makers will have to make such upfront investments for themselves. Latecomers or follower companies will be exempt from such investment for spreading FCEVs, and they will free-ride those infrastructures invested by first mover companies (Lieberman and Montgomery, 1988). Therefore, first mover FCEV manufacturers need to make this upfront investment as economically and effectively as possible.

HMG is working to solve this problem by joining networks of other early players. There are two types of the networks: consortiums composed of other

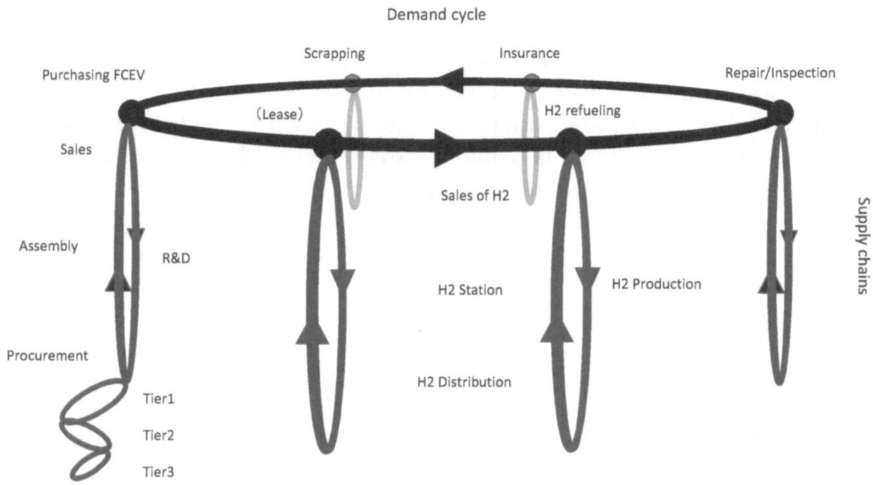

Figure 4.2 FCEV's value chain composed of a demand cycle and supply chains.

companies in the same and related industry with a loose couplings and strategic alliances with several companies that are complementary to each other. First, HMG participated in the Hydrogen Council, an international stakeholder group. The Hydrogen Council is a global initiative by leading energy, transportation equipment and industrial companies with a unified long-term vision of the spread of hydrogen as an energy source. It was launched in 2017 at the World Economic Forum in Davos as a coalition of CEOs from 13 participating organizations, including Hyundai and Toyota.

As of June 2019, the number of member companies has increased to 60 (Monthly Hydrogen Economy, 2019). In this way, it is thought that these first movers can save upfront investment by calling on governments to promote the hydrogen industry and by jointly conducting investment projects through the Hydrogen Council. However, since some of the Hydrogen Council members are possible competitors, the way they can cooperate with each other should be limited.

Second, HMG is developing a strategic alliance. We will introduce the example of a small value chain co-creation for the hydrogen truck mobility business that HMG is developing in Switzerland. In April 2019, HMG established Hyundai Hydrogen Mobility (HHM), a joint venture with a Swiss company, H2 Energy, to provide comprehensive commercial mobility, including leasing heavy hydrogen fuel cell electric trucks, in the way of Pay-Per-Use. This fee of mobility service covers all cost for refueling hydrogen, repair, insurance, and maintenance. Therefore, with a driver, HHM provides all other necessary mobility services. This makes it easier for users (truckers) to deal with strict government environmental regulations without investing hugely in buying eco-friendly trucks. To provide this emission-free mobility service, HHM has signed strategic alliances with HydroSpider for the supply of H2 and Auto AG Truck in the vehicle repair and inspection. Key customers of HHM are members of the H2 Mobility Switzerland Association. On July 6, 2020, 10 Xcients, the world's first mass-produced fuel cell electric trucks (34 tons), have been shipped. HMG plans to export 1,600 fuel cell trucks to HHM by 2025. This mobility business project in Switzerland is to capture FCEV market earlier by creating a small value chain through tight couplings such as international joint ventures and strategic alliances among its complementary partners. In the hydrogen mobility industry, where the establishment of the value chain is lagging at present, HMG is trying to increase its first mover advantage by capturing the future market in advance (Lieberman and Montgomery, 1988). At the same time, it is saving upfront investment by joining the loose couplings with partner companies.

4 Summary of HMG's green shift strategy and challenges post Covid-19

Currently, existing automakers have been facing an increasing pressure of the green shift in automotive industry. It does not seem that even Covid-19 is changing this trend of industry evolution. Currently, the delay in overall automobile production is not due to changes in electrification, but to a lack of supply of automotive semiconductors. Rather, investment for economic recovery is likely to go to new industries, not traditional ones in post Covid-19 world.

During this transition period of green shift, HMG has undergone a transformation from a follower to a first mover. We suggest HMG's emergent strategies, effective use of existing internal resources during the transition period, balancing the in-house development of core technologies and outsourcing complementary resources, and pioneering the future market by collaboration with external companies with saving first mover's investments should be significant factors in adapting smoothly to the green shift. What we have discussed on HMG's adaptive behaviors may provide a practical implication for existing automakers, including Japanese automakers that have a competitive advantage in HEVs to cope with this green shift.

Japan's automotive industry has an edge in decarbonization technology. Toyota and Honda, like HMG, have launched HEVs, PHEVs, BEVs and FCEVs. These automakers have concentrated on the production and sales of HEVs, which they have strengths in. For example, currently Toyota's HEVs account for about 20% of its global sales, and its sales are still strong. A significant increase in HEVs in new vehicle sales would be effective in meeting the CAFE regulations.

On the other hand, the strategy to focus on HEV adoption could not be enough to clear environmental regulations such as zero emission vehicle compulsory sales at a certain ratio or prohibiting the sale of conventional vehicles from some point in the future. In addition, the effectiveness of HEVs' response to green shifts will also change as the ratio of renewable energies in each country's power generation sources increases or the hydrogen economy ecosystem is built. Toyota and Honda may need to be prepared to flexibly change their priorities between HEVs, PHEVs, BEVs and FCEVs, depending on the changes in future environmental regulations, global eco-friendly car market trend and other environmental factors.

Therefore, flexible attitude that allows changes in eco-friendly car sales plans, sharing management resources for both conventional vehicles and eco-friendly vehicles and leveraging first mover's advantages, while saving first mover's investment derived from the case of HGM, can be significant for Japanese automakers to adapt to the green shift.

References

Choi, E. (2015). Hyundai's dynamics of styling-driven capability development: A historical analysis of the 1970s–1990s. *International Journal of Automotive Technology and Management*, 15(3), 292–310.

Chosun Biz. (2021). Last year EV sales increase 44%: Tesla first, HMG fourth. (March 11) (in Korean). https://biz.chosun.com/site/data/html_dir/2021/03/11/2021031101192.html (accessed April 28, 2021).

E-Daily News (2018). Intensifying competition for weight reduction: Aluminum emerging. (November 3) (in Korean). https://www.edaily.co.kr/news/read?newsId=01685926619402112&mediaCodeNo=257 (accessed April 28, 2021).

Hankyung. (2020). Hyundai invests 6 billion won: Acceleration of mobility. (December 10) (in Korean). https://www.hankyung.com/car/article/202012105104g (accessed April 28, 2021).

HMG. (2014). Hyundai-Kia's eco-drive acceleration: Do you know the "2020. 22. 2 project"? *HMG Journal*. (November 24) (in Korean). https://news.hmgjournal.com/Tech/Item/2020-22-2-project (accessed August 1, 2020).

HMG. (2020). Hydrogen/electric, Hyundai website. https://www.hyundai.com/kr/en/main, and Eco-friendly, Kia website. https://www.kia.com/kr/main.html (accessed August 1, 2020).

Inside EVs. (2020). Compare electric cars: EV range, specs, pricing & more. https://insideevs.com/reviews/344001/compare-evs/EVs (February 16). (accessed April 28, 2021).

Jo, H., Jeong, H. & Kim, C. (2016). Unpacking the 'black box' of a Korean big fast follower: Hyundai Motor Company's engineer-led production system. *Asian Journal of Technology Innovation*, 24(1), 53–77.

Ku, S. (2015). An introduction to Hyundai motor's growth and its factor analysis: Focusing on business systems. *Kyoto Management Review*, 24, 113–133. (in Japanese).

Kukmin Daily. (2021). Nexo defeats Mirai but Korean H2 economy has long way to go. (March 2) (in Korean). http://news.kmib.co.kr/article/view.asp?arcid=0015585078 (accessed April 28, 2021).

Lee, J. (2006). Management resources and organizational capacity building in developing enterprises. *Yamaguchi University Asian Economy Review*, 64(2), 44–55. (in Japanese).

Lee, J. (2013). Building global organizational capabilities of latecomer automakers: A case study of the Hyundai Motor Group. *Memories of Kyoto Tachibana University*, 39, 197–227. (in Japanese).

Lee, J. & Hirano, M. (2013). Pooling and learning in inter-organizational synergy management between car makers: Through comparison of Ford-Mazda with Hyundai-Kia. *The Annals of Japan Society for Applied Management*, 50, 13–23. (in Japanese).

Lieberman, M.B. & Montgomery, D.B. (1988). First-mover advantages. *Strategic Management Journal (Special Issue: Strategy Content Research)*, 9, 41–58.

Lim, J. (2010). *The endless challenge to quality: A study on the management spirit of the Hyundai Motor Group*, Korea Institute of Automotive Industry. (in Korean).

Maeil Business. (2020). Hyundai unveils four future business strategies: All production lines automated by 2040. (December 10) (in Korean). https://www.mk.co.kr/news/business/view/2020/12/1270471/ (accessed April 28, 2021).

Mizuno, J. (1997). *Automotive industry in Korea*, Institute of Developing Economies. (in Japanese).

Monthly Hydrogen Economy. (2019). Another six members join: Global News. (June 19) (in Korean). http://h2news.mediaon.co.kr/news/article.html?no=7619 (accessed April 28, 2021).

Nakanishi, T. (2018). *CASE Revolution: Automotive industry in 2030*, Nikkei Publishing Inc. (in Japanese).

Nikkei. (2020). Toyota confronts CASE. (January 11) (in Japanese).

Nikkei. (2021). Germany, France, and UK share up 7%, up 5 points last year, boosted by environmental regulations. (January 11) (in Japanese).

Shioji, H., Nakata, T., Tomiyama, E., Su, Y., Lee, T., Sun, F., Akaba, J., Noro, Y. & Inoue R. (2012). *Hyundai Motor's growth strategy*, Daily Automotive News (in Japanese).

Su, Y. (2014). Dynamics of the global knowledge network: A comparative analysis of Toyota motor corporation and Hyundai motor corporation. *Doctoral Dissertation of Tokyo University*, 1–228. (in Japanese).

Womack, J.P., Jones, D.T. & Ross, D. (1990). *The machine that changed the world*, Rawson Associates, New York.

5 Renewable energy for a sustainable future

Can Japan catch up?

Faith Hatani

1 Introduction

During the COVID-19 pandemic, the volatility of the fossil fuels market due to the stagnation of transport and other sectors, caused by preventive measures introduced for the pandemic, has contributed to the rapid growth of the renewable energy industry (IEA, 2021). Renewable energy refers to the energy that is generated from natural sources or processes that can constantly be replenished (e.g., solar, wind, hydropower, biomass, geothermal and ocean) (Shinn, 2018). While many businesses were hit hard by pandemic-related restrictions, the renewable energy industry has operated effectively and with even more resilience than other sectors (IRENA, 2020). Moreover, the increasing awareness of the need to tackle climate change has also accelerated the green transition across the world. Against this background, the *COVID-19 pandemic can be seen as a turning point for both countries and firms alike to take action to materialise* environmentally friendly economies based on renewable energies.

However, Japan is falling behind other major economies in terms of the market share of the renewable energy industry, as well as its utilisation of renewable energy sources. In the fiscal year 2019, the ratio of renewable energy in Japan's power sources was 18% (Agency for Natural Resources and Energy, 2021). If a traditional natural energy source, such as hydropower, is excluded, the share (comprising solar, wind, geothermal and biomass combined) was just over 10%, whereas the renewable energy ratio in Germany and the UK, for instance, was more than 30% in the same year (Agency for Natural Resources and Energy, 2021). Given these statistics, there is an urgent need for Japan to make renewable energy available for wider use by transforming its energy system and industries.

This chapter explores how Japanese firms have responded to the new competitive landscape of the renewable energy industry. Among renewable energy sources, this chapter will focus on solar power and wind power, especially offshore wind. This chapter then examines the strategies adopted by two leading Japanese companies that have been involved in these two types of renewable energy. Their activities are analysed in light of the global value chain (GVC) framework, especially the concept of "environmental upgrading". Subsequently,

DOI: 10.4324/9781003216049-6

this chapter outlines business implications that Japanese firms should take into account to ensure they make a positive contribution to sustainability.

2 Global value chains of renewable energy

The term "value chain" refers to the full range of activities carried out by various firms and workers in different locations, often across borders, to produce goods or services (Kaplinsky, 2004). Each value chain consists of intermediary phases such as design, production, assembly, marketing, delivery, maintenance and even disposal/recycling. The firm that coordinates and controls the functional integrations in a given chain is called the "lead firm" (Gereffi, 1999). The main dimensions of the GVC analysis include GVC upgrading, GVC governance and the institutional framework within which GVCs operate (Kano, 2018; Ponte, 2019), and the identification of different types of upgrading is the first step towards a better understanding of the value chain in question (Humphrey & Schmitz, 2002).

In the GVC research, various concepts have been developed to analyse the economic contribution and industrial competitiveness of value chains. With regard to sustainable development, however, the focus on traditional socioeconomic dimensions per se may be no longer adequate to examine a value chain's implications. It is imperative to ensure environmental protection alongside business growth, and this is particularly the case in the post-pandemic world. Business entities need to commit to post-pandemic recovery while promoting environmentally sustainable businesses, and a key concept of this theme is "environmental upgrading".

2.1 Environmental upgrading

In the GVC literature, upgrading refers to shifts that firms make in their activities by enhancing their competencies or entering a new market segment to increase their incomes and/or maintain their competitive edge (Humphrey & Schmitz, 2001). Traditionally, the analysis of GVC upgrading has focused on industrial upgrading (e.g., Gereffi, 1999; Humphrey & Schmitz, 2001). However, recent studies have paid more attention to the process of improving the environmental impact of activities in a value chain (Poulsen et al., 2018). De Marchi et al. (2013) define environmental upgrading as "the process by which economic actors move towards a production system that avoids or reduces environmental damage from their products, processes or managerial systems" (De Marchi et al., 2013; p. 65).

Drawing upon the types associated with industrial upgrading, three forms of environmental upgrading can be identified: (a) process improvement, by which firms achieve eco-efficiency by optimising their production systems or implementing more sophisticated technology; (b) product improvement, which is the development of more environmentally friendly product lines; and (c) organisational improvement, through which firms enhance their business and management to achieve (or by achieving) higher environmental standards and certifications (De Marchi et al., 2019). These three forms are not mutually exclusive but possibly have some overlaps. For instance, if a firm upgrades a product so that it is more environmentally friendly, its production system may also need to change. Firms may have different attitudes towards environmental upgrading, either proactively as part of their green growth strategy, or reactively in response to regulatory obligations or customer demands (Poulsen et al., 2018). To identify the form of environmental upgrading, several factors should be taken into account, such as the firm's motivation, its priority and the nature and degree of the change. In addition, the institutional setting of a given context is also a crucial factor because policies and regulations influence the norms and practices within and around each GVC (Ponte & Gibbon, 2005). This point is particularly important when we consider the business potentials of renewable energies in Japan.

3 Japan's renewable energy industry

Japan's energy policy is based on the concept of "3E+S", which refers to "energy security", "economic efficiency", "environmental protection" and "safety" (Agency for Natural Resources and Energy, 2020). However, Japan does not have an energy source that can adequately meet these objectives. The country relies heavily on the importation of oil and gas, and its self-sufficiency ratio of energy was 11.8% as of 2018, which meant it was ranked 34th of 37 Organisation for Economic Co-operation and Development nations (IEA, 2020a). In fact, during the winter of 2020–2021, Japan suffered a power shortage and a subsequent spike in electricity prices due to the turmoil of the global liquefied natural gas market.

Meanwhile, in the midst of the pandemic, the Japanese government made a carbon-neutral pledge, aiming to expand renewable energy as much as possible by 2050 in order to achieve net-zero greenhouse gas emissions (METI, 2020). As an island country with a notoriously scarce domestic production of fossil fuels (Moe, 2012), it is essential that Japan develops a range of energy types to generate an adequate supply of energy but in different proportions, the so-called "energy mix". To cope with the post-pandemic context, in which a bounce-back of economic activities and a stronger-than-ever demand for decarbonisation of energy are expected, Japan needs to stabilise its energy supply while promoting renewables.

Similar to other global industries, such as the automotive and information technology industries, the renewable energy sector has extensive value chains, including various actors that perform different functions across borders. Along with the rapid growth of the renewable energy market globally, large energy multinationals and their suppliers have been aggressively expanding their outreach, whereas the presence of Japanese firms in the renewable energy market has been weakening in recent years. The following sections examine how Japanese firms performed during the pandemic time.

3.1 Solar power

Solar power is one of the most widely used renewable energy sources in Japan, although its contribution to the country's primary energy supply is still small – only 6% in 2018 (Agency for Natural Resources and Energy, 2021). Some large Japanese manufacturers began developing solar photovoltaic modules – commonly known as solar panels – shortly after the oil shocks in the 1970s. Backed by government incentives, these companies steadily increased their market share over time until the early 2000s. However, as foreign solar energy manufacturers began to expand, the market share of Japanese firms rapidly declined. The global solar power market is now dominated by Chinese producers, along with companies from Canada and South Korea. The same players are also dominating the Japanese market (Table 5.1).

In fact, Japanese solar panel producers had lost their competitiveness even before the COVID-19 outbreak. For instance, Mitsubishi Electric halted production of its own-brand solar panels just before the pandemic struck in 2020. Moreover, in early 2021, Panasonic, a Japanese electronics giant, also announced that it would exit the solar battery market as a result of fierce price competition from foreign firms, especially those based in China. While many Japanese solar panel manufacturers left the business, Kyocera maintained sixth slot in the Japanese market. Yet, if Kyocera wishes to remain in the solar power market, it needs to find a way of upgrading its solar business amidst intense international competition.

3.1.1 Kyocera group

Kyocera has a long history in the field of solar power generation. Although its main business is the production of electronic devices and industrial components, the company began its solar business in 1975, just after the first oil shock. As a pioneer in this field, Kyocera has orchestrated the value chain of its solar power business, involving system design, equipment procurement, production, construction, operations and maintenance. Similar to other solar power firms in

Table 5.1 Top solar panel producers in 2019 (by shipments)

Global market			*Japanese market*		
Rank	*Company*	*Headquarters*	*Rank*	*Company*	*Headquarters*
1	Jinko Solar	China	1	Jinko Solar	China
2	JA Solar	China	2	Canadian Solar	Canada
3	Trina Solar	China	3	Hanwha Q Cells	South Korea
4	LONGi Solar	China	4	Trina Solar	China
5	Canadian Solar	Canada	5	JA solar	China
6	Hanwha Q Cells	South Korea	6	Kyocera	Japan
7	Risen Energy	China	7	Solar Frontier	Japan

Source: Sylvia (2020) and Nikkei (2020a).

Japan, however, Kyocera also *suffered* historic *losses* in 2019 and 2020 due to the Japanese government cutting the subsidy, as well as the harsh price war with Chinese firms, which had intensified by that time (ITmedia, 2021).

During the pandemic, between 2020 and 2021, Kyocera began a series of strategic collaborations with other Japanese firms. At the outset, in April 2020, Kyocera merged its subsidiaries, KYOCERA Solar Corporation (KSC) and KYOCERA Communication Systems (KCCS). Before this merger, KSC mainly engaged in the sale and construction of solar panels as well as in after-service, while KCCS specialised in information system integration. In this merger, KCCS was a surviving entity and retained its corporate name. In December 2020, the new KCCS played a key role in establishing a service contract with Tokyo Century Corporation and Kawasaki Heavy Industries (KHI). Tokyo Century is one of the largest leasing companies in Japan, and the aim of this tie-up is to provide comprehensive support services for industrial power generation to KHI. This joint project has been supported by Japan's Ministry of the Environment as one of the supply chain reform projects for the realisation of a carbon-free society (KCCS, 2020).

Then, in January 2021, Kyocera's other subsidiary, Kyocera EPA, began a joint business with NTT Telecon (NTT-TC). They will provide a remote meter-reading and monitoring service of solar power generation equipment (NTT TC, 2021). Kyocera EPA's main task in this joint business is to provide corporate clients with solar power generation systems, while NTT-TC will supply sensors to remotely monitor the operation of solar power generators and the usage of solar power. This joint work will enable Kyocera to provide more value-added services in the solar power sector.

The third collaboration was instigated by the parent company, Kyocera itself, with a start-up, Digital Grid. Digital Grid originated in the "electricity network innovation" course at Tokyo University. In February 2021, it launched an experiment to demonstrate new renewable trading systems (Kyocera, 2021). One of the ambitions of this joint project is to achieve 100% renewable energy. Moreover, through this project, Kyocera aims to achieve the Kyocera Group's long-term environmental goals (Digital Grid, 2020).

3.2 Offshore wind power

Wind energy exhibits the highest potential among renewable energy sources in the years to come. Wind power comprises two major types: onshore wind and offshore wind. In the international market, while onshore wind experienced some delay to projects due to COVID-19-related restrictions, the pandemic did not significantly impact the offshore wind market (GWEC, 2020). Most deals for offshore wind were executed as scheduled across the major markets, such as Europe and China, because offshore wind projects tend to have longer project timelines (IEA, 2020b).

Offshore wind energy also has high potential in Japan because of the country's geographical characteristics. As a mountainous island nation, Japan has a long coastline while there is limited land space suitable for onshore wind power generation. Despite this, the offshore wind industry is largely underdeveloped in Japan because of its rigid regional monopoly system for electricity supply. Although the Japanese government launched the liberalisation of the electricity market in 1995, progress was rather gradual. It was accelerated after the Fukushima nuclear disaster in 2011, and subsequently a full liberalisation of the electricity retail market in 2016. Nonetheless, Japan's offshore wind market is largely lagging behind other major economies. Notably, although Japan's offshore wind industry is still in its early stage, foreign firms have already taken control of the majority of the market share (Table 5.2).

Because of the decarbonisation targets set by many countries, there has been a global shift towards renewable energy in recent years. Against this background, foreign firms have been rapidly expanding their offshore wind business internationally. Moreover, given the recovery of industries after the pandemic, the demand for electricity is expected to increase. Before the COVID-19 pandemic, however, Hitachi and Japan Steel Works, which used to be the major players in the offshore wind business in Japan, announced that they were halting their production of wind turbines. Another Japanese firm, Mitsubishi Heavy Industries (MHI), found itself at a crossroads during the pandemic.

3.2.1 Mitsubishi heavy industries

MHI is one of the major engineering/industrial machinery producers in Japan. It entered the wind power business in the early 1980s by installing the country's first commercial wind power equipment. Since then, the company has delivered more than 4,200 units, equivalent to about 4.4 million kilowatts, in Japan and abroad (MHI company webpage, n.d.). Although MHI had previously produced onshore wind turbines, it exited the onshore wind market after a prolonged lawsuit against General Electric in the US between 2008 and 2013 (Smith, 2013). In the subsequent decade, MHI has specialised in offshore wind power.

Table 5.2 Top wind turbine producers in 2019 (by wind capacity)

Global market			*Japanese market*		
Rank	*Company*	*Headquarters*	*Rank*	*Company*	*Headquarters*
1	Vestas	Denmark	1	General Electric	US
2	Siemens Gamesa	Spain	2	Enercon	Germany
3	Goldwind	China	3	Vestas	Denmark
4	General Electric	US	4	Hitachi	Japan
5	Envision	China	5	Siemens Gamesa	Spain
6	Mingyang	China	6	MHI	Japan
7	Windey	China	7	Japan Steel Works	Japan

Source: BloombergNEF (2020) and Nikkei (2020a).

Note: *The rankings are based on data by fully commissioned wind capacity in both onshore and offshore wind. The data of Vestas do not include MHI-Vestas' capacity, because organisations must own more than 50% of a subsidiary to receive credit.*

In 2014, MHI formed a 50-50 joint venture (JV), MHI Vestas Offshore Wind (MHI-Vestas, hereafter) in Denmark, with a Danish offshore company Vestas. At that time, Vestas was on the verge of bankruptcy with a severe financial deficit (Johnsen, 2012). MHI's investment in Denmark to form MHI-Vestas was a significant remedy for Vestas, and also a chance for MHI to facilitate technology transfer from Vestas (Nishioka, 2020). Thus, forming MHI-Vestas was a new opportunity for both MHI and Vestas to boost their offshore wind business together internationally. Within six years of its establishment, MHI-Vestas became one of the major suppliers in the global offshore wind market.

However, when COVID-19 began to have a negative effect on the world economy, MHI was in a very different situation to that which it had enjoyed at the beginning of the JV. While MHI-Vestas thrived in an international market, MHI was unable to adequately absorb core competence from Vestas through the JV. Although MHI and Vestas had an equal ownership share, the technological and managerial decision-making remained with Vestas (Nikkei, 2020c). Furthermore, during the pandemic, MHI's non-energy business was affected by pandemic-related restrictions. As a diversified engineering conglomerate, MHI has other businesses, such as aircraft parts and shipbuilding/repair, and they were impacted by a sharp fall in demand (Nikkei, 2020b). This weakened the company's financial status. In this context, at the end of 2020, Vestas acquired MHI's share of MHI-Vestas. This signified MHI's withdrawal from the production and research and development (R&D) of wind turbines.

In the meantime, during the pandemic, the Japanese government made a step forward in the development of offshore wind by launching offshore wind auctions (GWEC, 2020). Eyeing the potential of Japan's offshore wind market, in 2021 Vestas formed another new JV with MHI, called MHI Vestas Japan Co. Ltd., in Tokyo. Vestas holds a 30% share while MHI has the 70% majority. Nonetheless, in this JV, MHI will primarily be in charge of selling and marketing for Vestas' wind power products without being involved in the production and R&D of wind turbines (Plechinger, 2021). Even though the impact of COVID-19 on the global offshore wind market has been limited, the pandemic period brought twists and turns for MHI, which caused the company to make a critical decision on its offshore wind business.

4 Strategic actions and prospects for environmental upgrading

Kyocera and MHI were once key Japanese players in their respective segments in the renewable energy industry. However, as outlined in Sections 3.1 and 3.2 above, both companies are facing the challenging situations in the new competitive landscape. Since solar power and offshore wind have different business contexts with different competitors, it is not surprising that Kyocera and MHI have taken different approaches to the renewable energy business. Nevertheless, there are some common issues that they need to address; one such issue concerns the question of what type of environmental upgrading they might have achieved so far or could potentially achieve in the post-pandemic world. In line with the concept of environmental upgrading, Table 5.3 summarises the actions taken by these two companies during the pandemic.

4.1 Kyocera: striving to become a system integrator

Kyocera's overall strategy appears to involve active collaborations with other Japanese firms. Initially, Kyocera consolidated its subsidiaries, KCCS and KSC, to combine their businesses of information system integration and solar power generation. This can be seen as an attempt at an *organisational improvement* that constitutes one of the three aspects of environmental upgrading. The new KCCS business consists of four main domains: information and communications technology, telecommunications engineering, environment and energy engineering and management consulting. This enables KCCS to provide its clients with a more comprehensive "one-stop service" drawn from Kyocera's management system. The challenge for Kyocera will be how it can increase its customer base and implement higher environmental standards in a wider market.

In terms of *product improvement*, Kyocera has shifted its focus from manufacturing solar panels to providing services for solar power generation. In the joint business with NTT-TC, Kyocera EPA leases solar power generation facilities to corporate clients, while NTT-TC will monitor the clients' electricity consumption and provide the data to them. By doing so, Kyocera EPA and NTT-TC aim to achieve a more efficient supply and usage of solar power (NTT TC, 2021). NTT-TC regards this as a part of their open innovation effort. Open innovation refers to the purposeful utilisation of knowledge exchange to accelerate internal

Table 5.3 Typology of the two firms' strategic actions during the pandemic period (2020–2021)

Types of upgrading	*Product improvement*	*Process improvement*	*Organisational change*
Kyocera (Solar power)	Begins remote services (via Kyocera EPA, with NTT-TC) Begins new services for industrial power generation (via KCCS with Tokyo Century)	Launching renewable P2P power trading systems (with Digital Grid)	Consolidation of subsidiaries (KCCS and KSC)
MHI (Offshore wind)	Withdrawal from production	Not known	Dissolved MHI-Vestas (in Denmark) Formed MHI-Vestas Japan (in Japan)

innovation and expand its market (Chesbrough et al., 2006). Similarly, the contractual agreement between KCCS and Tokyo Century is also this type of effort to combine both companies' existing resources and create a new value, although an aspect of technological innovation in this tie-up is rather limited. Still, their joint businesses can potentially contribute to the development of environmentally friendly service products in Japan. However, Kyocera's business tie-ups for solar power are, to date, primarily with Japanese firms targeting the Japanese market only, with little interaction with foreign entities. In a way, it is quite limited in terms of open innovation. Thus, it is uncertain to what extent they can maximise knowledge exchange to achieve further product improvement.

Kyocera's joint experiment with Digital Grid can be seen as a form of *process improvement.* This endeavour is an application of Kyocera's solar power batteries and Digital Grid's platform to explore the possibility of establishing a new supply system of renewable energy. The experimentation is an important step to optimise power trading systems in Japan. However, the main challenge for Kyocera is how an optimal system of solar power can be disseminated to make it an industry standard. Kyocera's recent strategy demonstrates its ambition to establish itself as a system integrator of the solar power business. However, while the international market of solar power still shows a growth potential, the Japanese market for solar panels has somehow already been saturated. In addition, solar power facilities have raised concerns about the environmental impact, such as land degradation. Given these factors, further innovation is indispensable to not only revive the market but also to achieve an impactful environmental upgrading.

4.2 MHI: environmental upgrading or downgrading?

During the seven years of the JV with Vestas, MHI had, in theory, direct access to Vestas' expertise in wind turbine manufacturing and sustainable energy solutions. Even during the pandemic period, MHI-Vestas completed the installation of a new turbine model at a floating wind project in Scotland. Floating offshore wind typifies *product improvement* of environmental upgrading; floating wind turbines are potentially more environmentally friendly and efficient because they can produce more energy with higher wind speed far offshore with greater spatial diversification than bottom-fixed turbines. Moreover, in 2020, MHI-Vestas reached an agreement for local assembly in Taiwan. It is planned to assemble power conversion modules for offshore wind projects in Taiwan in collaboration with Taiwanese firms (MHI-Vestas, 2020). This deal can be seen as a form of *process improvement.* It is an important step not only to promote sustainable localisation, but also to encourage knowledge transfer in Taiwan and facilitate the green transition internationally. Unfortunately, however, the dissolution of MHI-Vestas implies that MHI has lost these opportunities for further environmental upgrading.

Regarding *organisational improvement*, which can be any form of change to a company's managerial system or function in the value chain to realise higher environmental standards, MHI can maintain the partnership with Vestas through the new JV in Japan. However, it should be noted that MHI's main function in the new JV involves the sale of Vestas' products and technical support in the Japanese market. Having withdrawn from wind turbine production, MHI is now relying on Vestas for R&D of new products in wind power business. Thus, the managerial initiative that MHI can adopt to promote environmental upgrading in wind energy may be limited. Given these aspects, one would even argue that MHI appears to be downgrading rather than upgrading its contribution to environmental sustainability.

Besides its relationships with Vestas and the offshore wind business, however, there has been a notable move towards environmental upgrading at MHI. In 2020, the company announced that it would issue its first green bond, which can be utilised to fund projects related to renewable energies. To issue the green bond, MHI obtained a *second-party opinion* from Sustainalytics, a leading rating company in the field of environmental, social and corporate governance performance, which endorsed its conformity to the International Capital Market Association's Green Bond Principles and the Green Bond Guidelines of the Japan's Ministry of the Environment (Kudo, 2020). Environmental upgrading through organisational improvement such as this is indeed a key area where a large company like MHI can contribute effectively to promote green investment. Yet, a complexity at MHI is that, as a diversified firm, it has been operating in the oil and gas industry and also businesses related to nuclear power generation. While it might be necessary for MHI to maintain these businesses to respond to Japan's need for multiple energy sources to attain a realistic energy mix, a challenge for MHI will be how it will make decisions on which business the company will prioritise and how it will allocate resources to promote a comprehensive environmental upgrading in the coming years.

4.3 Opportunities and challenges ahead

Certainly, the business environments of solar power and offshore wind are not identical. The cases of Kyocera and MHI only exemplify how their renewable energy businesses have come through the pandemic in different ways. Nonetheless, there are some common issues that Japanese renewable energy companies need to take into account with regard to environmental upgrading. One key issue is the company's positioning in a renewable value chain. Today, Japanese firms are barely playing the leading role in global renewable energy value chains. Japanese firms should consider what business function they will engage within a given value chain and on which product segment they aim to focus in order to outperform competitors.

Japanese firms appear to have started pursuing different paths, depending on their core competence. For instance, while Kyocera is still in the solar power market, the company seems to be aiming to become a system integrator rather than enlarging its solar panel production. Another notable example in the solar power business may be Sharp, which is focusing more on solar batteries for home electricity and electric vehicles. Given the intensive cost competition with foreign solar panel producers, together with the uncertainty of the growth potential of Japan's solar power market, their strategic moves may be reasonable albeit less ambitious in terms of global reach.

However, in the offshore wind industry, effective positioning in a value chain is a more urgent task for Japanese firms. Japanese manufacturers are no longer active in the production of wind turbines. One of the options for Japanese firms will be to specialise in related services such as the sale and marketing of wind power solutions, as MHI does now. However, if MHI's function remains limited to these functions, it will be difficult for the company to take meaningful leadership in environmental upgrading. Toshiba, which has recently entered into partnership with General Electric's division, GE Renewable Energy, also exhibits a similar position in the value chain. Alternatively, another possibility is to strengthen a position in a value chain as a supplier of key components. Some Japanese firms are pursuing this strategy by expanding their supply parts business. For example, NSK Ltd., a large manufacturer of bearings, has been increasing the production of bearings for rotor shafts of wind turbines, while Toray Industries Inc. supplies carbon fibre materials for wind turbine blades (Nikkei, 2021). By playing a key supplier role, they could continue being in charge of *product* and *process improvements* for environmental upgrading.

A drawback is that, in most value chains, suppliers' market expansion and upgrading opportunities tend to hinge on a lead firm's competitiveness and power in a given chain. This is one reason why Japanese firms' exit from the production of key products relating to some renewable energies, such as solar panels and wind turbines, is a serious issue for Japan's renewable energy industry. Yet, since the renewable energy industry consists of large and highly complex value chains, there should be various new business opportunities that Japanese firms can explore and exploit. It is imperative, and urgent, for Japanese firms to identify their optimal position and target market to make a positive contribution to sustainability in the long term.

5 Implications

Drawn from the concept of environmental upgrading in the GVC framework, this chapter has considered Japanese companies' strategies for renewable energies. Despite the prolonged COVID-19 pandemic that has affected many companies in a variety of industries, the global renewable energy industry, especially with regard to solar power and offshore wind, has maintained a steady growth. With an increasing awareness of the need to tackle climate change, together with the anticipated post-pandemic economic boom, renewable energies are key areas for firms not only to make profits but also to contribute to sustainable growth. To achieve these, environmental upgrading should be an integral aspect of any business strategy.

Although this chapter has focused on an overall strategy for environmental upgrading, other factors, such as innovation to commercialise new technologies at a firm level, inter-firm relationships at a network level and regulatory factors at a national level, are all important, and they interact with each other in the complex structure of the renewable energy value chains. For instance, solar batteries and floating offshore wind can be seen as potential market segments, which Japanese firms can exploit to a larger extent in the future (Ministry of Economy, Trade and Industry, 2020). However, foreign firms have also been actively targeting these renewable energy businesses and some of these international competitors already have an established competitive advantage; Japanese firms need to envisage their strategies and take urgent action to compete or collaborate with them. At the same time, policy reform and government incentives are essential to improve business environments in Japan and facilitate companies' efforts. There are numerous topics that further research could investigate in the Japanese context.

Although Japan was once known for its competitiveness, especially in manufacturing, this is becoming a thing of the past in some industries, and the renewable energy industry poses a question for Japanese companies in both domestic and international markets. Japan is, in fact, reaching the turning point in relation to its sustainable future. Given this, it is not only the pandemic crisis but also the race for sustainability in the post-pandemic world that will be the real challenge for Japanese businesses.

References

Agency for Natural Resources and Energy, Japan. (2020). 日本のエネルギー 2020年度版. https://www.enecho.meti.go.jp/about/pamphlet/energy2020/ (accessed February 3, 2021).

Agency for Natural Resources and Energy, Japan. (2021). Japan's energy 2020. https://www.enecho.meti.go.jp/en/category/brochures/pdf/japan_energy_2020.pdf (accessed February 3, 2021).

BloombergNEF. (2020). Vestas still rules turbine market, but challengers are closing in. (February 18). https://about.bnef.com/blog/vestas-still-rules-turbine-market-but-challengers-are-closing-in/ (accessed April 30, 2021).

Chesbrough, H., Vanhaverbeke, W., & West, J. (Eds.). (2006). *Open innovation*. Oxford University Press, Oxford, UK.

De Marchi, V., Di Maria, E., & Micelli, S. (2013). Environmental strategies, upgrading and competitive advantage in global value chains. *Business Strategy and the Environment*, 22(1), 62–72.

De Marchi, V., Di Maria, E., Krishnan, A., & Ponte, S. (2019). Environmental upgrading in global value chains. In S. Ponte, G. Gereffi, & G. Raj-Reichert (Eds.). *The handbook on global value chains* (pp. 310–323). Elgar online. https://www.elgaronline.com/view/edcoll/9781788113762/9781788113762.00027.xml?rskey=tT16xf&result=2 (accessed April 30, 2021).

Digital Grid Corporation. (2020). RE100 を目指す、再生可能エネルギーを利用した 相対（P2P）電力取引について [Press release, December 9]. https://www.digitalgrid.com/pdf/article201209.pdf (accessed April 30, 2021).

General Electric. (2021). Press release: GE Renewable Energy and Toshiba announce strategic partnership agreement on offshore wind in Japan. (May 11). https://www.ge.com/news/press-releases/ge-renewable-energy-and-toshiba-announce-strategic-partnership-agreement-on-offshore-wind-japan (accessed May 21, 2021).

Gereffi, G. (1999). International trade and industrial upgrading in the apparel commodity chain. *Journal of International Economics*, 48(1), 37–70.

Global Wind Energy Council (GWEC). (2020). Global offshore wind report 2020. https://gwec.net/global-offshore-wind-report-2020/ (accessed September 8, 2020).

International Energy Agency (IEA). (2020a). World energy balances: Overview. https://www.iea.org/reports/world-energy-balances-overview (accessed March 28, 2021).

IEA. (2020b). Renewables 2020. https://www.iea.org/reports/renewables-2020 (accessed March 28, 2021).

IEA. (2021). Global energy review: CO2 emissions in 2020. https://www.iea.org/articles/global-energy-review-co2-emissions-in-2020 (accessed March 28, 2021).

International Renewable Energy Agency (IRENA). (2020). The post-COVID recovery: An agenda for resilience, development and equality. https://www.irena.org/publications/2020/Jun/Post-COVID-Recovery (accessed February 3, 2021).

ITmedia (2021). パナソニックの太陽電池生産終了　国内各社に逆風　システム開発で活路. (February 2). https://www.itmedia.co.jp/news/articles/2102/02/news063.html (accessed April 5, 2021).

Humphrey, J., & Schmitz, H. (2001). Governance in global value chains. *IDS Bulletin*, 32(3), 19–29.

Humphrey, J., & Schmitz, H. (2002). How does insertion in global value chains affect upgrading in industrial clusters? *Regional Studies*, 36(9), 1017–1027.

Johnsen, M. (2012). Vestas på randen af konkurs. (June 11). https://www.wind-watch.org/news/2012/06/12/vestas-pa-randen-af-konkurs-vestas-on-the-brink-of-bankruptcy/ (accessed September 10, 2020).

Kano, L. (2018). Global value chain governance: A relational perspective. *Journal of International Business Studies*, 49, 684–705.

Kaplinsky, R. (2004). Spreading the gains from globalization: What can be learned from value-chain analysis?, *Problems of Economic Transition*, 47(2), 74–115.

Kudo, S. (2020). 三菱重工が初のグリーンボンド、再エネ・水素を強化. (November 2). https://project.nikkeibp.co.jp/ms/atcl/19/news/00001/01272/?ST=msb (accessed April 23, 2021).

KYOCERA Communication Systems Co., Ltd. (KCCS). (2020). 「脱炭素社会の実現」に向けた産業用自家発電サポートサービス契約の締結について [Press release, December 17]. https://www.kccs.co.jp/news/release/2020/1217/ (accessed April 20, 2021).

Kyocera Corporation. (2021). Kyocera and Digital Grid begin joint demonstration of renewable peer-to-peer power [Press release, February 18]. https://global.kyocera.com/news/2021/0207_mawe.html (accessed April 20, 2021).

MHI Vestas Offshore Wind A/S. (2020). MHI Vestas secures footprint in Taiwan with waterside manufacturing facility. https://mhivestasoffshore.com/mhi-vestas-secures-footprint-in-taiwan-with-waterside-manufacturing-facility/ (accessed April 22, 2021).

Ministry of Economy, Trade and Industry, Japan. (2020). 2050年カーボンニュートラルに伴うグリーン成長 戦略: 資料1. https://www.meti.go.jp/press/2020/12/20201225012/20201225012-1.pdf (accessed February 3, 2021).

Ministry of Economy, Trade and Industry (METI), Japan. (2020). 2050年カーボンニュートラルに伴うグリーン成長戦略. https://www.meti.go.jp/press/2020/12/20201225012/20201225012.html (accessed April 1, 2021).

Mitsubishi Heavy Industries Group (MHI). (n.d.) 風力発電プラント. https://www.mhi.com/jp/products/energy/wind_turbine_plant.html (accessed March 22, 2021).

Moe, E. (2012). Vested interests, energy efficiency and renewables in Japan. *Energy Policy*, 40, 260–273.

Nikkei. (2020a). 再エネ外資、日本市場席巻 洋上風力や太陽光パネル. (November 7). https://www.nikkei.com/article/DGXMZO65954220W0A101C2EA5000/?unlock=1. (accessed November 10, 2020).

Nikkei. (2020b). 三菱重工 新型コロナで航空、船舶修繕事業に異変. (May 12). https://www.nikkei.com/article/DGXMZO58871650Y0A500C2000000/ (accessed March 19, 2021).

Nikkei. (2020c). 三菱重工、洋上風力開発から「撤退」自前路線を転換. (December 13). https://www.nikkei.com/nkd/company/article/?DisplayType=1&ng=DGXMZO66153040S0A111C2X13000&scode=7011 (accessed April 19, 2021).

Nikkei. (2021). 風力、日本は部材に活路. (March 23). https://www.nikkei.com/article/DGKKZO70220990S1A320C2TJ2000/ (accessed April 19, 2021).

Nishioka, A. (2020). 三菱重工、洋上風力開発から「撤退」自前路線を転換. (November 13). https://www.nikkei.com/nkd/company/article/?DisplayType=1&ng=DGXMZO66153040S0A111C2X13000&scode=7011 (accessed April 19, 2021).

NTT Telecon Co. Ltd. (NTT TC). (2021). 京セラEPA合同会社との協業による 太陽光発電量遠隔検針・発電設備監視サービスの提供開始について [News release, January 26]. https://www.ntt-tc.co.jp/2021/01/post.html (accessed April 19, 2021).

Plechinger, M. (2021). MHI og Vestas etablerer joint venture. (February 2). https://energiwatch.dk/Energinyt/Renewables/article12731491.ece (accessed April 19, 2021).

Ponte, S., & Gibbon, P. (2005). Quality standards, conventions and the governance of global value chains. *Economy and Society*, 34(1), 1–31.

Poulsen, R. T., Ponte, S., & Sornn-Friese, H. (2018). Environmental upgrading in global value chains: The potential and limitations of ports in the greening of maritime transport. *Geoforum*, 89, 83–92.

Shinn, L. (2018). Renewable energy: The clean fact. (June 15). https://www.nrdc.org/stories/renewable-energy-clean-facts#sec-whatis (accessed April 19, 2021).

Smith, P. (2013). GE settles five-year legal struggle with MHI. (December 16). https://www.windpowermonthly.com/article/1224869/ge-settles-five-year-legal-struggle-mhi (accessed April 19, 2021).

Sylvia, T. (2020). Jinko Solar the world's biggest module provider again in 2019. (February 12). https://www.pv-magazine.com/2020/02/12/jinko-solar-the-worlds-biggest-module-provider-again-in-2019/ (accessed April 19, 2021).

6 Current status and issues of metal 3D printing business in Japan

Yukako Harata and Nobutaka Odake

1 Introduction

1.1 New manufacturing with additive manufacturing

The worldwide spread of COVID-19 has led to lockdowns and states of emergency in the world, which has had a major impact not only on people's health and livelihoods, but also on the economy. In the manufacturing industry, there were cases where production and logistics functions were suspended, the supply chains were disrupted, and factories were forced to stop operations. The value of 3D printing/additive manufacturing (AM) has been reaffirmed and is accelerating changes in business models. AM is used to manufacture medical equipment, such as respirators, which are in serious shortage, swabs for virus testing, and personal protective equipment (PPE), such as medical masks and face shields (MONOist, 2021). The integration of product development and information technology based on a design philosophy that focuses on the connection of devices via networks has led to the development of "connected factories" or "smart factories" that utilize cyber physical systems (CPS). AM is one of the tools used to promote digital manufacturing and stands out from other digital technologies as it goes into the processing method itself (Tech Factory, 2021). The American Society for Testing and Materials (ASTM International), one of the world's largest standards organizations, defines AM as "a process of joining materials to make objects from 3D model data, usually layer upon layer, as opposed to subtractive manufacturing methods". AM makes it possible to create unibody structures and custom products of complex shapes, reduce modeling cycle times, and improve yields. In AM, the shape is created by placing and joining materials, so there is no problem of interference between the tool and the part in the removal process or between the mold and the part in the forming process, and any shape can be processed. This is one of the features of AM, which is the rapidity with which parts can be processed from shape data without complicated processing (Niino, 2020). Also, AM is expected to be the core manufacturing technology for mass customization. Compared to conventional mass production using molds, AM enables flexible and rapid high-mix, low-volume production without molds. Because of these features, AM is expected to change the existing business

DOI: 10.4324/9781003216049-7

model for the industry (Rayna and Striukova, 2016). AM has made a presence with the COVID-19 pandemic in the face of supply chain vulnerabilities. As the flow of decentralization of parts suppliers and production bases accelerates, direct manufacturing by AM becomes an effective means for a flexible production system as needed (MONOist, 2021). ASTM International classifies AM as shown in Table 6.1. In this study, we focus on the field of metal AM, which has been growing rapidly.

1.2 Metal additive manufacturing

In the field of metal AM, the market has evolved from a prototype and single-product market to a mass production (i.e., small- and medium-volume production) market. Although the market for metal AM products is not necessarily large yet, these are expected to be used in a wide range of fields such as aerospace, medical, and automotive (Table 6.2). In Japan, efforts are underway to produce individual products with complex shapes, particularly for molds and medical parts (MONOist, 2020). Aluminum alloys are widely used as materials, but it is expected that the use of titanium alloys will expand in the future

Table 6.1 Classification of Additive Manufacturing (AM)

Process type	*Process methodology*
Sheet Lamination (SHL)	AM process in which sheets of material are bonded to form an object
Vat Photopolymerization (VPP)	AM process in which liquid photopolymer in a vat is selectively cured using light-activated polymerization
Material Extrusion (MEX)	AM process in which material is selectively dispensed through a nozzle or orifice
Binder Jetting (BJT)	AM process in which a liquid bonding agent is selectively deposited to join powder materials
Material Jetting (MJT)	AM process in which droplets of built material are selectively deposited
Powder Bed Fusion (PBF)	AM process in which thermal energy selectively fuses regions of a powder bed
Directed Energy Deposition (DED)	AM process in which focused thermal energy is used to fuse materials by melting as they are being deposited

Table 6.2 Market for AM products

Industry	*Application examples*
Aerospace	Weight reduction, complex shape
Medical	Custom products
Automotive	Custom parts, spare parts, reduced storage, cost for molds
Machinery/facilities	Difficult-to-form materials
Railway/logistics	Maintenance or spare parts, service business using warehouses or delivery bases

(ODEC CO., LTD., 2021). It is expected that the combination of technological innovation in fabrication methods and the diversification and sophistication of materials will lead to a wider application of AM in end products (The Nikkei, 2020).

The number of machines sold in Japan has been on an upward trend since 2012, with a remarkable 180% year-on-year increase in 2017 (TSC Foresight 32, 2019). In Europe and the United States, major manufacturers are acquiring and spinning off service bureaus (companies engaged in contract processing using 3D printers) and moving to a full-scale mass production system. In Japan, the number of service bureaus has increased rapidly in recent years. In case it is difficult to own the machines due to the installation cost or space, utilizing the modeling service by the service bureaus could be effective (MONOist, 2021). Among the methods listed in Table 6.1, binder jetting (BJT), powder bed fusion (PBF), and directed energy deposition (DED) are mainly used for metal AM. In the past, PBF and DED were the main methods used, but in recent years, BJT has also attracted attention which is suitable for mass production. In BJT, the powder bed is sprayed with resin to produce compacts, which are then dewaxed and sintered. Because the powder bed is used, the flowability, spreadability, and filling properties of the powder are important. These factors affect the density of the compact and the final sintered product (Kyogoku and Ikeshoji, 2017).

The most important aspects of metal AM are design, materials, and machines. Design issues include topology optimization, customization, design of highly functional geometries, and exploitation of the unique alloy structure of AM. The design for AM (DfAM) involves determining the machine and materials, stacking direction and conditions, and using different methods and components. In addition to these design capabilities, the service bureaus must also consider the total process design, including pre- and post-processing design. In terms of materials, the challenges include powder modification, compounding, granulation, powder manufacturing, and powder bed formation. In addition to the high level of complexity of the fabrication technology, the high cost of the machines is one of the factors raising barriers to market entry (Matsushita, 2019). In addition, there are many factors that increase the running cost, such as the cost of materials, the power consumption during fabrication, and the installation and maintenance costs of related software (Tech Factory, 2020).

2 Focus on the service bureaus

Many service bureaus provide services based on 3D computer-aided design (CAD) data brought in by their customers. The most important factors that determine the performance of a model are the modeling conditions such as the energy output, scanning speed, modeling trajectory, temperature in the modeling chamber, and powder spreading conditions (Kyogoku and Ikeshoji, 2017). The difficulty of metal AM is much higher than that of resin, and there are many non-automated areas where the engineers have to predict the thermal deformation from their experiences and set the forming conditions (MONOist, 2019).

Kyogoku and Ikeshoji (2017) pointed out that it is important to find the optimum conditions for producing a high-quality object, and that the optimum laser powder and scanning speed, optimum scanning pitch, and stacking pitch should be considered for each fabrication. It is also important to keep track of many parameters during the actual fabrication process, and this constitutes the know-how of each company. Because the shapes and properties that can be formed vary, depending on the performance of the equipment and the characteristics of the powder, it is desirable to be able to fully grasp and accumulate modeling data and recipes that have been handled by the company and utilize these when forming other products.

A service bureau can improve the quality and range of the services that can be developed by taking advantage of its position as a "brokerage" company connecting users, designers, and manufacturers, and by building a "library" that stocks and utilizes modeling data and recipe information. There are also service bureaus that develop more advanced services by combining technologies and external resources cultivated in existing businesses. However, some machine manufacturers in Europe sign maintenance contracts with their customers and provide them with the optimal modeling condition recipes for the powder materials they use or sell condition recipes for each material (TSC Foresight 32, 2019). In some cases, the recipes are sold at high prices (Watari et al., 2020) or restrictions are placed on the machine, and the condition parameters cannot be set freely (TSC Foresight 32, 2019). These make it difficult to conduct original development research. While there is a lack of openness in terms of intellectual property, it is important for service bureaus to consider the knowledge of recipes as a company asset and to practice "retention" and "retrieval" in the organizational memory process, as described by Walsh and Ungson (1991). The business that utilizes the knowledge accumulated via such networks is now becoming a mainstream. With regard to the data utilization via such networks, Hashiguchi et al. (2017) discussed the case of applying AM to printed circuit production, concluding that the local cloud production method, which collects operational status data and product data from various production sites on a single platform, is a production method that can be expected to improve efficiency with machines. In addition, as shown by Taki (2020), "AM as a service" has also been proposed, in which 3D data are exchanged via a network, and on-demand modeling is performed, and the products are delivered. At the moment, however, engineers who are familiar with AM make various adjustments based on their experience, so it is still difficult for anyone to create a model without failure. As pointed out by Niino (2020), AM is not just a processing technology, but a "system technology" that utilizes the adhesion of materials. Similarly, Dietrich et al. (2019) also see AM as "a series of technologies" and emphasize the need for the cooperation of different disciplines to solve the problems. In order to realize modeling services by AM, it is necessary to drastically change the conventional organizational structure and relationships between companies, and it is important to review such structures and relationships from the viewpoint of the ecosystem. Iansiti and Levien (2004) state that the essence of innovation in business ecosystem is "integration and adaptation" and point out the importance of the ability to integrate to "pull together new and old competencies, internal and external assets" and "constantly evolve and extend a firm's role in its ecosystem by tying together previously disconnected elements". Takeuchi (2019) stated that in order to solve problems in AM, not only the machine but also many other hurdles to business planning, design, materials, modeling, finishing, quality assurance, standards, and data management must be overcome. In that paper, the machine manufacturer is introduced which established an AM ecosystem related with external partners to compensate for issues that cannot be solved by the machine alone. Further, the paper points out that similar movements are expanding both in Japan and overseas. In this chapter, we take up case studies of service bureaus that use PBF and BJT machines of metal AM and summarize the current status of and issues regarding the realization of digital manufacturing.

3 Case study of the metal AM service bureau

3.1 Company A

Company A, a ferrite magnetic annealing and heat treatment business for aluminum die casting molds, was founded in 1960. The company introduced a metal AM machine in 2001 and is now engaged in a wide range of industries, including aerospace, energy, automotive, and medical equipment, and offers integrated contract manufacturing from design to production based on elemental technologies such as metal heat treatment, hot isostatic pressing (HIP) treatment, diffusion bonding, brazing, and precision machining. The aircraft parts that Company A has been working on for a long time require a reduction in the number of parts and weight, and the use of AM is highly anticipated in this field. Company A has established an extensive design support system by selecting machines and modifying shapes to suit the customer's desired shape. Specifically, Company A proposes 3D lattice structures that are difficult to fabricate using existing methods, such as component-integrated structures using topology-optimized structures and lightweight structures, and provides support to customers for more advanced modeling studies. The lattice structure can be placed at any location with the intended line diameter and grid pitch according to the customer's desired complex shape. In addition, Company A has two types of PBF machines; it is therefore able to select and offer the best system according to the required shape and application of the final product. As mentioned earlier, in metal AM, it is necessary to consider a modeling method that includes peripheral processes after understanding the advantages and disadvantages of the machines and the characteristics of the materials. In some cases, the existing shape must be changed and a shape suitable for AM has to be recreated. Therefore, it is essential to have abilities similar to consulting, such as careful coordination and fine-tuning with the customer. Since this is a new field for which there is no manual, Company A emphasizes the necessity of accumulating experience by modeling and getting a feel for the fabrication; it is also making efforts to develop human resources within the company. In the past, as the parts were fabricated according to the drawing without sufficient consideration of the support material and thermal balance, quality requirements could not be met and product evaluation could not be carried out because of the lack of support material removal and finishing. However, Company A utilizes the strength of its existing heat treatment technology to handle the entire process in-house, from pre-verification to modeling, heat treatment, finishing, and quality inspection (Figure 6.1).

The modeling process is tended to be focused on, but it is also necessary to follow the process before and after, including quality assurance. Since AM is manufactured by layering one layer at a time, there is a possibility of quality variations and defects in each product. In particular, when the internal structure is also manufactured, inspection of the internal shape is also necessary, and depending on the application, inspection of all products may be required. In terms of quality inspection, Company A discusses control methods with customers at the time of design and ensures traceability by designing shapes that can be inspected. In January 2021, one of the Company A's plants obtained ISO 13485 certification, an international standard for quality management systems in medical devices, in order to expand this technology to medical device manufacturing. By using HIP treatment, a core technology of the company, in combination with the post-process, defects inside the modeling body and fatigue fractures that occur from defects are suppressed. Company A believes that appropriate measurement and evaluation are important not only for preventing defective products from being released into the market, but also for reviewing the modeling process and improving the quality of the modeling data.

3.2 Company B

Company B was established in 2017 for the purpose of mass production and sale of metal AM products, a joint venture between Company D, a general trading company, and Company E, a company engaged in the casting business. Company E was established in 1973, and is engaged in the manufacture and sale of prototype and mass-produced castings and metal powder laminated parts, and non-destructive testing using CT and laser scanning non-contact measuring

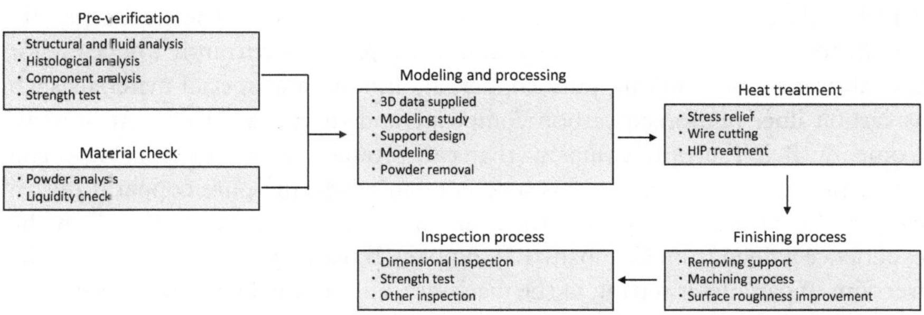

Figure 6.1 Metal AM process at Company A.

equipment. Company D, a general trading company, is engaged in the sale and trading of goods, planning of various projects, and investment in various fields such as automobiles, plants, aviation, medical infrastructure, and energy. Company E introduced 3D CAD in 1998 and started digital manufacturing; the company became the first in Japan to provide one-stop services from design to commercialization through introducing a sand 3D printer in 2007. In 2012, it became the first company in Japan to start contract manufacturing using metal AM. In 2003, Company E started a new project for the introduction of a new medium- to long-term technology with a wider use. Company E has received numerous certifications from the Ministry of Economy, Trade and Industry and Kanagawa Prefecture, and has been involved in a number of support projects. The company was asked by its customers to establish a system to accumulate the method modeling and data technology necessary for casting. In the field of metal AM, the sharing of information and collaboration between different departments in the manufacturing process is very important. Company E believes that concurrent engineering is only possible when the technology to handle 3D data, AM technology that can create a product according to the data, and non-destructive inspection technology are all in place (Hito to system 54, 2009). In addition to the experience of Company E, Company B's strengths include the know-how provided by the institute for materials research at University A, which provides technical support based on academic research, and the global network and information capabilities of Company D. Company D supports Company B's business development by utilizing its network as a general trading company and its expertise in a wide range of businesses, and also responsible for expanding sales of the metal powders and metal products developed by Company B. Company B is the first company in Japan that provides a full range of services, from powder materials development and manufacturing to prototype fabrication, mass production and support for certification by combining the strengths of both Company D and Company E. Company B offers three types of services: contract manufacturing, powder material development support, and product development support. As for mass production, they can estimate the cost of mass production and support the development of parameters to reduce the cost. It is also possible to evaluate and give advice on quality control during mass production. Company B owns two types of PBF machines, which enables it to handle and mold a wide range of steel types. Some of the steel types are unique to Company B, and research and development is currently underway for the fabrication of titanium, pure copper, aluminum, and special materials such as carbon fiber-reinforced carbon composite and tungsten carbide. At present, Company B is the only company that can produce pure copper using metal lamination equipment, and it has succeeded in producing pure copper using an electron beam method by improving the production parameters based on the experience gained from Company E. Company B places great importance on the freedom of parameter setting of the machines, and original parameters are often adopted. In addition, Company B can optimize the fabrication recipe and improve the quality based on the results of evaluation and analysis after fabrication, which is supported by academic research. By repeating the process of prototype fabrication, evaluation and analysis, and recipe optimization, Company E can now aim to manufacture practical products and parts by metal AM. At present, the service bureaus are compensating for the lack of machines and processing technology, and it is recognized that autonomy, which can be achieved by software, is yet to be realized.

3.3 Company C

Company C was established in 1956 for the sale of steel plates and pig iron. The cast steel products handled by Company C are special steels used under severe conditions, and are often used in nuclear, thermal, and hydroelectric power plants. Forged steel products are important parts that have both high hardness and high fatigue and are used in the engines of large ships and in rolls for rolling steel. The machinery business handles a wide range of products, including chemical, industrial, and hydraulic machinery, while the metals business handles a wide range of materials, including metal powders and Metal Injection Molding (MIM) products. It offers a modeling service using machines from Company F, a manufacturer of BJT machines. Company F's machines are characterized by the types of powder materials that can be used, the cost, and the scale of the parts they can produce. BJT involves sintering and has been specialized for small products, but it can also be applied to the mass production of large products. Company C receives product drawings in the form of 3D data from customers and handles everything from molding to sintering. In some cases, sintering is performed by the customer. Company C has been involved in various types of modeling, but stainless steel and cemented carbide account for approximately 50% and 20%, respectively, of the materials applied. In the field of products, industrial products account for less than 50%, cemented carbides for 20%, while automotive products for less than 10%. Non-disclosure agreement (NDA) contracts have currently been signed with more than 40 customers and the company is considering the introduction of prototypes and machines. The objectives of the customers vary, but the main objectives are described below. For example, by installing a BJT machine and distributing product data on demand, it is possible to reduce tooling costs and design change costs in the molding of low-volume, high-mix production products. In addition, a customer who faces problems with surface roughness in the molding of thin-walled and complex-shaped products can now secure a density of 99% or higher and solve shape problems. For a customer who had a problem with the type and cost of powder materials used in the fabrication of a mold, Company C was able to use powder supplied by the customer and improve the practicality of the molding process by using inexpensive powder. Likewise, for a customer who needs to create products using powder materials developed by the customer, Company C has achieved a high degree of freedom in forming shapes that differentiates from other companies. The physical properties of the raw material powder used for metal AM are reflected in the quality of the formed product. In order to understand the characteristics of the AM and the object, it is necessary to understand not only the difference in the process types but also the powder manufacturing technology used as the raw material and the powder characteristics. The knowledge of powder materials is beyond the expertise of Company C. Company G analyzes the physical properties of the powder materials. The filling used in the powder bed is strongly related to the density of the formed object. It is therefore necessary to optimize and predict the mechanical properties of powder materials, as the lack of technical information about the raw powder can be an obstacle in the manufacturing process. Because powder materials deteriorate without proper management, it is essential to constantly monitor the condition of materials to ensure stable production, especially in case of mass production. Periodic evaluation and management are also necessary when using recycled powders, and specialized skills are required to apply advanced powder property measurement technology to AM. In particular, when using powder materials brought in by customers, as described above, various knowledge and skills are required to understand the mechanical properties of the materials. In addition, collaboration with chemical manufacturers is required for the binder used in the BJT. The examples discussed in this section are shown in Figure 6.2. Company H is a manufacturer of powder materials and powder manufacturing equipment, and also owns Company F's machine. Company I is a sintering furnace manufacturer that accounts for 70–80% of the sintering furnaces for MIM in China. The modeling service provided by Company C is made up of players from different industrial fields collaborating across the organizations.

4 Discussion

The value of AM was reaffirmed by the COVID-19, and it became indispensable for the growth of the manufacturing industry and the creation of innovation, but the core was the service bureau. As AM is a "system technology", it is extremely

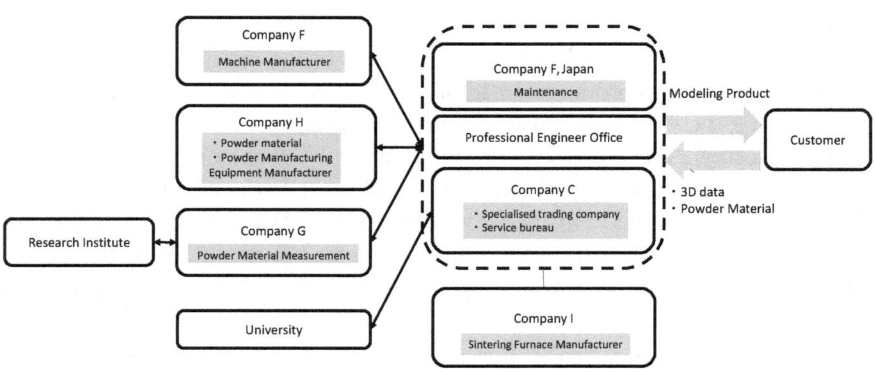

Figure 6.2 Ecosystem of Company C.

difficult for a single company to provide the entire service. At the present stage, there are only a limited number of types of machines and not many examples of modeling, so the service can be operated using analog operation management that relies on a specific engineer. However, if the market expands in the future, and the number of machine types and modeling requests increase and diversify, such an individualized operation will not be sufficient. The case studies discussed here highlight the importance of building an internal "library", collaborating with external players, and integrating skills and capabilities, both within and outside the company, with an eye to the future. It is important to be able to build a "library" (organizational memory) that can accumulate, store, and retrieve design data in-house. For example, in the case study of Company A, the need to accumulate experience through repeated modeling cases by focusing on consultation and coordination with customers is emphasized. Company A already possesses HIP processing technology and has the strength to propose total process solutions. It can be called a functional integration. By combining technologies and related processes in other fields through existing businesses, it will be possible to respond beyond specific industries and applications. As regards collaboration with outside players, it is clear that Company B's joint management with Company D enabled them to expand their network, which Company E could not have done alone. The case of Company C is an example of a service system that crosses various specialized technologies and includes manufacturers and research institutes; this type of collaboration is aimed at building long-term business relationships with customers by providing a back-up system equipped with specialists in each field during the initial phases of digital manufacturing. It can be called an organizational integration. This is also what differentiates Company F from other BJT machine manufacturers. As a contact point, the service bureau has the potential to build information and utilize advantages. With these advantages, it can develop a service business that leverages the strengths of the existing businesses of each player outside the company, and to function and grow as an ecosystem. The impact of COVID-19 and the acceleration of digital manufacturing will mean that more and more customers will be considering the introduction of AM machines and mass production. The role of the service bureau will be to integrate internal and external organizations and functions so that it can handle not only the processing, but also the front-end processes such as design and material development and the back-end processes such as post-processing, inspection, and production scale-up.

As described above, the thorough accumulation and utilization of knowledge by the service bureau will lead to the enhancement and expansion of its own library, while the integration of internal and external skills and capabilities will lead to the expansion and sophistication of its modeling services (Figure 6.3).

Because the three factors of design, materials, and machines are closely related, it is thought that the knowledge accumulated by the service bureaus will become multilayered. The cycle is a loop, and because metal AM is a field with many unknown factors, it is thought that the current stage is a test of a company's strength to turn the cycle over and over again. As the trend toward high-mix,

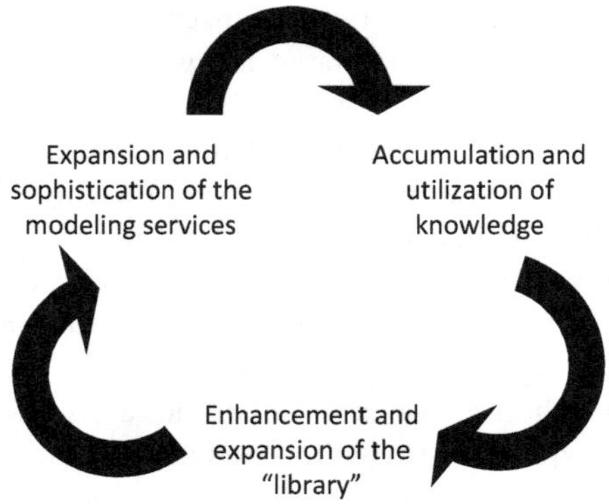

Figure 6.3 Growth cycle of the service bureaus.

small- and medium-volume production and decentralization of parts suppliers and production bases accelerates with the COVID-19 pandemic, the need for direct manufacturing using AM will increase, but the cost of installing a machine, the difficulty of modeling, and the hurdles to conception and design are high. The shortages of human resources with the establishment of quality assurance technology and design skills are also issues. In order to shift the paradigm from the conventional method to AM, it is necessary to overcome these issues. In direct manufacturing, the design base and manufacturing base do not have to be in the same factory but can be in remote locations, such as overseas. At the design base, 3D design data is converted to AM data, and at the manufacturing base, manufacturing is performed based on the sent data. The construction of an in-house "library" based on the design data accumulated in this process could be a powerful incentive for service bureaus to work on.

5 Summary

Digitization is driving the development of AM. The value of AM, which was re-recognized under the COVID-19 pandemic, is expected to increase further in a wide range of industries in the future. In the field of metal AM, in addition to the conventional PBF and DED, BJT has also attracted attention in anticipation of mass production. As mentioned above, the cost of introducing AM machines is still high, and there are many problems in introducing AM, such as advanced design technology and severe powder material management systems. For companies that are hesitant to introduce AM on their own, the ecosystem of service bureaus that provide support from consideration of introduction to application in mass production will be very attractive. Service bureaus have, so far, mostly been involved in AM prototyping. However, their expertise and high level of technology in AM will help manufacturers to introduce and apply AM machines in the future. Rather than doing everything on their own, it is becoming more and more common to consider the application of AM machines together with the help of professional service bureaus. The case studies discussed in this chapter highlight the importance of building a "library" for storing and retrieving "knowledge" such as modeling data and recipes, and of building a service system that crosses various specialized technologies involved in the modeling service by the service bureaus. Although the case studies presented in this chapter are only a small part of the picture, but it is hoped that this study will contribute to the realization of digital manufacturing using metal AM.

References

Dietrich, D. M., Kenworthy, M. & Cudney, E. A. (2019). *Additive Manufacturing Change Management Best Practices*, Boca Raton, Florida: CRC Press.

Hashiguchi, N., Kodama, K. & Mitsufuji, T. (2017). Ryousankoutei ni okeru 3D printer ni kansuru innovation (Innovations on 3D printers in mass production processes), *Nenjigakujutsutaikai kouenyoushisyu (Abstracts of Annual Academic Conference)*, 32, 82–85 (in Japanese).

Hito to system 54 (Human and system 54). (2009). 次世代の鋳造技術には EOSINT Sが必須. (July 1) (in Japanese) https://www.nttd-es.co.jp/magazine/backnumber/no54/no54-koiwai.html (accessed May 30, 2021).

Iansiti, M. & Levien, R. (2004). *The Keystone Advantage: What the New Dynamics of Business Ecosystems Mean for Strategy, Innovation, and Sustainability*, Boston, MA: Harvard Business School Press.

Kyogoku, H. & Ikeshoji, T. (2017). *Zukai kinzoku3Dsekisouzoukei no kiso (Basics of Metal Additive Manufacturing)*, Tokyo: Nikkan Kogyo Shinbun, Ltd. (in Japanese).

Matsushita, T. (2019). Sangyouyoukinzoku 3D printer no hukyu heno sogai youin to taiousaku ni kansuru ichikousatsu (Inhibiting Factors for Diffusion, and Countermeasures for the Industrial Metal 3D Printer), *Sankaikenronsyu (The Economic and Business Review)*, 31, 11–23 (in Japanese).

MONOist. (2019). 金属3Dプリンタ活用3つのハードルと日本のモノづくりの今後. (January 8) (in Japanese) https://monoist.atmarkit.co.jp/mn/articles/1901/08/news069.html (accessed May 30, 2021).

MONOist. (2020). 広がる金属3Dプリンタと工作機械の融合、それぞれの技術方式の特徴. (December 14) (in Japanese) https://monoist.atmarkit.co.jp/mn/articles/2012/14/news050.html (accessed May 30, 2021).

MONOist. (2021). コロナ禍で生まれた3Dプリンタ活用の流れが、デジタル製造を加速. (January 14) (in Japanese) https://monoist.atmarkit.co.jp/mn/articles/2101/14/news021.html (accessed May 30, 2021).

The Nikkei. (2020). 矢野経済研究所、3Dプリンタ材料の世界市場調査結果を発表. (January 7) (in Japanese) https://www.nikkei.com/article/DGXLRSP526349_X00C20A1000000/ (accessed May 30, 2021).

Niino, T. (2020). Innovation in Products and Services through Additive Manufacturing Technologies, *Chemical Engineering of Japan*, 84(4), 171–174 (in Japanese).

ODEC CO., LTD. (2021). 金属3Dコラム　第39回　新型コロナ禍、金属３Dプリント市場の状況（世界市場予測）. (n.d.) (in Japanese) http://3d.kinzoku-kakou-odec.com/column/column-702/ (accessed May 30, 2021).

Rayna, T. & Striukova, L. (2016). From Rapid Prototyping to Home Fabrication: How 3D Printing Is Changing Business Model Innovation, *Technological Forecasting & Social Change*, 102, 214–224.

Takeuchi, N. (2019). Kinzoku 3D printer ga hiraku monodukuri: hukaseizou no senshing-ijutsu (New Manufacturing through Additive Manufacturing: Advanced Technology in Additive Manufacturing), *Kikaigijutsu (Mechanical Engineering)*, 67(12), 38–41 (in Japanese).

Taki, K. (2020). Additive Manufacturing as a Service (AMaaS), *Chemical Engineering of Japan*, 84(4), 175–178 (in Japanese).

Tech Factory. (2020). 3Dプリンタニュースまとめ——2020年7月〜9月. (October 26) (in Japanese) https://wp.techfactory.itmedia.co.jp/contents/50367 (accessed May 30, 2021).

Tech Factory. (2021). 治具や部品製造への適用も実現、製造現場を変革する次世代3Dプリンタとは. (January 13) (in Japanese) https://wp.techfactory.itmedia.co.jp/contents/52584 (accessed May 30, 2021).

TSC Foresight 32. (2019). 金属積層造形プロセス分野の技術戦略策定に向けて. (February 8) (in Japanese) https://www.nedo.go.jp/content/100888376.pdf (accessed May 30, 2021).

Walsh, J. P. & Ungson, G. R. (1991). Organizational Memory, *Academy of Management Review*, 16(1), 57–91.

Watari, N., Ogura, Y., Yamazaki, N. & Watanabe, T. (2020). Two-Fluid Model to Simulate Metal Additive Manufacturing, *Chemical Engineering of Japan*, 84(4), 191–198 (in Japanese).

Section 2
Services

Hiroki Ishikura and Anshuman Khare

The percentage of workers engaged in the tertiary industry already exceeds 70%. Japan, which has an image that manufacturing is the leading industry, is no exception to this. Service industry is the largest sector in Japan consisting of various kinds of businesses and plays an important role in its economy. To prevent the spread of COVID-19 infection, it was essential to control the flow of people, and face-to-face work switched to telework. In this shift towards digitalization of work, the consequence of delays in digital transformation in Japan in recent years became clear. The seven chapters in this section touch on a number of issues triggered by the pandemic and the move towards digitalization.

Japanese service industry was lagging behind in digitalization. While digital innovation continues to develop unique technologies such as AI and robots, it also promotes the development of IT infrastructure and improves the efficiency of services. In Chapter 7, it is pointed out that the Japanese way of working makes it difficult to adopt business innovation necessary in the Internet society. It has not been able to produce the same results as when the Japanese achieved results by manufacturing.

Chapter 8 examines the problems and issues of communication inside and outside the organization due to the switch to working from home. It focuses on the physical and mental health of employees and staff and discusses the possibility of breaking away from long-standing practices and changing management styles.

"Horenso" is discussed in Chapter 9. It can be recognized as part of Japan's decision-making process and means reporting, contacting, and consulting. The chapter re-examines horenso, which is challenging to apply internationally, especially during the COVID crisis and while global business transitions to the digital age.

Cashless payments are addressed in Chapter 10. In Japan, cash payments were still widespread until the spread of COVID-19. Even now, in cashless payments, credit cards that can be infected are still standard. Non-contact cashless payment methods are explained and recommended.

Chapter 11 presents a commentary on the new challenges being faced by the Japanese travel and tourism industry which has been forced to a paradigm shift because of the COVID-19 pandemic. People in the travel and tourism industry

DOI: 10.4324/9781003216049-8

have been working hard to discover new values in tourism, foster the civic pride in the local people, and develop new business models. In some cases, technology is used as a channel to deliver services. There is a lot more to come in this business sector.

Chapter 12 presents the challenges in an international industry-academia collaboration between Japan and Bangladesh – the Miyazaki-Bangladesh model is introduced. In recent years, however, Japanese companies with a shortage of IT engineers have provided IT education for international students from Bangladesh. The COVID-19 pandemic has damaged this project. Measures necessary to keep the model in play are discussed.

The final chapter of this section, Chapter 13, deals with companies, universities, and collaborative research. It focuses on trust relationships and describes how strong ties of trust lead to better outcomes and a higher likelihood that additional joint research will be initiated by partner organizations. It touches on how joint research initiatives are proceeding with private companies during the pandemic.

7 Expectations for escape from restraints on Japanese digital transformation during COVID-19

Hiroki Ishikura and Anshuman Khare

1 Introduction

Japanese economic regression in the information age is noteworthy (Ishikura & Khare, 2020). Why has Japan, which had outperformed the rest of the world in manufacturing, lost its competitive edge in the information age? Japan's declining birthrate and aging population may be losing its competitiveness. Khare, Khare and Baber (2020) depicted the digital transformation (DX) of Japanese business in terms of key technologies, impact finance, retail, manufacturing, services, agriculture, and elder care. Generally, it is observed that Japanese workers cannot use English sufficiently enough to compete in the modern global society, or even that excessive regulation hinders free competition in the economy. Ikegami and Iijima (2020) explored key strategic themes for Japanese enterprises regarding DX. They applied directed content analysis for the interviews and obtained detailed descriptions that explain the insufficiency of DX in Japanese enterprises. Customer Experience, Strategic Intent, and Ecosystem were pointed out as critical points. It is also thought that these reasons cannot wholly explain the decline of Japan in recent decades. We argue that the root cause of this regression is the way Japanese people view work.

This conclusion was reached by comparing the productivity of workers, the amount of value added by a company, and the profits of those services compared to those of Western companies competing with Japanese companies while incorporating a view utilizing the history of how the Japanese view work. Without making the most of IT in society, the Japanese work ethic has not been able to increase the productivity of businesses, i.e., a poor DX (Ishikura & Khare, 2020). This is the reality in Japan today. Will the productivity of Japanese companies cause them to lose competitiveness in the face of digital progress? The definitions of digitization and DX can vary slightly from author to author. In this chapter, IT utilization functions are referred to as digitalization, and digitization aimed at improving productivity is referred to as DX.

It seems that there is currently an opportunity for Japan to move forward. Until now, digital societies have expanded business opportunities using the Internet. However, in recent years, parallel with the expansion of Internet businesses, competition to use vast collections of big data amassed through the years has

DOI: 10.4324/9781003216049-9

begun. Japan is also behind in the fields of data science and AI utilization. However, there is one possibility that makes the best use of the characteristics of the Japanese workers' view of labor.

Japanese people do not pursue a dramatically changed society. They tend to accept only the reality in front of them and think about how to improve it. So, what is the difference between reality and thought? The five senses accept objective reality, but thought is shared by language (Yoro, 2005). Fact is essential in Japanese work ethic, and computerization and DX do not feel natural because nature is analog. At least, only sight and hearing are fully digitalized, but tactile, taste, and smell cannot be said to be digitized (Spence et al., 2016). It could be one reason why the Japanese have not tackled DX seriously.

2 Broad overview of the situation

2.1 Japanese industry regression in the IT society

Figure 7.1 shows the changes in nominal GDP per capita in major countries, extracted from the International Monetary Fund data (Global Note, 2021), showing the relative decline in personal wealth in Japan since its peak in 1995 when Windows 95 and Internet Explorer were launched and ordinary people began to conduct significant daily activities online.

As shown in Table 7.1 (based on ILO, 2021), in the developed countries of the world, people engaging in tertiary industries like health care, education, or other services accounted for three-fourths of all workers. Unless the labor productivity of the service industry increases, the country will not be enriched. Regarding fast fashion companies and the restaurant industry, representing the

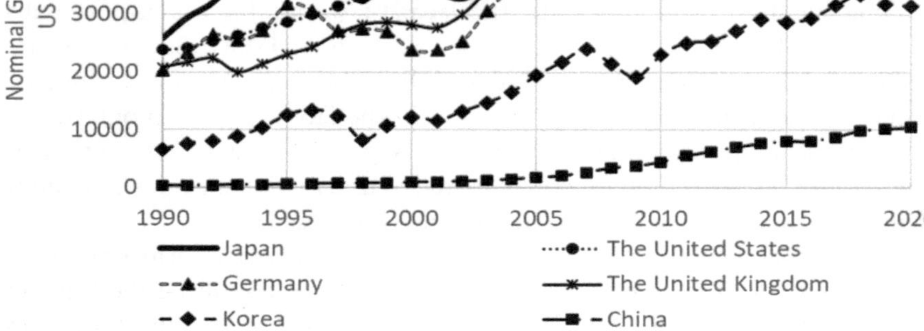

Figure 7.1 Nominal GDP per capita.

Table 7.1 Percentage of employees by industry in 2019

	Primary industry	*Secondary industry*	*Tertiary industry*
Korea	5.1	24.5	70.4
China	25.1	27.5	47.4
Japan	3.3	23.7	73.0
Germany	1.2	27.2	71.6
United Kingdom	1.0	18.1	80.9
United States	1.4	19.9	78.7

Data Source: ILO (2021).

modern Japanese service industry in the book, Japan has relatively high service productivity per worker. However, value-added productivity is used to measure the labor productivity of services. Value-added productivity is lower than service productivity, indicating that the profits were not as strong as they could be due to lower labor productivity.

In Switzerland's IMD World Competitiveness Ranking 2020 (IMD, 2020), Japan is ranked 34 (down four places from 2019). It is below Singapore (the top ranked country), China, South Korea, and Thailand in Asia, according to the IMD World Digital Ranking (IMD, 2020).

Figure 7.2a shows the labor productivity growth rate between 1995 and 2018 in the wholesale, retail, food and beverage, and accommodation industries in Japan, the United States, and the United Kingdom (Japan Productivity Center, 2020). The United States and the United Kingdom show growth rates of about 1% annually, but Japan is barely growing. Figure 7.2b shows the labor productivity growth rate in the financial insurance industry (Japan Productivity Center, 2020). The growth rate in the United Kingdom is greater than the United States. It can be seen that the United Kingdom is growing steadily as a center of finance. Japan is also different from other countries in the financial insurance industry as the IT age continues to progress. It can be seen that Japan is lagging behind both countries in the financial insurance industry as digital technologies continue to proliferate. Everyone must recognize the importance of the DX in finance, such as the shift to cashless economies during and after the COVID-19 pandemic as well as the widespread use of virtual currencies.

Figure 7.2c shows the labor productivity growth rate for the information and telecommunications industry, which is directly related to DX (Japan Productivity Center, 2020). The growth of productivity in the United States in this sector is remarkable. Japan's growth rate is one-third that of the United States and two-thirds that of the United Kingdom.

For reference, compare the productivity growth rates in the manufacturing industries during the same time period in these three countries, as shown in Figure 7.2d. The growth rate of the United States is high here, but the growth rate of Japan is nearly comparable, demonstrating a higher growth rate than the United Kingdom. It can be seen that the reason why the Japanese economy

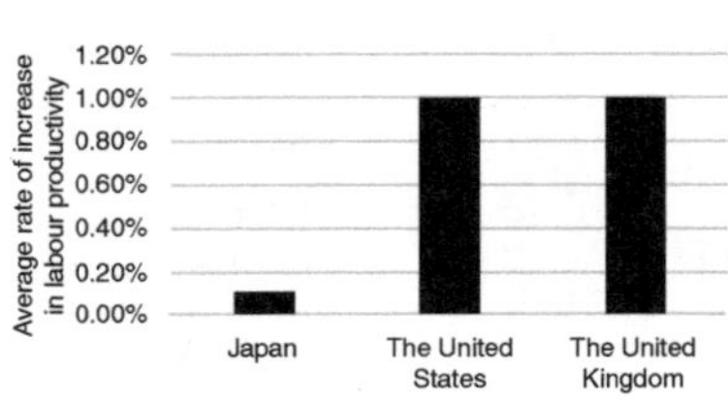

Figure 7.2a Labour productivity in wholesale and retail, food, beverage, and accommodation industries 1995–2018

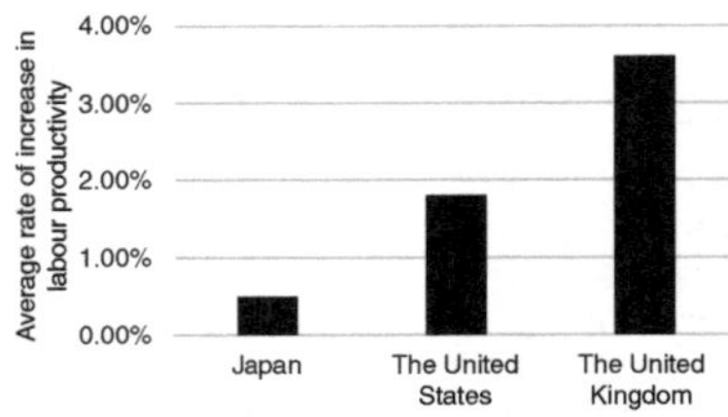

Figure 7.2b Labour productivity in the financial insurance industry 1995–2018

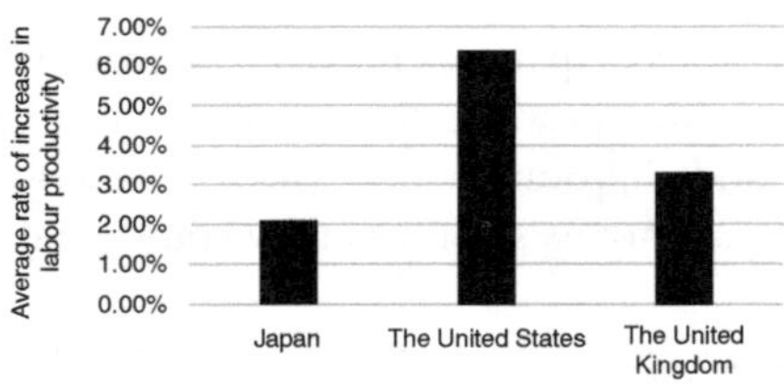

Figure 7.2c Labour productivity in the information and telecommunications industry 1995–2018

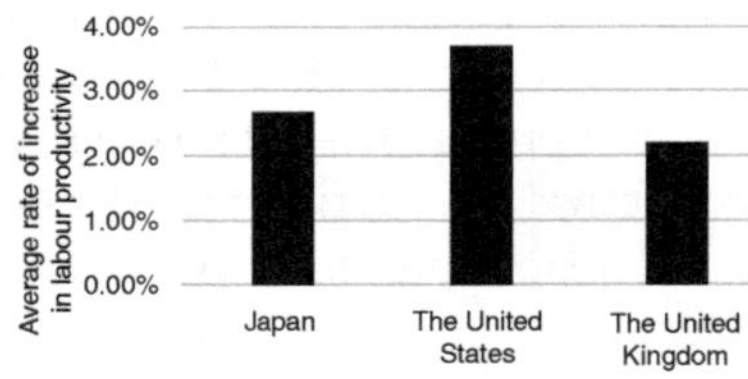

Figure 7.2d Labour productivity in the manufacturing industry 1995–2018

Figure 7.2 Labor productivity.

has not grown over the past two decades is that the productivity of the service industry has not increased.

2.2 Why labor productivity in the services sector in Japan is not improving

The labor productivity in the service sector cannot improve because the ability of labor to utilize IT is not increasing, and there is a lack of new services with high productivity. To explore this question, consumer prices in Japan and the United States were examined.

Figure 7.3a shows that the consumer price index for services in Japan has remained flat in stark contrast to the consumer price index in the United States (e-Stat Japanese Government Statistics, 2021; US Bureau of Labor Statistics, 2021).

By comparing the consumer price indexes of products in Figure 7.3b (e-Stat Japanese Government Statistics, 2021; US Bureau of Labor Statistics, 2021), it can be seen that inflation in both Japan and the United States has remained stable. In other words, although the labor productivity of the commodities sector has increased, the price index has not risen, indicating that the labor productivity of this sector has grown in both countries. Regarding service productivity in the

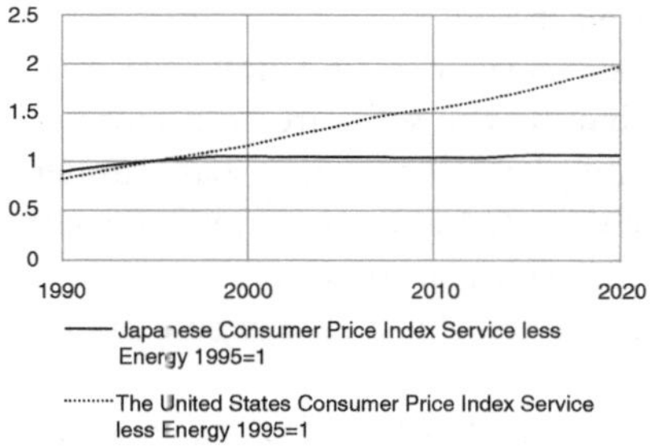

Figure 7.3a Changes in the consumer price index for Japanese and the United State services

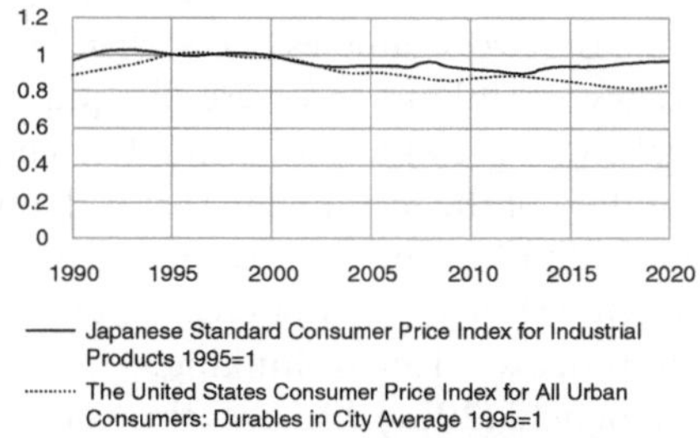

Figure 7.3b Changes in the consumer price index for Japanese and the United State products

Figure 7.3 Changes in the consumer price index.

United States, value-added labor productivity and the consumer price index are rising and new high value-added services are being created. In Japan, neither the value-added labor productivity nor the consumer price index have risen. The fact that they have not increased indicates that new advanced services have not grown in the last 20 years or more.

Nominal GDP per capita in Japan has been declining compared to other countries since 1995; one reason might be that productivity improvements using IT were not as widespread as in other developed countries and China.

2.3 *Weak state of Japanese digital technology revealed by COVID-19*

The fact that DX is not progressing in Japan became clear to the public in response to the COVID-19 pandemic that started around April 2020. In many local governments, COVID-19-related benefits were paid earlier to those who applied via physical mail, while those who applied online received them later. Applying online using "My Number", a system for numbering all registered people in Japan, was possible, but My Number and the Basic Resident Register system, an identification number for administrative purposes, were not linked in many municipalities. This work had to be done manually, and the manual processing of mail applications was completed faster than the online applications could be processed (Nikkei, 2020). This is a classic example of underdeveloped DX.

Another example happened with Japan's COVID-19 Contact Confirmation Application (COCOA), which had been out of order for over four months (NHK, 2021) and no one was aware of it. COCOA uses Bluetooth and records other smartphone terminals when they stay within one meter of each other for at least 15 minutes. However, Android users were not notified of contact with infected individuals during that four-month period. Even when COCOA was properly installed for Android users, when the user came into close contact with a person who had Covid-19, the program did not notify them. The development team was unable to achieve its development objectives.

These two examples show that Japanese IT developers did not have goal-oriented thinking and were ill-equipped to handle the software and hardware challenges presented to them. The engineers probably had only a basic understanding of the technology that is the basis of COCOA and could not cope with the realities of different operating systems. Simply incorporating IT without a targeted strategy cannot create a DX. By all accounts, this is an example of inferior process-oriented thinking.

Noguchi (2021) discusses the relationship between Japan's delay in a widescale DX and the decline in Japan's economic competitiveness. As shown above, Japan has fallen from the top to 34th in international rankings, according to the MDI (2020) survey. Noguchi (2021) analyzed the causes of falling competitiveness, and believed this to be due to the legacy of the old mainframe computer era. Even if Japan tried to improve a computer system that became too complicated, it could not figure out what kind of effect it would have if things did not happen as planned, and the situation meant being in a state of "scary and out of hand". As a result, Japan has managed to continue using the old system. The long-term affect has been that the computer system has become complicated and obsolete. In these legacy systems, the programming language used is COBOL, which was used in the 1980s. The programming language has changed since then and engineers who understand COBOL are now retiring. Japan has the potential to be in a situation where current computer systems will become a mystery to the new generation. The explanation provided by Noguchi (2020) is concrete and compelling. The dependency on old mechanisms and systems will possibly delay the digitalization of Japan as a whole.

2.4 *Japanese work ethic and incompatibility of new Internet business*

Japan was by no means indifferent to the introduction of IT and the DX it creates to improve productivity (Prime Minister's Office, 2021). In July 2000, when the delay in economic competitiveness became apparent, the Information and Communication Technology (IT) Strategic Headquarters for the Promotion of an Advanced Information and Telecommunications Network Society "IT nation" was established. At the first Strategic Headquarters meeting on January 22, 2001, the "e-Japan Strategy", based on the "IT Basic Strategy", was announced to be the national IT strategy. The goal of the "e-Japan Strategy" was to promptly promote the transition to become the world's most advanced IT society.

According to a report compiled by the Ministry of Economy Trade and Industry in 2018 (METI, 2018), existing IT systems were ageing and bloated, requiring enormous costs for operation and maintenance, and management's commitment was thin, as corporate DX was not thought to be important. It states that there has been no progress in modernization. It has been pointed out that if DX progresses at its current rate, economic losses of up to JPY 12 trillion may occur yearly starting in 2025. The Ministry of Economy, Trade and Industry describes this as the "cliff of 2025". On June 17, 2019, the government's IT Strategic Headquarters approved the "Most Advanced Digital Nation Declaration and Public-Private Data Utilization Promotion", which will be the new IT strategy for the first year of the Reiwa Period (2019).

Priority Initiatives of the plan include:

1 Social implementation projects of pioneering initiatives that lead the world
2 Utilization of data that allows users predict the benefits in people's lives
3 Implementation of Digital Government throughout Japanese society
4 Improvement of social infrastructure

The Suga Cabinet, established in 2020, aims to present the Digital Agency in September 2021. Even though the hope is to improve productivity by promoting IT and the DX it will bring throughout the country and plans have been put in place, why is Japan's digitalization still lagging?

Considering Japan's success in manufacturing, it cannot be assumed that the country's ability to adapt is low. It is perhaps an unconscious problem that has caused the Japanese people to believe in the importance of IT and DX yet has prevented progress.

It seems that there is no survey that has investigated the penetration rate of personal computers (PCs) in developed countries. However, the approximate penetration rate can be estimated from the annual sales volume of PCs and the average usage period calculated against the total population. At the end of 2019, before the Covid-19 pandemic spread, the United States had on average one PC per capita, the United Kingdom had 0.8, and Japan had 0.5 (Kaya, 2019). Many Japanese think PCs are not needed if people have smartphones or mobile phones, but while smartphones and mobile phones are effective tools for communication and play, those tools are not as useful for increasing work productivity.

In the early Edo period at the beginning of the 17th century, when it is said that the Japanese view of labor was established, the most important thing was to strive for doing one's work well. It was explained that working hard became a practice in Buddhism and that this practice freed one from all worldly desires. This is encapsulated well in a tale about Shosan Suzuki, a former samurai monk. A farmer said to him, "I want to pray to the Buddha for religious training but farming in the rice fields leaves me no time for religious training. What should I do"? Shosan replied, "Do your work. What you do thoroughly is a religious practice. Do not worry and work hard for your rice field". This thinking can still be found in the Japanese view of labor that continues to this day. People believe that you must do the work in front of you and you must do your best (Yamamoto, 2006). It is probably the reason why the Japanese succeeded in making things. This attitude may have been what produced a rapid succession of technological advancements starting around the turn of the 20th century. Japan was effective in creating improvements seen in the quality and functionality of automobiles and consumer electric products invented in Europe and the United States. The improvements were created through process-oriented thinking. However, with computerization, looking at the business goals of companies like Amazon and Google and that these companies continue to develop business goals that Japanese companies do not share, it seems that the Japanese have been unable to set similar goals to meet the challenges of the 21st century.

To utilize IT in an advanced Internet business, programming technology superior to that found in other countries is required. It is desirable for Japan to develop an internationally standardized program, but many engineers need to master the same standardized program even if it cannot be created domestically.

Shichihei Yamamoto (1989) stated in "Study of Faction" (Bungei Shunju) that "Japan is not a country that complies with the law, but a country where the reason for an action is more critical. It matters if people understand your actions, even if they are illegal". In other words, IT that requires keeping many rules which do not allow individual interpretation is not suitable for Japanese labor (Yamamoto, 1989).

The Japanese do not have a work ethic that follows standardized rules and acts with enthusiasm. When Japanese have to follow directions, they are concerned about the attitudes and perceptions of others, so they follow the rules set for them; however, at such times, there is no enthusiasm and no competitiveness. Improvement in industrial products depend on individual ingenuity, and that is when results were obtained. It seems that common tacit knowledge was born from individual effort. However, it is difficult to demonstrate this enthusiasm for computerization to craft immense goals given an immutable rule base.

It is difficult to find research that shows that Japanese work ethics may not apply to the information society centered on the Internet. We assume that when businesses try to respond to this Internet-centric information society, new businesses do not succeed unless they set clear goals. The Internet is now the most important infrastructure, and the power of the Internet has to be assessed by examining the potential benefits and how it can be leveraged in business situations. However, the Japanese are only interested in improving the problem at hand and no idea of setting a big goal. As expressed in the words of Shosan Suzuki (Yamamoto, 2006), this is the fundamental outlook on life that if you keep working hard every day, you will be able to realize your potential, and only those who can realize their potential will be able to become happy.

At least in Japan, the status of IT engineers is not well respected. Japanese Software Engineers (SEs), in many cases, are seen as field engineers in companies, while American IT engineers are located closer to corporate management. Japan has not developed any significant programming language. The percentage of SEs who graduates from computer science programs or graduate schools is not as high compared to SEs overseas. The underlying reasons may be the unconscious resistance from the work ethic mentioned above or intrinsic Japanese values that cannot be easily evaluated.

In the competition to expand Internet business in the first 30 years of the digital age, the Japanese fell far behind due to their lack of goal orientation.

2.5 Comparison of specific major service industries in Japan and the United States

It is important to compare the service industry sectors of Japan and the United States. The number of specialized service industries in the science and technology sectors is increasing in the United States. Still, since these service industries are not found in Japan, conventional supermarkets and Internet shopping companies were compared. Aeon is Japan's top-selling supermarket and Rakuten is Japan's top-selling e-commerce shopping center (EC malls). There is no significant difference in per capita sales between traditional retailers Wal-Mart in the United States and Aeon. Regarding EC malls, the productivity rate per employee of Rakuten, which manages retail stores, is higher than Amazon, which sells individual products. Figure 7.4 shows net sales per employee of each company. Figure 7.4a shows net sales per employee of these companies (Amazon, 2020; Edinet, 2021; Walmart, 2021).

Figure 7.4b shows net sales (Amazon, 2020; Edinet, 2021; Walmart, 2021). The sales volume of these two companies in the United States is significant. When comparing the sales volume of the entire company, Wal-Mart is overwhelming. The scale of Amazon is also large, and the growth rate is much higher than the other three companies. When it comes to IT investment, the two American companies have economies of scale, and it is advantageous.

Net income per total assets of each company is shown in Figure 7.4c (Amazon, 2020; Edinet, 2021; Walmart, 2021). The two American companies have high net profits per total assets, and they make effective use of their assets to make profits.

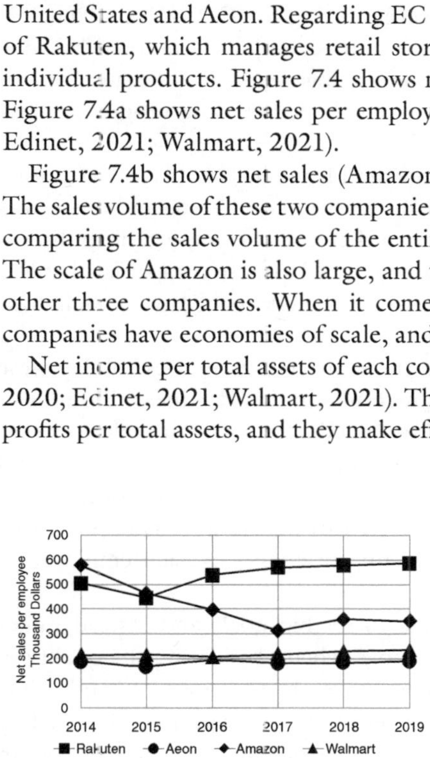

Figure 7.4a Net sales per employee

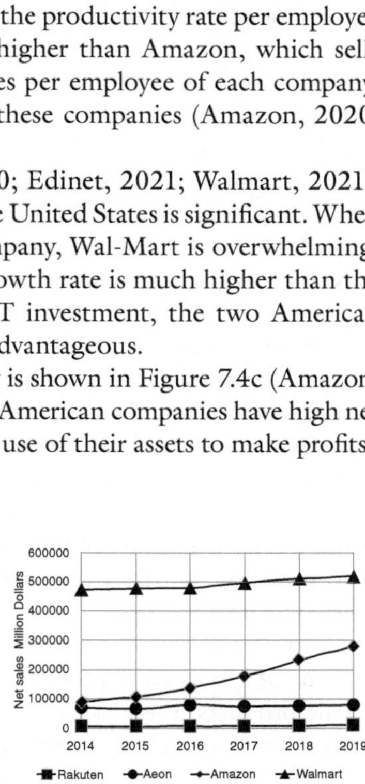

Figure 7.4b Net sales

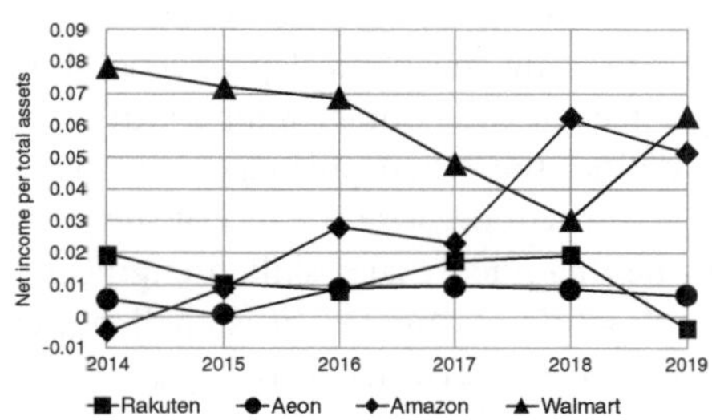

Figure 7.4c Net income per total assets

Figure 7.4 Representative retail stores and EC Malls in Japan and the United States.

3 Discussion – can Japanese industry regain its competitiveness in the digital society

The possibilities for Japanese companies to develop in the information age are going to be discussed. First, COVID-19 has to be a trigger to awaken Japanese people to the importance of IT. As is well known, Japanese people are sensitive to external pressure. It may have something to do with their work ethic. They are focused on immediate improvements and do not like significant changes. COVID-19 is a substantial external pressure. In the past, Japanese people tended to think that there is no need to spend money on IT for specific jobs because those jobs can be done without IT. However, during the COVID-19 pandemic when human contact was not possible, the number of jobs that could be done without using IT and without human contact was small. It is because of this environment that IT is developing in Japan. It is hoped that this progress will lay the foundations for DX.

In other words, business competition in the IT age in Japan is in a changing stage. At present, Japan's inadequacy is apparent in data science and AI sectors as well. However, there is promise for Japan there, so it is important to discuss this. It is necessary to consider the development of Japanese companies that was triggered by the shock of COVID-19, in which the effects of Japan's digitalization delay became apparent.

With the spread of the Internet, are there any opportunities for Japanese companies that have failed to produce any results in their business? From businesses that require clear goals for Internet-based economies of scale to work, businesses are moving toward finding answers that suit the values of each and every consumer using large amounts of data. In deep learning AI construction using neural networks, the efficiency of the entire community is improved by incorporating the detailed ingenuity and improvements of each employee as training data.

Japan's business culture appears unable to set big goals and instead values fine-tuned services and products. For example, when considering the quality of textile products, there is a difficult property to evaluate known as hand value. Hand value is related to the physical properties of the textile product. It is mainly a mechanical property, but the description of its mechanical properties is as an anisotropic non-linear viscoplastic. Only one textile product has had its scientific properties accurately described; however, it was not an easy process (Das & Alagirusamy, 2010). Not only mechanical properties but also other physical properties such as the feel of the contact temperature were involved. It was a difficult property to define, but when ordinary consumers buy clothes online, they often want to return them because the feel of the garment is not what they had imagined. It can be imagined that a skilled engineer can objectively judge a given property in a short time; however, it is challenging to make a scientific judgment even with advanced instruments. In Japan, there are many such skills in services and manufacturing that are hard to explicitly evaluate. However, in order to use any of these skilled techniques as they are presently known is inefficient because each person has to deal with them one by one. This utilization is not competitive in a highly efficient digital society unless customers are willing to pay high prices. It is possible to utilize these skills more efficiently by embracing DX. Using the digitalized data of these experts as training data, we believe that a large number of answers can be given in a short time by utilizing deep learning in neural network or similar environments. In Japan, there are many complex non-linear services and manufacturing techniques. While these data, often tacit and non-digitized, can be used by individuals, we believe that by recording them in an AI system as training data, we can use them efficiently and contribute to the world.

It can improve a company's efficiency across the community by incorporating fine-tuned ingenuity and employee improvements into AI building. These tasks are similar in design and may be suitable for the Japanese work ethic.

Jozuka (2015) reports that Yumi Wakao, a researcher at the Nomura Research Institute, did the same kind of analysis in Japan that the Oxford University researcher Michael Osborne did in the United Kingdom and the United States, attempting to find out how many jobs robots could take over in Japan over the next 20 years. The report concludes that up to 49% of jobs could be automated in Japan. Previous research had indicated this to be lower at 35% in the United Kingdom and 47% in the United States. Naturally, simple repetitive tasks will be replaced by robots and AI. It will take time for robots and AI to perform creative work. With current technology, it could be possible for AI to learn many jobs that skilled workers can perform (see Figure 7.5).

The five senses are needed to use the improved services and manufacturing data that the Japanese have found through painstaking efforts, to create better AI, which is more efficient and faster than ever before and also mass-produces services and manufacturing products more proficiently. Providing higher-quality and higher-performance services and manufacturing at a lower price as well as valuing tastes, smells, and respecting the digitizable data is more important than pursuing immediate profits. If we can achieve this, the importance of the Japanese industry will be reaffirmed both globally and in Japan.

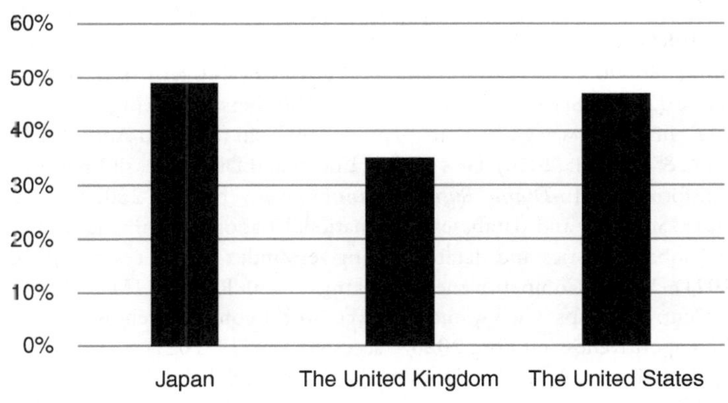

Figure 7.5 Percentage of working population that is likely to be replaced by AI or robots.

4 Conclusion

Japan's per capita nominal GDP peaked in 1995 and is declining year by year compared to other developed countries. The Japanese economy has been stagnant since the beginning of the information age in the mid-1990s. This shows that Japan could not adapt to the information age. In developed countries, more than three-quarters of workers are engaged in tertiary industries. It is essential to increase the value added by the service industry. The Japanese service industry has not been able to increase productivity or add value to its services. An advanced service industry has not been born due to the delay in Japan's DX. It is thought that companies that utilize economies of scale with clear goals have an advantage in digitization. The main reason for decline is that the Japanese work ethic does not aim to clarify goals and dramatically exceed them, but only to find the immediate purpose of the work in order to improve what is immediately in front of the worker. In the future, as digital innovation continues to develop unique technologies such as AI and robots, Japanese companies will promote the development of the IT infrastructure because of the external pressures such as COVID-19, international politics, and current globalization trends. They will be compelled to improve the efficiency of their services and manufacturing products through the use of AI.

References

Amazon (2020). Amazon Annual Reports. Proxies and Shareholder Letters. https://ir.aboutamazon.com/annual-reports-proxies-and-shareholder-letters/default.aspx (accessed April 26, 2021).

Das, A., & Alagirusamy, R. (2010). Kawabata Evaluation System. Science in Clothing Comfort. Science Direct. https://www.sciencedirect.com/topics/engineering/kawabata-evaluation-system (accessed May 26, 2021).

Edinet (2021). Electronic Disclosure for Investors NETwork. (In Japanese). https://disclosure.edinet-fsa.go.jp/EKW0EZ1001.html?lgKbn=1&dflg=0&iflg=0__(accessed April 26, 2021).

e-Stat Japanese Government Statistics (2021). Shohisha Bukkashisu. (In Japanese). https://www.e-stat.go.jp/stat-search/files?page=1&layout=datalist&toukei=00200573&tstat=000001084976&cycle=0&tclass1=000001085995&tclass2=000001085936&tclass3=000001085996&tclass4=000001085997&tclass5val=0 (accessed April 26, 2021).

Global Note (2021). Sekai no Meimoku GDP Kunibetsu Rankingu. Suii (IMF). (In Japanese). https://www.globalnote.jp/post-1409.html (accessed April 26, 2021).

Ikegami, H., & Iijima, J. (2020). Unwrapping Efforts and Difficulties of Enterprises for Digital Transformation. In *Digital Business Transformation* (pp. 237–250). Springer, Cham.

ILO (2021). Statistics and databases. International Labor Organization. https://www.ilo.org/global/statistics-and-databases/lang--en/index.htm (accessed April 26, 2021).

IMD (2021). World Competitiveness Rankings 2020 Results. IMD World Competitive Centre. https://www.imd.org/wcc/world-competitiveness-center-rankings/world-competitiveness-ranking-2020/ (accessed May 23, 2021).

Ishikura, H., & Khare, A. (2020). Does the Japanese Work Ethic Conflict with the Needs of Retail in the Digital Era? In Transforming Japanese Business (pp. 71–87). Springer, Singapore.

Japan Productivity Center (2020). Kokusaiseisansei no kokusaihikau 2020 (December 23). (In Japanese). https://www.jpc-net.jp/research/assets/pdf/report_2020.pdf (accessed April 26, 2021).

Jozuka, E (2015). Robots Could Take Over Nearly 50 Percent of Jobs in Japan in the Next 20 Years. *Vice Newsletter*. (March 12). https://www.vice.com/en/article/4xaddj/robots-could-take-over-nearly-50-percent-of-jobs-in-japan-in-the-next-20-years (accessed April 26, 2021).

Kaya, K. (2019). Nihon ha mohaya kousinnkoku (pp. 81–99). Shuwasisutemu. (In Japanese).

Khare, A., Khare, K., & Baber, W. W. (2020). Why Japan's Digital Transformation Is Inevitable. In Khare, A., Ishikura, H. & Baber, W. W. (Eds.). *Transforming Japanese Business* (pp. 3–14). Springer, Singapore.

METI (2018). DX Report. Ministry of Economy, Trade and Industry. (September 7). (In Japanese). https://www.meti.go.jp/press/2018/09/20180907010/20180907010-2.pdf (accessed May 5, 2021).

NHK (2021). Kokoa no Chinmoku. (February 12). (In Japanese). https://www3.nhk.or.jp/news/html/20210212/k10012859871000.html (accessed April 26, 2021).

Nikkei (2020). Jyuman yen shikyu jyunbi ni kosetsu. (June 27). (In Japanese). https://www.nikkei.com/article/DGKKZO60877170W0A620C2EA3000/ (accessed April 29, 2021).

Noguchi, Y. (2021). The Decisive Factor that caused a Big difference in "IT" between Japan and China Toyokeizai. (In Japanese). https://toyokeizai.net/articles/-/402691 (accessed April 26, 2021).

Prime Minister's Office (2021). Koudo Jyoho tsushin netowaku shakai senryaku suiisin honbu. (In Japanese). http://www.kantei.go.jp/jp/singi/it2/index.html (accessed April 26, 2021).

Spence, C., Obrist, M., Velasco, C., & Ranasinghe, N. (2017). Digitizing the Chemical Senses: Possibilities & Pitfalls. *International Journal of Human-Computer Studies, 107*, 62–74.

US Bureau of Labor Statistics (2021). Consumer Price Index. https://www.bls.gov/cpi/data (accessed April 26, 2021).

Walmart (2021). Walmart Inc 2020 Annual Report. https://corporate.walmart.com/media-library/document/2020-walmart-annual-report/_proxyDocument?id=00000171-a3ea-dfc0-af71-b3fea8490000_(accessed April 26, 2021).

Yamamoto, S. (1989). Habatsu no kenkyu. Bungei Shunju. (In Japanese).

Yamamoto, S. (2006). Nihonnjin toha nanika. Shodensha. (In Japanese).

Yoro, T. (2005). Mushiso no Hakken. Chikuma Shinsho. (In Japanese).

8 The impact of Covid on office work in Japan

Kieran Gane and Ayaka Saito

1 Introduction

In the early stages of the pandemic, companies in Japan took extraordinary measures to change the way their employees work in the office, but in many companies these measures were only temporary. This chapter will leverage numerous surveys by the Japanese government and private companies, most only available in Japanese, to explain to a foreign audience which measures are likely to outlast the pandemic and permanently change office work in Japan. Since these surveys often use different channels and target groups and were carried out at different times, there can be some inconsistencies in their results, and so some interpretation is occasionally required.

This chapter begins with a brief outline of the pandemic in Japan and continues by giving some relevant background to the country, including actions taken by the Japanese government. These actions are partly in reaction to the pandemic, but also in a bid to catch up with other developed nations and are relevant to changes adopted by Japanese companies.

The main content starts by examining the level and impact of the implementation of working from home measures taken by companies and will move on to the challenges of working from home in Japan, the impact on productivity, and the preference of workers. This is followed by a look at how companies adapted to the pandemic, including the digitalization of approvals, moving to online training, and reviewing their office space. Last, it will look at other impacts, starting with the impact on women, on mental health, recruitment and retention, workforce flexibility, and business travel.

2 Background

2.1 Timeline and impact in Japan

COVID-19 was first identified in Japan in January 2020. On January 28, the Prime Minister, Abe, Shinzo, named the novel coronavirus a designated infectious disease under the Infectious Diseases Control Law and a quarantinable infectious disease under the Quarantine Act (Government of Japan, 2020a).

DOI: 10.4324/9781003216049-10

The virus started spreading slowly throughout Japan during the year with a low infection rate compared with most nations, particularly those in the West (Worldometer, 2021). While the exact reasons for this difference are not fully understood, the ubiquitous wearing of masks and high level of compliance to government guidelines are thought to be important factors.

In April, Abe declared the first state of emergency in seven prefectures, including Tokyo, but said that there would be no lockdown as services must continue to enable the economy and society to function (Government of Japan, 2020b). The government urged the public to stay at home and there was a high level of compliance for an initial period, after which many people returned to work, as can be seen by the level of train usage (Government of Japan, 2021a). Declarations were retracted and renewed during 2020 and early 2021, as the rate of infection rose and fell and Japan began the vaccination of its citizens in April 2021.

2.2 Background on Japan

Japan has a tendency to change only when it must, and Covid may well be the catalyst to trigger or accelerate a number of changes that were long overdue. The working culture is generally traditional with most people going to the office, working diligently for the company, and often working extra hours. Peer pressure can be very strong and 12-hour days are not uncommon. At the extreme are so-called "black companies" (a "black" company being one with poor working conditions), in which workers may work up to 15 hours per day, sometimes working the weekend also. There are even annual awards for the most "black" company, with many household names regularly appearing in the top 10 (Smart Tenshoku, 2020).

Like many developed countries, Japan has a low birth rate, an aging population, and suffers from depopulation of the countryside. While successive governments have tried to mitigate the extent and impact of these demographics, they have had little success.

2.3 Japanese government actions

The government took numerous financial and social measures to reduce the immediate impact of the virus, including incentives to promote telework among small and medium companies (Government of Japan, 2021b). The new Prime Minister, Suga, Yoshihide, elected in September 2020, also began the process of setting up a new digital agency, planned to open in September 2021 (Government of Japan, 2020d). The enacted law had three main principles: to automate all processes and services, to ask for information once only, and to enable one-stop processing for services (Government of Japan, 2020e). It is reported that this agency will be led not by a government official, but someone with business experience, and that workers will not have to wear suits, will have flextime, and be able to work from home.

This new law is driven by the fact that Japan is still largely paper-based, with only 7.5% of the approximately 56,000 government services accessible online, possibly due to the fragmented nature of government IT infrastructure at both the national and local levels (*The Economist*, 2021). The government also declared its intention to digitalize all but 83 of its 14,992 approval processes in an effort to increase productivity and resilience (Government of Japan, 2020f; p. 53). However, the use of "hanko" (physical seals used for the approval of documents) will be retained for services such as real estate, company and vehicle registration as well as inheritance tax declaration. The new digital agency and plan to become paperless are the latest of several such attempts by the Japanese government, so success is not guaranteed.

3 Working from home

In this section, the terms "working from home" and "telework" will be treated as equivalent, since the majority of telework is done at home.

3.1 Work from home implementation

Surveys on the extent to which companies implemented work from home measures give varying results, but the change was large and lasting. A survey of employees in Tokyo found that from a base of less than one in five in December 2019, over half were working from home in April 2020 (Tokyo Metropolitan Government, 2020; p. 2). It also showed that the larger the company, the more likely they were to have implemented work from home.

According to a survey of companies by Keidanren, Japan's biggest business lobby, 90% of its members had made efforts to implement work from home, a huge increase from pre-Covid levels (Keidanren, 2021; p. 1). However, the level of success differed greatly, with only 37% in prefectures under a state of emergency having met the government's target of cutting commuters by 70% or more. Excluding essential workers, this led to a 65% reduction in the amount of commuting to work. The survey also showed that, on average, the smaller the company, the lower the rate of telework was likely to be.

By comparison, in a survey of workers in April 2020, over half of the respondents said that their company had not implemented a work from home system (Kaonavi, 2020a). This discrepancy is probably due to the fact that smaller companies, where most workers in Japan are employed, are less likely to join Keidanren or have the time to answer surveys. This survey also showed a higher rate of implementation in urban areas.

The proportion of workers working from home decreased over the course of the pandemic from the high in April/May 2020. A survey of all workers showed the number working from home in Tokyo peaked at 48.4% in May 2020 and dropped to 42.8% by December (Government of Japan, 2021c; p. 30). Across the whole of Japan, the drop was from 27.7% to 21.5% over the same period. This survey found that the industries with the highest rate of working from home were telecommunications and utility companies, and that the probability of teleworking increased with income.

Another survey found the proportion of those working from home falling to one in five by April, 2021 (Japan Productivity Center, 2021a; p. 17). Tokyo continued to have the highest proportion of teleworkers, at almost one in three, but the proportion in Osaka was less than one in five and was likely much lower in rural areas. These levels are still significantly higher than they were before the pandemic.

3.2 *Working from home challenges*

Japanese working from home faced many of the same issues as workers in the rest of the world, but there were some more prevalent in Japan, starting with the home environment. Over half of those working from home reported doing so from their living room, probably due to the tendency for smaller houses in Japan (Recruit Sumai, 2020; p. 10). Another survey found that almost half of respondents had issues with their chair, desk, lighting, or internet connectivity (Japan Productivity Center, 2021b; p. 16).

The processing of physical documents was also a barrier to working from home. These included approvals in general (Japan Productivity Center, 2021b; p. 16), and the approval of contracts and handling of physical mail (Gekkan Soumu Online, 2021). The use of "hanko" for approval was a particular issue for smaller companies (TSR, 2020; p. 3) and physical invoices were also a problem (Sansan, 2021).

Communication with managers and colleagues was found to be an issue (Japan Productivity Center, 2021b; p. 16), as was communication with vendors (Government of Japan, 2021c; p. 35). Half the respondents in one survey said that it was difficult to communicate with colleagues (Kaonavi, 2020b) and another survey identified management concerns that the relationship between the employee and the company could break down (Gekkan Soumu Online, 2020a). Indeed, many managers were not comfortable with their team working from home because they could not see what they were doing, and workers were worried whether they would be fairly evaluated when they couldn't be seen (Kaonavi, 2020c).

Mental health was also impacted by the pandemic. One survey found that almost 70% of workers in Japan said that Covid had a negative impact on their mental health, with younger workers more likely to say they were impacted (Oracle, 2020; p. 6). Many of these people said that mental health issues caused sleep deprivation, poor physical health, reduced happiness at home, suffering family relationships, or isolation from friends. Another survey showed that three-quarters of workers were feeling anxious about Covid, their own productivity, communication difficulties, and their contribution to the team (Kaonavi, 2020d).

Working from home itself was also a concern, with younger workers more likely to have concerns than older workers (Persol, 2020a). Difficulties in working from home reduced during 2020 as workers got used to the new way of working, but that there was a tendency to work longer hours as the distinction between work and home life became blurred.

Many of these issues persisted into 2021 (Japan Productivity Center, 2021a; p. 19), including those regarding the physical environment and connectivity at home, the use of physical documents and approvals, and communication issues, albeit at reduced rates.

3.3 Work from home productivity

The picture on productivity when working from home is complex and depends heavily on the industry and type of work. In one survey remote workers reported that productivity when working from home was on average only 84.1% of that when working in the office (Persol, 2020a). On the other hand, in another survey over half of respondents felt that their productivity had increased while working from home, more than those who felt that it had decreased (Japan Productivity Center, 2021b; p. 7). The number of workers saying that productivity had improved while working from home continued to increase over time to three-fifths by April 2021 (Japan Productivity Center, 2021a; p. 18).

A survey of companies found that productivity varied greatly by industry with Information and Communication Industry having the highest at 80.3% and Retail having the lowest at 62.6% (Morikawa, Masayuki, 2021). It reported that the top four factors affecting the adoption and productivity of working from home were issues with the home telecommunication environment, the unsuitability of some types of work, requirements that some work only be done in the office, and communication difficulties due to the inability to have face-to-face interactions. The analysis concluded by saying that productivity could be improved by the resolution of those issues as well as by changes to relevant laws and regulations, but that for the foreseeable future further adoption is likely to be restricted.

3.4 Working from home popularity

While there are many challenges to working from home and questions remain about productivity, there are also many benefits which make it popular with workers. In one survey almost nine out of ten of those working from home wanted to continue to do so in some form, and even of those not working from home, two-thirds wanted to have the option to do so (Government of Japan, 2021c; p. 37). Apart from reducing the risk of infection, benefits included not spending time on commuting, the ability to use breaks efficiently, the ease of taking breaks and relaxing, the reduction in interpersonal stresses, and the ability to concentrate.

It is not surprising that more women than men want to continue working from home (Kaonavi, 2020e) since they take on the majority of housework and child-rearing responsibilities (Government of Japan, 2021d; p. 55), and working from home makes balancing the two easier.

There also seemed to be benefits for the companies that allowed working from home. One survey found that there was a stronger feeling of attachment and gratitude to the company amongst teleworkers compared to those working in the office (Persol, 2020b). There was a correlation between the measures taken by companies to protect the health of their workers and the commitment of workers to the company.

3.5 Going forward

It is clear that working from home is a tool, just like any other, suitable only for certain types of jobs and tasks. While many companies in Japan at the start of the pandemic promoted working from home, the proportion has gradually reduced over time and will no doubt drop further once the risk of infection disappears.

However, there seems to be a core of progressive companies that are not only fully embracing working from home, but taking it further. Fujitsu announced work from home measures in July 2020 and stated the intention to make them permanent (Fujitsu, 2020). The Fujitsu press release said it as redefining the working style for its employees in Japan to realize employee well-being. It went on to explain three core principles: Smart Working (realizing optimal working styles), Borderless Office (reassessment of the ideal office environment), and Culture Change (transforming corporate culture). Other major companies such as Hitachi, Nomura and Dentsu seem to be following suit to a lesser extent. This is good for workers, but also for society as a whole since commuting is inherently inefficient taking up a significant amount of the working day.

However, personal relationships are very important in business in Japan and meetings in person are the glue that maintain those relationships. In one survey three-quarters of respondents said that the lack of face-to-face meetings had caused them problems (Kaonavi, 2020d). Another survey of new graduates and their managers showed a preference for face-to-face meetings (JMAM, 2020). Therefore, it is likely that while progressive companies adopt a variation of Fujitsu's hybrid model, traditional companies will probably return to the pre-pandemic working in the office norm.

4 Company adaptation

4.1 Permanent change

A government survey confirmed what we have seen previously that many companies made changes to internal meetings, approval processes, system access, meetings with customers and vendors, and started becoming paperless (Government of Japan, 2021c; p. 33). Whether companies had been planning this or not, action was taken due to Covid that would not have been taken otherwise. These actions, once taken, are not likely to be reversed.

Keidanren also found that the vast majority of their member companies had modified their IT environment, business content and/or processes to enable telework, and listed three requests to the government to further enable working from home (Keidanren, 2021; p. 7). These were: to update government guidelines on the labor management of telework, to give subsidies and tax cuts for information technology capital investment, and to digitalize government offices and reduce the use of "hanko" in public documents.

Workers were also confident that some of the changes that were implemented would become lasting. In particular, there was a belief that the necessity of work processes would be reviewed, flexible working hours and web meetings would be continued, and that approvals would be digitalized, as will be discussed in the next section (Japan Productivity Center, 2021a; p. 21).

4.2 Digital approval

Seals, or "hanko", became popular during the Meiji Era and are ubiquitous in personal and business life in Japan, and this is one of the challenges to working from home as we have seen previously. We have also seen that the government is taking action to digitalize its approval processes and that this is welcomed by the companies of Keidanren. In a country prone to natural disasters, enabling digital processes is a very practical step toward resilience and the alignment of government and business raises the likelihood of success.

There is also much support for abolishing the use of "hanko" and some progress has been made. In a large online survey 85% of respondents said that they thought they should be abolished (GMO Internet Group, 2020), and this support seems to be leading to concrete action. Another survey found that one-fifth of companies had already implemented digital contracts due to Covid and a further quarter were planning to do so (Persol, 2020c).

However, not everyone is convinced that it is possible. A survey of senior managers and directors found that over four-fifths of companies were still using "hanko" for some of their processes (Adobe, 2020). While most of the respondents thought it would be good to abolish the use of "hanko" to improve efficiency, half said that they didn't think eliminating them would be easy in their company since they were required for legal reasons, for the convenience of the other party in a contract, or for security.

4.3 Training

The majority of companies did not have online events, including training, in 2019 (Gekkan Soumu Online, 2020b). In 2020 the situation had completely reversed, and the most popular online event was training with over half of companies having adopted it in some form. A later survey confirmed this, finding that Covid had been the direct cause of the shift to online training for most companies and that a fifth of companies carried out all training online (Gekkan Soumu Online, 2020a). Three-quarters of the companies said that online training was a success, with over half having adapted the content for online delivery. Benefits of online training included no travel time, no limitations on training space, and cost savings.

However, the same survey found that three-fifths of the companies performing training online wanted to move back to face-to-face delivery. Reasons given for this included the lack of opportunity for workers to interact, the difficulty of practical hands-on training, and the passive nature of online training. Despite this desire to revert, now that online training has been trialed at scale, it seems unlikely that there will be a complete return to pre-Covid practices as the cost and time overhead may not always outweigh the benefit.

4.4 Office space

The press release by Fujitsu mentioned previously included plans to allow employees to choose where they work depending on what they need to do, be that at home, in a satellite office, or in a main office (Fujitsu, 2020). The company also stated plans to reduce its office footprint by 50% by the end of the 2022 fiscal year.

According to a Reuter's poll, a third of firms were reassessing their office use due to large decreases in utilization (Kajimoto, 2020). Of the companies reassessing office use, almost half said that they were looking at satellite offices, while a third were looking to downsize, and one in ten looking at shared workspaces.

A later survey of companies in Tokyo found that although three-quarters of companies had implemented work from home due to Covid, most expected that the majority of their staff would work in the office post-Covid (Mori Building, 2020; p. 1). A quarter of companies responding had plans to change their offices, largely unchanged from 2019, but while in 2019 more companies had been looking for somewhere larger, in 2020 more companies were looking for somewhere smaller. Interestingly, the reasons given for wanting to move were not directly related to Covid, but were wanting to move to cheaper offices, a desire for a better location, and wanting a building with better earthquake-proofing.

5 Other impact

5.1 Impact on women

In the 2021 Global Gender Gap Report, Japan places 120th of the 156 nations surveyed and 117th in the Economic Participation and Opportunity subindex (World Economic Forum, 2021; p. 37). The report also notes that well under a fifth of senior roles are taken by women. This is reflected by Japan's political and business leaders who are renowned for their ill-chosen remarks about the role of women. Japan's governing party in 2021 famously invited women to a key meeting on the condition that they did not speak (BBC News, 2021). Indeed, Kanji, the Chinese characters which are used in the written language, contain traditional views of the role of men and women, with women often being associated with the home. It may be necessary to reform the written language in order to fully change mindsets around gender.

Although there was a greater fall in the number of female workers than male workers in April 2020, the number of female workers seemed to have mainly recovered by February 2021 (Government of Japan, 2021d; p. 4). The greater fall is due to the fact that more women are in non-permanent jobs, and so part of the flexible work force which is at risk in economic downturns (Government of Japan, 2021d; p. 7). The same survey also found that those in non-permanent jobs felt more insecure than those in permanent roles, with younger people feeling the most insecure, which shows that young women felt the most insecure (Government of Japan, 2021d; p. 11).

Women's income was also impacted: 18.7% of men said that there had been some change in their employment compared with 26.3% of women and 21.9% of women had their income reduced by more than 30% compared with 15.6% of men (NHK, 2020). This does not help the wage gap between men and women, which is already the second largest in the developed world (Government of Japan, 2021d; p. 19).

Successive Japanese governments have attempted to enable greater participation of women in the workforce. The Covid pandemic has shown that systemic and cultural issues remain and would need to be addressed before the full potential of Japanese women can be realized.

5.2 Mental health and automation

An increase in process automation was driven by Covid, with a fifth of companies having started implementation and another fifth in the planning stage (Persol, 2020c). One particular use for automation is in tackling mental health issues which we noted previously have increased during the pandemic. Interestingly, there is a strong preference for talking to a robot about mental health rather than to a person, since robots are considered judgement-free, unbiased, and quick to respond (Oracle, 2020; p. 8). Demand is also high for other technology to support mental health, including wellness or meditation apps, and proactive health monitoring tools, and on-demand counseling, chatbots, or self-service resources.

The same survey found a majority desiring AI support for their work to enable the automation of administrative tasks, provide information to work more effectively, automate tasks and decrease workload, prevent burnout, and help prioritize tasks. Bottom line benefits of AI were perceived to increase employee productivity, improve job satisfaction, improve overall well-being, a shorter working week, and the ability to take longer vacations.

5.3 Recruitment and retention

There have been immediate impacts on recruitment and the recruitment process. A press release from the JAL Group (2021) announced that there would be a large reduction in the number of employees due to Covid, and so they would not recruit new graduates in 2022. In fact, many other companies also planned to reduce or stop recruitment of new graduates in 2022, and mid-career recruitment plans were also reduced (Persol, 2020a). This is likely to be temporary, until the overall economy recovers.

The recruitment process also changed as interviews moved online. A survey of companies on the recruitment of new foreign graduates found that not only the interviews of those outside of Japan, but also of those in Japan, had moved online, particularly for the first interview (DISCO, 2020; p. 11). However, as the candidate proceeded through the recruitment process, there was a greater chance of being invited for an in-person interview.

Both recruitment and retention are likely to be impacted by worker desire to have the option to work from home. Indeed, one survey found an increased desire of almost one in five workers to change to a company or type of work that could be done from home (Persol, 2020a). As we have seen, working from home is not only a useful tool to balance work and personal life, but also an indication of the focus of employers on the well-being of their workers. Given that, working from home may well be the latest battleground for key skills where the power lies with the worker in choosing the employer.

It does not seem likely that companies will change their policies to recruit from anywhere, but given a hybrid working model and the reduced frequency of going to the office, some workers may choose to live further away. The level of migration to Tokyo has reversed slightly in 2020, but the change does not indicate a mass exodus from cities and repopulation of the countryside (Tokyo Metropolitan Government, 2021), and workers themselves do not believe that many people will do so (Japan Productivity Center, 2021b; p. 21).

5.4 Workforce flexibility

A 2020 survey by the Ministry of Health, Labor, and Welfare showed that 9.7% of the working population had side jobs, continuing the increasing trend of recent years (Government of Japan, 2020c; p. 7). Interestingly, the pandemic seems to have increased workers' desire for a side job even further (Persol, 2020a). There has also been an increased desire of workers to improve their employability, with many wanting to learn more specialist skills or take some form of retraining (Japan Productivity Center, 2021b; p. 12).

A flexible workforce will be important since Japan faces a large skills shortage, in particular of IT workers due to the declining population (nippon.com, 2021). While companies in other countries might look to offshore for the work, language becomes a barrier in Japan at some point in any service. It is likely then that companies will have to be flexible, perhaps relying more on temporary, on-demand workers.

5.5 Business travel

International travel during the pandemic has decreased dramatically to only a small fraction of the pre-Covid level. It will not recover greatly in 2021, and whether it will recover fully or not is unclear. However, the fact that companies continued to work during Covid with no major issues has shown that in the short to medium term, business travel is not essential. Given that and the increasing awareness of the impact of the climate crisis, peak international travel, including business travel, may well be behind us.

A study of the impact of business travel on the development of industries hypothesized that business travel is the force that drives the diffusion of know-how, which was defined as being the knowledge in people's brains, not just on paper (Coscia, Neffke, & Hausmann, 2021). This would mean that countries will grow industries if they are visited by people from countries that specialize in those industries. The study proved the hypothesis, concluding that business travel actually causes economic growth.

Intuitively, this makes sense. The extra time spent together, over coffees and at lunches and dinners, helps to build a more complete picture by enabling the discussion of the abstract and conceptual as well as the practical, and the development of personal relationships which can be leveraged in the future. So, going forward, business travel is likely to recover, but only time will show us the extent of the recovery.

6 Summary

Covid has impacted all industries in Japan, and thus all companies, domestic and international, for an extended period of time. It has highlighted the importance of physical and mental health of workers, and shown the vulnerability of women in particular to economic downturns. In the office it has triggered a minor revolution, including the expansion of working from home, and accelerated the use of web meetings, the digitalization of processes, approvals, and services. Many companies are reviewing their use of offices, and changes made to training and recruiting are likely to persist to some extent. Finally, it has galvanized the government to again attempt to modernize the way it works.

There is broad support for these changes, as they give workers more flexibility in their personal and work life. Companies also benefit as they become more efficient and enhance their resilience. Of course, not all companies have adapted, and the challenge is greater for smaller companies even with government incentives. However, it is possible that progressive companies in each industry will force others to follow their example.

As the pandemic subsides, the drive for Japan to change will reduce. How far the momentum of change that built up during Covid will take the country may well depend on the success of the government's digital agency and changes at major companies such as Fujitsu. The inertia of traditional companies and practices that they need to overcome is considerable, and success is not guaranteed.

7 Acknowledgements

Thanks to those who REVIEWED early drafts of the chapter, in particular Stefan Voss and David Klan. Also, thanks to Yamamoto Coffee for providing the perfect place to write.

References

Adobe (2020). アドビ「中小企業経営者に聞いた判子の利用実態調査」の結果を発表. https://www.adobe.com/jp/news-room/news/202006/20200615_adobe-seal-usage-survey.html. (accessed March 11, 2021).

BBC News (2021). Why Japan Can't Shake Sexism. https://www.bbc.com/worklife/article/20210405-why-japan-cant-shake-sexism (accessed April 8, 2021).

Coscia, M., Neffke, F., & Hausmann, R. (2021). What would Happen if Business Travel Stopped? https://growthlab.cid.harvard.edu/academic-research/business-travel. (accessed April 8, 2021).

DISCO (2020). 「外国人留学生／高度外国人材の採用に関する調査」. https://www.disc.co.jp/wp/wp-content/uploads/2021/01/2020kigyou-global-report.pdf(accessedApril 8, 2021).

The Economist (2021). Japan's New Prime Minister Drags Government into the Digital Era. https://www.economist.com/asia/2021/01/02/japans-new-prime-minister-drags-government-into-the-digital-era (accessed April 8, 2021).

Fujitsu Limited (2020). Fujitsu Embarks towards 'New Normal', Redefining Working Styles for Its Japan Offices. https://www.fujitsu.com/global/about/resources/news/press-releases/2020/0706-01.html (accessed April 8, 2021).

Gekkan Soumu Online (2020a). 73.4%が対面研修のオンライン化に着手したが、うち59.0%がオンライン研修を対面に戻したいと回答. https://www.g-soumu.com/linkage/2020/12/employeetraining-questionnaire.php (accessed April 8, 2021).

Gekkan Soumu Online (2020b). テレワークで「会社の方向性を伝えにくくなった」が79.1%。そのうち95.7%が社員のエンゲージメント低下を実感. https://www.g-soumu.com/linkage/2020/11/motivationquestionnaire.php (accessed April 8, 2021).

Gekkan Soumu Online (2021). コロナ対策やテレワーク推進の影響で、約9割が2020年度に会社全体のデジタル化が進んだと回答。2021年度の総務体制に求めることも「デジタルツールの導入」が最多. https://www.g-soumu.com/linkage/cat656/. (accessed April 8, 2021).

GMO Internet Group (2020). 日本の脱ハンコを後押しする「さよなら印鑑キャンペーン」終了！. https://www.gmogshd.com/news/info/201001_3088.html. (accessed April 8, 2021).

Government of Japan (2020a). National Printing Bureau. 特別号外 第4号. https://kanpou.npb.go.jp/old/20200128/20200128t00004/20200128t000040002f.html. (accessed April 8, 2021).

Government of Japan (2020b). Prime Minister's Office of Japan. 新型コロナウイルス感染症対策本部（第２７回）. https://www.kantei.go.jp/jp/98_abe/actions/202004/07corona.html. (accessed April 8, 2021).

Government of Japan (2020c). Ministry of Health, Labor, and Welfare. 副業・兼業に係る実態把握の内容等について. https://www.mhlw.go.jp/content/11201250/000660780.pdf. (accessed April 8, 2021).

Government of Japan (2020d). Prime Minister of Japan and His Cabinet. デジタル手続法. http://www.kantei.go.jp/jp/singi/it2/hourei/digital.html. (accessed April 8, 2021).

Government of Japan (2020e). Prime Minister's Office of Japan. デジタル改革. https://www.kantei.go.jp/jp/headline/tokushu/digital.html. (accessed April 8, 2021).

Government of Japan (2020f). Cabinet Office. 地方公共団体における押印見直しマニュアル（参考資料集）. https://www8.cao.go.jp/kisei-kaikaku/kisei/imprint/document/manual/201218reference_ver01.pdf. (accessed April 8, 2021).

Government of Japan (2021a). Ministry of Land, Infrastructure, Transport and Tourism. 鉄道利用者の皆様へ（新型コロナウイルス感染症対策の利用者向け情報）. https://www.mlit.go.jp/tetudo/tetudo_fr1_000062.html. (accessed April 8, 2021).

Government of Japan (2021b). Ministry of Health, Labour and Welfare. 2働き方改革推進支援助成金（新型コロナウイルス感染症対策のためのテレワークコース）. https://www.mhlw.go.jp/stf/seisakunitsuite/bunya/koyou_roudou/roudoukijun/jikan/syokubaisikitelework.html. (accessed April 8, 2021).
Government of Japan (2021c). Gender Equality Bureau Cabinet Office. コロナ下の女性への影響と課題に関する研究会. https://www.gender.go.jp/kaigi/kento/covid-19/siryo/pdf/11-1.pdf. (accessed April 8, 2021).
Government of Japan (2021d). Gender Equality Bureau Cabinet Office. コロナ下の女性への影響と課題に関する研究会報告書. https://www.gender.go.jp/kaigi/kento/covid-19/siryo/pdf/post_zuhyo.pdf. (accessed May 18, 2021).
JAL Group (2021). 年度入社JALグループ新卒採用について. https://press.jal.co.jp/ja/release/202102/005962.html. (accessed April 8, 2021).
Japan Productivity Center (2021a). 第 5 回 働く人の意識に関する調査. https://www.jpc-net.jp/research/assets/pdf/5th_workers_report.pdf. (accessed May 12, 2021).
Japan Productivity Center (2021b). 第4回「働く人の意識調査. https://www.jpc-net.jp/research/assets/pdf/4th_workers_report.pdf. (accessed April 8, 2021).
JMAM (2020). 【新型コロナによるビジネスパーソンの意識・行動変化に関する調査結果】. https://www.jmam.co.jp/topics/1260357_1893.html. (accessed April 8, 2021).
Kajimoto, T. (2020). Some Japan firms Rethink Traditional Office as Pandemic Boosts Working from Home: Reuters Poll. https://www.reuters.com/article/us-japan-companies-office-poll-idUSKCN25E2Y8. (accessed April 8, 2021).
Kaonavi (2020a). カオナビHRテクノロジー総研調査レポート. https://ri.kaonavi.jp/20200526/. (accessed April 8, 2021).
Kaonavi (2020b). カオナビHRテクノロジー総研調査レポート. https://ri.kaonavi.jp/20200610/. (accessed April 8, 2021).
Kaonavi (2020c). カオナビHRテクノロジー総研調査レポート. https://ri.kaonavi.jp/20201001/. (accessed April 8, 2021).
Kaonavi (2020d). カオナビHRテクノロジー総研調査レポート. https://ri.kaonavi.jp/20201022/. (accessed April 8, 2021).
Kaonavi (2020e). カオナビHRテクノロジー総研調査レポート. https://ri.kaonavi.jp/20200624/. (accessed April 8, 2021).
Keidanren (2021). 緊急事態宣言下におけるテレワーク等の実施状況調査. https://www.keidanren.or.jp/policy/2021/011.pdf. (accessed April 8, 2021).
Mori Building (2020). 2020年 東京23区オフィスニーズに関する調査. https://www.mori.co.jp/img/article/201223.pdf. (accessed April 8, 2021).
Morikawa, Masayuki (2021). The Productivity of Working from Home: Evidence from Japan. https://voxeu.org/article/productivity-working-home-evidence-japan. (accessed April 8, 2021).
NHK (2020). 新型コロナ 働く女性への影響は. https://www3.nhk.or.jp/news/special/coronavirus/difficulty/detail/detail_01.html. (accessed April 8, 2021).
nippon.com (2021). A Worsening Labor Shortage. https://www.nippon.com/en/japan-topics/g01044/digital-shift-japanese-recruiter-turns-to-india-amid-it-engineer-shortage.html. (accessed April 8, 2021).
Oracle (2020). As Uncertainty Remains, Anxiety and Stress Reach a Tipping Point at Work. https://www.oracle.com/a/ocom/docs/applications/hcm/2020-hcm-ai-at-work-study.pdf. (accessed April 8, 2021).
Persol (2020a). 第四回・新型コロナウイルス対策によるテレワークへの影響に関する緊急調査. https://rc.persol-group.co.jp/research/activity/data/telework-survey4.html. (accessed April 8, 2021).

Persol (2020b). パーソル総合研究所 - テレワークによる組織の求心力への影響に関する定量調査. https://rc.persol-group.co.jp/research/activity/data/telework-organizational-commitment.html. (accessed April 8, 2021).

Persol (2020c). 【業務のデジタル化に関する意識・実態調査】 デジタル化が進んでいるのは「Web会議の導入」 コロナ前後で3割から9割に迫る。「FAXの撤廃」の動きは他よりも遅れている。. https://www.persol-pt.co.jp/news/2020/12/17/4841/. (accessed April 8, 2021).

Recruit Sumai Company (2020). 「新型コロナ禍を受けたテレワーク×住まいの意識・実態」調査. https://www.recruit.co.jp/newsroom/recruit-sumai/data/upload/1c89c428b47ca0906f27259f7f648242.pdf. (accessed April 8, 2021).

Sansan (2021). 「請求書に関する業務の実態調査2021」. https://jp.corp-sansan.com/news/2021/survey_report_bill_one_2021.html. (accessed April 8, 2021).

Smart Tenshoku (2020). ブラック企業大賞の歴代受賞&ノミネート企業まとめ【過去8年分】. https://tensyokubu.net/2020/07/27/black-company-award-summary/. (accessed May 10, 2021).

Tokyo Metropolitan Government (2021). 「東京都の人口（推計）」の概要. https://www.metro.tokyo.lg.jp/tosei/hodohappyo/press/2021/01/28/01.html. (accessed April 8, 2021).

Tokyo Metropolitan Government. Bureau of Industrial and Labor Affairs Employment Division. (2020). テレワーク「導入率」緊急調査結果. https://www.hataraku.metro.tokyo.lg.jp/hatarakikata/telework/cyousagaiyou0511.pdf. (accessed April 8, 2021).

TSR (2020). 第8回「新型コロナウイルスに関するアンケート」調査. https://img03.en25.com/Web/TSR/%7Bd07e9c91-6739-49c7-95df-6ffe7bb82fef%7D_20200915_TSRsurvey_CoronaVirus.pdf. (accessed April 8, 2021).

World Economic Forum (2021). Global Gender Gap Report 2021. http://www3.weforum.org/docs/WEF_GGGR_2021.pdf. (accessed April 8, 2021).

Worldometer (2021). Coronavirus, World, Countries, Japan. https://www.worldometers.info/coronavirus/country/japan/. (accessed April 8, 2021).

9 Japanese business communication in the COVID crisis

A study of horenso and its implications

Kanji Kitamura

1 Introduction

Since the outbreak, many research efforts have been made worldwide to gauge the impacts of COVID-19 and establish strategies to cope with the pandemic. One strategy to contain the spread of the virus is social distancing, which has inevitably hampered social activities in most sectors across the world. Under these circumstances, teleworking has gained popularity more than ever. In most cases, it is forcibly introduced to employees with no prior remote work experience (Waizenegger et al., 2020). The massive expansion of teleworking may be considered a global-scale experiment (Sostero et al., 2020). In the USA, the Telework Enhancement Act of 2020 provides the federal definition: "The term telework or teleworking refers to a work flexibility arrangement under which an employee performs the duties and responsibilities of such employee's position, and other authorized activities, from an approved worksite other than the location from which the employee would otherwise work" (United States Government Publishing Office, 2010; p. 1). The definition gives general ideas on the term.

The extent to which an employee can work offsite is often referred to as teleworkability: it is a newly emerged term defined as "the technical possibility of providing labor input remotely into a given economic process", according to European Commission's working paper (Sostero et al., 2020; p. 29). Teleworkability varies, depending on various factors. At the macro level, it correlates with the industry, to which the employer belongs. The top three sectors with the highest teleworkability are IT and communication, knowledge-intensive services, and education (Sostero et al., 2020; p. 10). Besides sectorial classification, the type of work can be the determinant. Labor-intensive occupations, such as nurses and production line workers, cannot be performed remotely with the available technologies (Sostero et al., 2020). This chapter focuses on occupations in business sectors with a reasonable level of teleworkability.

As for Japanese businesses, local scholars have carried out a series of studies on the challenges that the Japanese companies have been facing. The main findings include the significance of difficulty communicating between employees in organizations (Hara et al., 2020; Hattori et al., 2020; Sasaki et al., 2020). Research

DOI: 10.4324/9781003216049-11

shows that Japanese companies see it as a major challenge, or at least something critical despite the availability of internet-based communication tools. This finding seems to have important implications because communication difficulty generally does not appear to be as equally critical in studies administered outside Japan; instead, the issue of mental and physical health is frequently discussed as the major theme (Waizenegger et al., 2020). This cross-country difference has become the origin of research interest for this study.

In Japan, the Ministry of Health, Labor and Welfare[1] provides a comprehensive portal website dedicated to teleworking. One of the Q&A descriptions in their webpage for frequently asked questions offers a clue to the cross-country difference of communication. The question reads: how can I do houkoku, renraku, and sodan when teleworking (Ministry of Health, Labor and Welfare, 2020)? Similarly, Japanese media features the issue: *Nikkei*, the prominent newspaper in the nation, writes that when teleworking, you should be mindful of houkoku, renraku, and sodan more than usual (Nihon Keizai Shimbun, 2020; p. 1). The keywords, houkoku (reporting), renraku (contacting), and sodan (consulting), are usually called horenso, which is an acronym consisting of the first syllables of the three words (Kameda, 2013). Horenso is a widely known term in Japan, yet under-researched system of communication specific to the nation. This chapter focuses on horenso: its significance in the context of Japanese business and its implications that may help gain insights into the future trajectory of the communication system. The aim of this study is to envisage Japanese-style communication in the post-COVID era by investigating their current practice during the pandemic.

The literature suggests that horenso is a regionally peculiar system coexisting with the locally shared values of preference (Kameda, 2013). Such regional values are often referred to as cultural constructs at the individual level (Thomas and Peterson, 2017). This chapter will begin with a review of relevant concepts and position horenso as an attribute of the wider context of Japanese employment connected with the regionally shared ways of thinking. Supported by interview data available to the public, the case examples will reveal that the system of horenso can be perceived as part of the Japanese decision-making process. By bridging business studies, cultural studies, and Japanese studies, this chapter will develop the concept of horenso and predict that horenso will remain in the post-pandemic era alongside the internet-based video conferencing platforms that have already gained popularity today.

2 Literature review

Originally coined in the business sector, the term horenso is frequently and especially heard in empirical settings. The history of horenso dates to at least Japan's boom times and possibly further back. Tomiji Yamazaki, President of Yamatane securities at that time, first wrote a book about horenso in the late 1980s (Yamazaki, 1989). It is considered groundbreaking work, in the sense that it conceptualized the term and made it popular. While Yamazaki can be the father of the term, some form of horenso is likely to have existed in Japan. Before Yamazaki wrote his book, many scholars carried out research on Japanese business in the past. Early prominent researchers include James Abegglen, Michael Yoshino, and Peter Drucker, to name a few who introduced Japanese-style management in English to the West.[2] Citing Abegglen (1958), Yoshino (1968), Cole (1971), and Dore (1973), Beechler et al. (1996; p. 3) write of the following critical differences found in Japanese business as compared to their Western counterparts: "more frequent use of consultative decision-making practices, higher frequency of communication, lifetime employment (LTE), long-term planning horizons, generalist career paths, quality control circles, and implicit informal control mechanisms". Among these, consultative decision-making and frequent communication appear to be practically what is now called horenso. The idea here is similar to how the practice of kaizen attracted attention in the West: Masaaki Imai first wrote a book about kaizen in English (Imai, 1986). This book is considered the groundbreaking work worldwide that made it popular. While Imai's work is an important milestone, the Japanese have been practicing kaizen before the publication of Imai's work. This chapter refers to Japanese communication with the long-standing features as horenso for discussion purposes. Another feature of horenso is that Japanese businesses do not require it for all decisions, as Beechler et al. (1996; p. 3) point out "more frequent use" of horenso than the West. The difference of frequency is relative yet significant. For instance, the IT societies are often required to make quick decisions on the spot in accordance with the available technology in most countries, including Japan.

Literature concerning horenso is limited. Among available works, Kameda (2013) offers helpful discussions on the concept: it can be described as "a continual and collaborative communication process between superiors, subordinates, and colleagues over the course of a project" (Kameda, 2013; p. 9). This chapter provisionally borrows this description and attempts to develop it. Regarding the three words that constitute the term, houkoku means "reporting to supervisors on the progress, changes, if any, and result of your work in a timely manner when and if instructions and/or orders are given by supervisors" (Kameda, 2013; p. 9). This description appears reasonable, but suggests one way of communication from subordinates to supervisors. On the other hand, Yamazaki's original work promotes honest information sharing regardless of job titles (Yamazaki, 1989). This chapter does not reject Kameda's description, but presupposes that horenso may involve two-way communications between supervisors and subordinates or between employees across the organization.

The preceding description of horenso probably makes sense and poses nothing foreign to most professionals regardless of their national origin. However, Kameda (2013; p. 10) adds, "Horenso is a typical business communication practice peculiar to Japanese culture", suggesting that horenso or some elements of it are specific to Japan and the precise equivalent(s) may not exist in other countries. This important point needs to be addressed before proceeding. Literature offers cautionary notes regarding translation of and discussion on regionally specific practice. Miyashita and Russell (1994; p. 7) provide a useful example: "The word keiretsu does not translate neatly into English, and that is the beginning of the problem". It does not translate neatly because there is no exact equivalent of the form keiretsu in the English-speaking countries. It is problematic in a cross-national setting because the lack of a precise equivalent makes discussion harder. This chapter refers to this issue as the lack of mutual knowledge. The closest equivalent of keiretsu in English can be strategic alliance, which may be used for explanatory purposes. Nevertheless, strategic alliance in the English sense is "far from being Japanese-style horizontal keiretsu" (Miyashita and Russell, 1994; p. 208). As discussed earlier, the word horenso is an acronym consisting of the first syllables of three words: houkoku (reporting), renraku (contacting), and sodan (consulting). Each of these English translations of the Japanese words gives ideas on the concept but may not perfectly convey what horenso is. Regionally specific terms may be translated as guidance into English, but their semantic fields are not always identical to the closest possible translations. To tackle the challenging issue, the following section will establish a theoretical foundation for this research.

3 Theoretical framework

Arie de Geus (2002) writes about the useful concept of an entity's persona, originally coined by a famous German psychologist, William Stern, who developed the intelligence quotient formula. "To Stern, each living being has an undifferentiated wholeness, with its own character, which he called the persona" (de Geus, 2002; p. 84). To explain the concept, de Geus introduces a vertical ladder that William Stern drew in 1919. The ladder has five levels, namely Deity/Divinity/Godhead being on the top row, followed in descending order by Nation, Tribe, Family, and Individual placed on the lowest row, each of which is "a persona in its own right" (de Geus, 2002; p. 87). Borrowing Stern's idea, de Geus illustrates a company's organizational structure, using a ladder with seven levels, namely Society being on the top, followed in descending order by Corporation, Company, Division, Work Group, Team, and Individual. The idea of a ladder with multi-level personas corresponds with prevalent concepts in the literature. For example, Williams and Zumbansen (2011) write about "embeddedness" that signifies the connection between the levels of personas in the whole. According to Williams and Zumbansen (2011), institutions and markets are embedded in a society and manifest social values, and that is why those cannot be discussed in isolation from social values. Social values include regional values of preference and locally normative ways of thinking that generally belong to an individual-level persona. Institutions and markets are considered constituents of personas sitting at the higher levels than the individual level. Stern's idea is 100 years old, yet appears to stand today. This chapter refers to the idea of a ladder as intrinsic connection (Kitamura, 2020) and assumes that the personas mutually support each other for their coexistence. For this reason, the whole is in equilibrium and the personas are stable though not immutable.

Japanese-related studies, broadly conceived, offer the following examples of the "institutions and markets" (Williams and Zumbansen, 2011) in the nation:

LTE, the form of keiretsu, and the main bank system (Abegglen, 2006). All these stand with the intrinsic connection, not supported by legal contracts. For instance, the system of LTE is "better understood as a long-term commitment between workers and employers rather than a permanent employment contract", since in Japan, "the employment contract includes no explicit clause regarding this policy, and employers are under no obligation to guarantee employment" (Ono, 2010; p. 2). Peter Drucker, the renowned scholar in the field of business management, once discussed Japanese-style management with reference to LTE:

> Suppose that we have a gathering of Westerners and Japanese. When asked what one does, a Westerner usually answers, 'an accountant' while a Japanese would most probably say '[I am working for] Toyota'. Introducing not one's profession, but one's organization shows that each individual member of a Japanese organization has a kind of family consciousness. Here lies the greatest strength of Japan.
>
> (Drucker, 2005)

This comment has three topics: (1) Japanese professionals ascribe their identity to their employer rather than their profession, (2) the idea of family consciousness is generally shared within the nation, not just Toyota, and (3) Japanese family consciousness is their value of preference that is considered their strength. This interpretation never means that Japanese business is unconditionally stronger than others. This chapter presupposes that, like humans with character, societies have personas that come with unique strengths and weaknesses. Kameda (2013; p. 12) elaborates on the idea of family consciousness: "These words aptly describe Japan's collectivist culture". This country-level view corresponds with the cultural concepts, including individualism and its opposite, collectivism ("I/C"), much discussed in cultural studies (Thomas and Peterson, 2017). The term culture calls for careful handling, but research indicates that the Japanese generally prefer their collectivistic values of preference. A plain way of expressing collectivism is the primacy of collective interest (Livermore, 2015). The value of family consciousness can be described as the primacy of collective identity of Toyota. This primacy coexists with the system of LTE. On the other hand, in the English-speaking countries, professionals generally prefer such attributes as an accountant and an engineer. This value of preference suits the system of arm's-length employment ("ALE"), where individuals ordinarily change their jobs (Riordan, 2014). The employer's name is naturally unlikely to be an individual's identity with the ALE preference or the primacy of individualistic interest of job freedom. This chapter refers to the existing values of preference as cultural values. This term includes "social values" (Williams and Zumbansen, 2011) in the preceding discussion. Cultural values are subsumed under the cultural constructs, including I/C, which is this study's focus. Individualism and collectivism are two extremes of a linear scale for capturing and comparing the actual specificities – regionally shared ways of thinking – sitting on the scale between the extremes. Cultural specificities, such as LTE and ALE linked with the local cultural values, are referred to as culturally driven. Examined earlier, identity is a culturally driven attribute of the persona. I/C is one of the individual-level persona's characteristics. Cultural values are diffused ways of thinking that do not strictly nor equally apply to all individuals in the respective societies. Cultural values and personas are interlinked in the respective societies, as mentioned earlier. The term cultureless is used for any specificity, irrelevant to the cultural constructs reported in cultural studies. Cultureless factors include regulatory changes and technological advances. Cultureless practices tend to be internationally uniform because they are remote from the cultural values that make a difference of practice. Culture is not the sole determinant of social activities but can function as an influential driver alongside cultureless factors in the respective societies. With this force, the varieties of personas, including LTE and ALE, exist across societies. Culturally driven practices and cultureless practicalities are dynamic. This study focuses on culturally driven practices and regards the intrinsic link between the levels as its core element of theoretical framework. Having established the theoretical foundation, the following section will explore the related organizational systems and practices.

4 Case illustrations

This section will examine two short case examples: before and after COVID. The two examples do not relate to each other, but share the theme of horenso. The focus of this comparison is what has remained rather than what has changed before and after the pandemic in the context of Japanese businesses. With this focus, this section will examine what is likely to remain and envisage the future of the Japanese communication system. The first example narrates an unsuccessful story about a newly hired CEO at the Dutch office of a Japanese conglomerate. The purpose of this example is to have a reasonable understanding of horenso by knowing about the differences of communication. Created from a real story (Japan Consulting Office, 2021), this example is short yet contains several important implications:

> A major Japanese company's European operation hired their first non-Japanese CEO to replace incumbent Japanese CEO. New CEO, James, had only worked for American and European companies prior to this appointment. Soon after hiring James, the Japanese company's head office in Japan started receiving much less information than before. The head office and the Japanese expatriates ("expats") working at the European office kept asking James for information. James did not share information as requested because he had never done so in his years of professional life. The requested amount of information was too much for him. For the Japanese, it was necessary to know what and how he was doing. The head office became suspicious that James was not transparent about information sharing. At the same time, James became more and more frustrated with the Japanese company's micromanagement. James believed that he could do his job in his

> way. He was confident about the European office's progress that would be shown in the upcoming financial report. However, his relationship with the head office became worsened without mutual trust. The head office let him go before the fiscal end.

This example highlights three differences of communication: (1) the required amount of information, (2) the frequency of information sharing, and (3) the purpose of information sharing. The required amount and frequency are relatively larger and higher, respectively, in the Japanese communication system. The Japanese purpose of information sharing appears to be a status update, which is generally not required in Europe or the English-speaking countries. These characteristics illustrate the horenso system.

The next example is created from a peer-reviewed article (Suematsu, 2020) in a Japanese business magazine about a Japanese start-up, Daftcraft. Established in 2018, this company is small with seven employees (Daftcraft, 2021). The company is featured in the article for their unique and timely feature: they have no physical office. This example narrates their story based on the interview with Wataru Hanashima, founder and president:

> I established this company with my friends. All employees work remotely. We offer technology-oriented services including visualization solution and extended-reality content development. We create interesting and inspiring products. One of our employees enjoy having two places in different cities for living. Before the pandemic, we rented an office room or gathered in a nice park to have a meeting. I foster different lifestyles that we have. We trust each other but we cannot do our job without good communication. Horenso is vital for telework. We have minimum necessary rules: a mandatory weekly online meeting. Prior to the meeting, everyone writes in Google Hangouts Meet about what is done this week and what to do next week. Besides this, each team has a weekly meeting of their own. We use Slack for daily communication and Jira for progress management. There are many digital tools available for communication. What is important is how to use them, rather than which one to use. Horenso is most important for remote work. Full-time employees share an update with everyone else at least once a day. For sodan (consultation), I step in and have a one-on-one online meeting, as necessary.
>
> (Suematsu, 2020)

This short example underscores the same points as the first one from a pre-pandemic time: the amount of information, the frequency of information sharing, and the purpose of horenso that seems to pertain to the process rather than the outcome. These shared points may help envisage the future of Japanese business communication.

There is a useful work to synthesize the preceding examples. Yoshihiko Masuda, a Japanese national who served as CEO for two of the Fujitsu conglomerate's

Table 9.1 A summary of the case examples

	Horenso communication	*Arm's-length communication*
Amount	Much information shared	Less information shared
Frequency	Updates frequently shared	Status updates hardly shared
Purpose	To be on the same page for everyone involved	To escalate an issue absolutely necessary to be reported

American affiliates between 2004 and 2019, contributed a short article to a Japanese magazine locally published in the United States. Written from a Japanese viewpoint, this work offers lessons and tips for Japanese expats regarding how to manage business operations in the United States. The following is abridged from the article in Japanese by Masuda (2014):

> In Japan, horenso is important. In the United States, it is not. Sometimes they come to you but it is not for horenso. You get a request for a pay raise or a notice of resignation instead. American employees believe that horenso (frequent reporting and consulting) is a waste of time for your boss. If they find themselves unable to fulfill the professional responsibility on their own, they will eventually come to you. This is called an escalation.

This quote effectively explains why horenso is not necessary in the United States. The cross-national differences of communication seem to correspond with the shared elements from the first two examples. Table 9.1 summarizes the elements of communication in the respective societies:

The standard communication system in the English-speaking societies is referred to as arm's-length communication following the concept of ALE. The case examples suggest that the communication features are likely to remain after COVID-19 since they are present during the pandemic. The following section will discuss the future trajectory based on the critical elements of communication.

5 Discussions

The previous section reported on the case examples that support the multi-level framework with the intrinsic connection to link the personas in the respective societies. This section will discuss this chapter's contribution: developing the concept of horenso and predicting its position in the post-pandemic era. Table 9.2 is a summary of the relevant concepts from the case examples and prior literature:

Horenso can be positioned as an important attribute of the persona of Japanese institutions. More precisely, the features of horenso – reporting, contacting, and consulting – are the representative features of Japanese decision-making that respects a group consensus. These features correspond with relevant literature.

Table 9.2 A summary of the pertinent concepts

Personas	*The Japanese*	*English-speaking societies*
Practice level		
Employment system	Lifetime employment	Arm's-length employment
Communication system	Horenso communication	Arm's-length communication
Decision-making system	Group consensus	Individual decision-making
Individual level		
Expectation	Job security in collectives	Job freedom for individuals
Orientation	Group harmony	Efficiency
Underlying belief	Collectivism	Individualism

In "Decision-Making and Japan", Taplin (1995) examines the intrinsic connection between the cultural values and the decision-making process:

> In Japan, action or implementation of ideas takes place before the formal decision is announced. This occurs because the impact stage happens before action is announced formally. The informal decision-making stage in a Japanese organization is a continuous process in which information is gathered and discussed.... Such forms of all-encompassing communication allow both greater individual participation in the solution and an increased likelihood that action will be implemented effectively because there is a group consensus. Such behavior, which derives from groupism and egalitarian ranking, is contra-distinction to the Western decision-making method in which a quick decision, usually involving very few people, tends to be followed by implementation and then evaluation. Within the Japanese context, extensive evaluation occurs first in an egalitarian corporate group process that eventually leads to action.
>
> (Taplin, 1995; p. 25)

In this quote, the term groupism is theoretically identical to collectivism. The term egalitarian ranking, also referred to as vertical egalitarianism in her book, denotes the one "in which people tend to be seen both in a ranked hierarchy and with a great emphasis on discipline, on serving, with the customer ultimately being the most important person" (Taplin, 1995; p. 46). Vertical egalitarianism is one way of describing the typical Japanese corporate structure organized under the system of LTE. It tends to have a tall hierarchy resulting from being a quasi-eternal community with relatively low employee turnovers. A group consensus can be expressed as the primacy of collective interest of respecting all collective members' opinions for decision-making. In this description, collective members primarily refer to those who are involved in it and who belong to any teams potentially relevant to the decision, depending on the significance of the decision. The point here is that horenso takes place to reach a group consensus before the decision is officially made. Taplin's analysis mirrors the intrinsic connection between the Japanese cultural value of collectivism and the decision-making process as a culturally driven practice. As for the Western system, "the company tends to be managed by objectives rather than consensus" (Taplin, 1995; p. 25). The arm's-length principle ("ALP") best explains it. The shared preference of the ALP is their cultural value.

The case examples show that the horenso communication system has remained. What has changed is the mode of communication. Due to the pandemic, face-to-face communication has greatly decreased and digital tools, such as Zoom, have grown to replace it. Persol Research and Consulting Co., Ltd. ("Persol"), a major consulting firm in Japan, has carried out research pertinent to horenso in the context of this transition. Conducted in March 2020, their research collected 2,700 responses from 1,000 teleworkers, 1,000 non-teleworkers who have teleworking colleagues, and 700 managers who oversee teleworkers. Their research results are shown in Table 9.3:

Table 9.3 is useful in that the results analyze the frequency of communication channels used for each purposes of communication: houkoku, renraku, and sodan. Face-to-face communication is most suitable for horenso. This explains the Japanese view examined at the outset: The pandemic has posed a relatively high level of communication challenges from the Japanese standpoint. Their results show that email and telephone are mainly used for horenso in the early stage of the pandemic. On the other hand, web or video conferencing channels are not primarily used for horenso. This result seemingly contradicts the current popularity of web conferencing. The web platforms might have not been as pervasive at the time of their research. Horenso usually comes with delicate topics. One possible implication is that telephone and email, possibly combined, may better suit horenso, which entails intensive two-way communication. Video/web conferencing may be suitable for one-way communication or soft two-way communication; for example, a CEO's speech remotely made for satellite offices. Another potential reason is that telephone and email are possibly considered real as opposed to virtual means. However, this conjecture may be overturned as the web platforms gain further popularity. To sum up, horenso has remained today, and face-to-face communication best suits it.

Table 9.3 Communication means by purpose (created by author based on Persol, 2020)

Communication purpose	*Houkoku (reporting)*	*Renraku (contacting)*	*Sodan (consulting)*
Face to face	Most frequent	Often	Often
Non-face to face			
Email	Most frequent	Frequent	Sometimes
Online chat	Sometimes	Sometimes	Sometimes
Telephone	Often	Often	Sometimes
Web/video conferencing	Sometimes	Rare	Rare

Most frequent: 70% or above; Frequent: 65% – 69%; Often: 50% – 64%; Sometimes: 40% – 49%; Rare: 39% or below.

Abegglen (2006) provides helpful insights into how Japanese businesses have changed and will change: "Where people matter, adaptive change has occurred but within very clear cultural constraints" (2006; p. 9). Abegglen's idea suggests that culturally driven practices will not radically change as the stable cultural values function as constraints. The idea supports this study's concept of intrinsic connection. It also functions as cultural constraints as it presupposes that the personas are interconnected between the levels for their coexistence. The concept here appears to suggest that face-to-face communication is likely to be the primary means for horenso in the future. While so, cultureless activities, including non-horenso communication, will likely foster web conferencing as it is seen at present. Taken together, culturally driven practices, such as horenso, are likely to remain in the future. Cultureless practices can change into the "new normal", according to the technological developments without cultural constraints.

6 Concluding remarks

This study has developed the concept of horenso as Japan's culturally driven communication system specific to the nation. The horenso system is considered part of the Japanese decision-making process, which belongs to the nexus of intrinsic connections between the personas. Horenso typically involves timely and frequent status updates on favorable and unfavorable matters, so team members and their manager(s) are always on the same page. Horenso is likely to remain in the future with the local values of preference that support the system for mutual coexistence.

The local values of preference in this research can be seen as culture in a broad sense. Cultural research inevitably comes with the methodological issue of measuring a construct at the individual level. To mitigate the issue, this study has established the theoretical framework, in which horenso functions as tangible evidence. The framework supports the idea that cultural values at the individual level become observable when it is contextualized with evidence of a culturally driven practice obtained at a higher level. This approach can be used for future research into culture-related subjects.

The proposed framework suggests that it is effective to differentiate culturally driven and cultureless specificities for envisaging the future trajectory in the post-pandemic era. Culturally driven specificities, including regionally specific practices and values of preferences, are the constituents of the personas and are generally stable though not immutable. Cultureless specificities, including system changes ensuing technological developments, can relatively easily change without cultural constraints. The future is likely determined with intricate dialectic of the two contrasting realms. The current "new normal" may be, in a sense, a snapshot of Japan's temporary transition to cope with the ongoing pandemic. The future state may involve more face-to-face communication than present in the long run.

Notes

1 Translated by the author. No official English translation is available. All Japanese materials are translated to the best knowledge of the author.

2 The terminologies *West* or *Western* and *East* or *Eastern* are used for discussion purposes only, as they can be further subcategorized in many ways. Refer to the J-system (the Japanese corporate system) versus the W-system (the corporate system found in the West) in Aoki and Dore (1994) for similar use.

References

Abegglen, J. (1958). *The Japanese Factory: Aspects of Its Social Organization.* Glencoe: The Free Press.

Abegglen, J. C. (2006). *21st-Century Japanese Management: New Systems, Lasting Values.* Hampshire and New York: Palgrave.

Aoki, M., and Dore, R. (Eds.). (1994). *The Japanese Firm: Sources of Competitive Strength.* New York: Oxford University Press.

Beechler, S., Najjar, M., Stucker, K., and Bird, A. (1996). Japanese-Style versus American-Style Human Resource Management Overseas: Examining Whether the Data Support the "Facts". Working Paper No. 105. New York: Center on Japanese Economy and Business, Graduate School of Business, Columbia University.

Cole, R. (1971). *Japanese Blue Collar: The Changing Tradition.* Berkeley: University of California Press.

Daftcraft. (2021). Kaishagaiyoo. https://daftcraft.co.jp/company/ (accessed April 20, 2021).

de Geus, A. (2002). *The Living Company: Habits for Survival in a Turbulent Business.* Boston: Harvard Business Review Press.

Dore, R. (1973). *British Factory, Japanese Factory: The Origins of Diversity in Industrial Relations.* Berkeley: University of California Press.

Drucker, P. (2005). My Personal History, Nihon Keizai Shimbun (December 28, 2005).

Hara, Y., Imagawa, T., Otsuka, H., Okajima, Y., Kanki, N., Kudo, H., Koh, Y., Sasaki, M., Shionoya, G., TaKebe, R., Terahara, M., Nakazono, H., Hattori, Y., Fujimoto, M., Misaki, H., Miyao, M., Yatagai, T., Nakagawa, K., and HR Institute. (2020). An Urgent Survey of Japanese Companies' Organizational Responses to COVID-19: A First Report. IIR Working Paper WP#20-10. Institute of Innovation Research, Hitotsubashi University. (In Japanese).

Hattori, Y., Okajima, Y., Kanki, N., Fujimoto, M., Imagawa, T., Otsuka, H., Kudo, H., Koh, Y., Sasaki, M., Shionoya, G., TaKebe, R., Terahara, M., Nakagawa, K., Nakazono, H., Miyao, M., Misaki, H., Yatagai, T., Hara, Y., and HR Institute. (2020). An Urgent Survey of Japanese Companies' Organizational Responses to COVID-19: A Second Report. IIR Working Paper WP#20-11. Institute of Innovation Research, Hitotsubashi University. (In Japanese).

Imai, M. (1986). *Kaizen: The Key to Japan's Competitive Success.* New York-London: McGraw-Hill.

Japan Consulting Office. (2021). Why Is Reporting So Different in Japanese Companies? https://www.japanconsultingoffice.com/reporting-different-japanese-companies/ (accessed April 19, 2021).

Kameda, N. (2013). Japanese Global Companies: The Shift from Multinationals to Multiculturals. *Global Advances in Business Communication*, 2(1), 3.

Khare, A., Ishikura, H., and Baber, W. W. (Eds.) (2020). *Raising to the Digital Challenge: The Transforming of Japanese Business.* Singapore: Springer Asia.

Kitamura, K. (2020). The Future of Fintech in the Context of the Japanese Main Bank System. In Khare, A., Ishikura, H., and Baber, W. W. (Eds.) *Raising to the Digital Challenge: The Transforming of Japanese Business* (pp. 247–260). Singapore: Springer Asia.

Livermore, D. (2015). *Leading with Cultural Intelligence: The Real Secret to Success.* 2nd ed. New York: American Management Association.

Masuda, Y. (2014). Horenso no nai amerika de umaku buka to shigoto wo suru hoohoo. Lighthouse. https://www.us-lighthouse.com/business/e-15044.html (accessed October 11, 2020).

Ministry of Health, Labor and Welfare. (2021). Terewaaku soogo pootaru saito. https://telework.mhlw.go.jp/qa/qa3-6/ (accessed March 15, 2021).

Miyashita, K., and Russell, D. W. (1994). *Keiretsu: Inside the Hidden Japanese Conglomerates.* New York: McGraw-Hill.

Nihon Keizai Shimbun. (2020). Zaitaku Kinmu no chiimu waaku horenso wo ishiki: mokuhyoo nayami wo mieruka. May 19, 2020. https://www.nikkei.com/nkd/company/article/?DisplayType=1&ng=DGKKZO59276200Z10C20-A5EAC000&scode=8056&ba=1 (accessed October 11, 2020).

Ono, H. (2010). Lifetime Employment in Japan: Concepts and Measurements. *Journal of the Japanese and International Economies*, 24(1), 1–27.

Persol Research and Consulting Co., Ltd. (2020). Terewaaku ni okeru fuankan kodokukan ni kansuru teiryoo choosa. https://rc.persol-group.co.jp/thinktank/research/activity/data/telework-anxiety.html (accessed March 8, 2021).

Riordan, E. (2014). Where the Heart Is: Amending the Fair Labor Standards Act to Provide Wage and Overtime Pay Protection to Agency-Employed Home Health Aides. *St. John's Law Review*, 85(2), 15, 837–868.

Sasaki, M., Imagawa, T., Shionoya, G., Hara, Y., Okajima, Y., Otsuka, H., Kanki, N., Kudo, H., Koh, Y., Takebe, R., Terahara, M., Nakazono, H., Nakagawa, K., Hattori, Y., Fujimoto, M., Miyao, M., Misaki, H., Yatagai, T., and HR Institute. (2020). An Urgent Survey of Japanese Companies' Organizational Responses to COVID-19: A Third Report. IIR Working Paper WP#20-12. Institute of Innovation Research, Hitotsubashi University. (In Japanese).

Sostero, M., Milasi, S., Hurley, J., Fernández-Macías, E., and Bisello, M. (2020). *Teleworkability and the COVID-19 Crisis: A New Digital Divide?* Seville: European Commission, JRC121193.

Suematsu, S. (2020). Kanzen remootowaaku demo horenso wo tettei surutameni mouketa ruuru towa? Mainichi Doda 2020–04–24. https://mainichi.doda.jp/article/2020/04/24/1862 (accessed October 11, 2020).

Taplin, R. (1995). *Decision-Making and Japan: A Study of Corporate Japanese Decision-Making and Its Relevance to Western Companies.* Surrey: Japan Library.

Thomas, D. C., and Peterson, M. F. (2017). *Cross-Cultural Management: Essential Concepts.* 4th ed. Thousand Oaks: Sage Publications.

United States Government Publishing Office. (2010). Sections 6501 through 6506 of title 5, United States Code, as added by Public Law 111–292 (also known as the Telework Enhancement Act of 2010). https://www.telework.gov/guidance-legislation/telework-legislation/telework-enhancement-act/ (accessed March 14, 2021).

Waizenegger, L., McKenna, B., Cai, W., and Bendz, T. (2020). An affordance perspective of team collaboration and enforced working from home during COVID-19. *European Journal of Information Systems.* DOI: 10.1080/0960085X.2020.1800417.

Williams, C. A., and Zumbansen, P. (2011). Introduction: Corporate Governance After the End of History: Investigating the New Great Transformation. In Williams, C. A., and Zumbansen, P. (Eds.). *The Embedded Firm: Corporate Governance, Labor, and Finance Capitalism*. Cambridge: Cambridge University Press.

Williams, C. A., and Zumbansen, P. (Eds.). (2011). *The Embedded Firm: Corporate Governance, Labor, and Finance Capitalism* (pp. 477–482). Cambridge: Cambridge University Press.

Yamazaki, T. (1989). *Horenso ga kaisha wo tsuyokusuru: boukoku, renraku, Soudan no keieigaku*. Tokyo: Goma Shoboo.

Yoshino, M. (1968). *Japan's Managerial System: Tradition and Innovation*. Cambridge: MIT Press.

10 Research on promoting cashless payments in Japan to cope with COVID-19

Midori Takao and Shigetsune Yamoto

1 Introduction

Under the COVID-19 pandemic, studies are being conducted that discuss the risks associated with cash and in physical stores payments and changes in consumer behaviour. It has been confirmed that the possibility of infection by contact with devices such as credit card terminals and PIN pads is higher than that by cash. A review of the state of cashless payments in Japan shows that the country has a low level of cashless payments compared to major countries in the world.

After the COVID-19 pandemic, there was a growing momentum about the security of in-store payments, and Auer et al. discuss the risk of infection and the role of cash, as there was initially widespread speculation that the coronavirus could be transmitted by cash (Auer et al., 2020). In another study, Wisniewski et al. conducted a questionnaire survey of people in 22 European countries to ascertain the impact of cash use during the COVID-19 pandemic. The results of the survey revealed that those who considered cash to be "relatively risky" opted for cashless alternatives in shops (Wisniewski et al., 2021). Eger et al. demonstrated in relation to COVID-19 that fear appeals were associated with changes in customer behaviour and influenced in-store and online shopping (Eger et al., 2021). There are also several studies on in-store contact at the time of payment: Daqar et al. (2021) found in their questionnaire that people believe that avoiding physical contact with cash or any means of payment helps to prevent the spread of COVID-19 (Daqar et al., 2021). Hartoneva (2020) also found that a survey in Finland led to the result that consumers prefer to use their own devices rather than external devices to reduce the risk of infection. Auer et al. (2020) argue that contact with devices such as credit card terminals and PIN pads is more likely to cause infection than cash. Thus, studies have been conducted discussing the risks and changes in consumer behaviour regarding cash and physical stores payments under the COVID-19 pandemic.

As mentioned above, COVID-19 and cashless payments are being discussed in many countries, but the situation of cashless payments in Japan is low compared to other major countries in the world. In contrast, as shown in Figure 10.1, the situation in major countries around the world (FY 2017) was in the 40%–70%

DOI: 10.4324/9781003216049-12

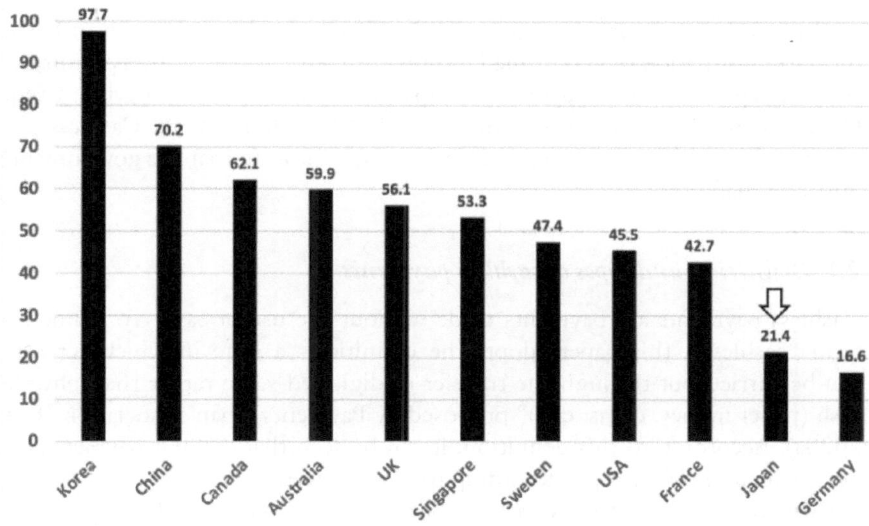

Figure 10.1 Percentage of cashless payments in each country during FY 2017.
Source: PJA (2020a).

range, with China at 70.2%, Canada at 62.1%, the United Kingdom at 56.1%, the United States at 45.5%, and France at 42.7% (PJA, 2020a). In Japan, the percentage of cashless payments was 21.4% in FY 2017, a low level compared to other major countries (PJA, 2020a). Cashless payment ratio, which refers to the ratio of annual amounts paid by cashless payment methods, as compared to the country's private final consumption expenditure.

In Japan, the government has been promoting cashless payments for some time in order to strengthen the national economy. In addition, after the COVID-19 pandemic, the government has set out to strengthen the promotion of cashless payments in order to reduce person-to-person contact.

Based on these previous studies, the question arises as to whether Japan can really just promote cashless payments and whether cashless payments in Japan are safe. Previous studies have discussed the contact between "people and objects" in shop payments, but none have identified the sequence of the payment process in shops and clarified the contact between "person to person" and "people and objects". In this paper, in order to confirm the safety of the transaction, we identify the process of the payment operation in terms of the contact and clarify the problem. Then, in order to find out how to solve the problem, we discuss and propose a solution to the problem based on the background of the study, such as the current spread of cashless payment and the government's efforts to promote cashless payment.

2 Current status of cashless payments

In this chapter, in order to understand the issues of cashless payment in Japan, the current situation was confirmed by literature research. First, it was confirmed that the types of cashless payments in Japan are classified into four types: Credit Cards, Debit Cards, Electronic Money, and QR Code Payment. Cashless payments in Japan have accelerated in recent years, indicating that the government's initiatives had some success.

2.1 Definition and types of cashless payments

Cashless payments are payments made without the use of cash. To define the term "cashless", this paper adopts the definition "a state in which activities can be carried out through the transfer of digitized value rather than physical cash (paper money, coins, etc.)" proposed by Payments Japan Association (PJA, 2020a). According to this definition, it can be seen that cashless payments can be classified into four types according to usage patterns.

Payment methods that enable cashless transactions include prepayment, immediate payment, and post-payment, depending on when the funds are contributed, i.e., their timing. In addition, the main devices used for payments are cards and smartphones. Furthermore, the two types of payment methods are contact and contactless, depending on whether or not the payment terminal and the device come in contact. Table 10.1 lists the timing of funding, devices, and methods of major cashless payments used in Japan.

An explanation for each payment method listed in Table 10.1 is provided as follows: (1) A "credit card" is a method in which no funds are contributed at the time of payment, but after a certain period of time, funds are contributed by the cardholder to settle. (2) A "debit card" contributes the amount of the payment at the time of payment. (3) "Electronic money" is sometimes used as a generic term for electronic means of payment, but in this paper, it refers to a method in which funds are contributed (charged, etc.) to a payment in advance and payments are deducted within the range of the amount contributed. (4) "QR code payment" is a method of exchanging the information necessary for payment in stores via QR code by consumers' smartphones. QR code payments allow users to choose the timing—prepayment, immediate payment, or post-payment—of the contribution of funds for payment.

Table 10.1 Classification of major cashless payments

Devices	*Methods*	*Timing of funding*		
		Pay before	*Pay now*	*Pay later*
Cards	Contact	—	(2) Debit cards	(1) Credit cards
	Contactless	(3) Electronic money		
Smartphones	Contactless	(4) QR code		

The cards listed in the payment device column of Table 10.1 are equipped with integrated circuit (IC) chips, and depending on the type of IC chips, consumers make payments either by inserting or by holding the card over a payment terminal at a store. Similarly, in the case of smartphones, with the exception of QR code payments, the IC chip built into the smartphone is held over the payment terminal at the store. Although electronic money, as well as credit and debit cards, can be used in the form of both cards and smartphones, the majority of people hold cards. In terms of methods used at the time of payment, electronic money is contactless, and although credit and debit cards are available in both contact and contactless formats, currently the majority of transactions are contact-based. In addition, QR code payment is a contactless method.

2.2 Current status of cashless payments and payment methods

This section describes the current status of cashless payments in Japan and the prevalence of each of the four cashless payment methods.

As shown in Table 10.2, Japan's cashless payment ratio was 24.1% in 2018. It grew by just over 1% during 2008–2017, but increased by 2.8% from 2017 to 2018, indicating that cashless payments are accelerating (PJA, 2020a).

Table 10.3 shows the settlement amounts and the number of cards issued for major cashless payments in Japan. The following sections describe the spread of this technology.

The number of credit cards issued in Japan was 290 million as of March 2020, which in terms of the ratio of the adult population means that each person holds 2.8 credit cards (JCCA, 2020). In 2019, the credit card shopping transaction volume was approximately ¥64,454.4 billion, an increase of 10.4% over the previous

Table 10.2 Ratio of cashless payments to private final consumption expenditure

Year	*2008*	*2009*	*2010*	*2011*	*2012*	*2013*	*2014*	*2015*	*2016*	*2017*	*2018*
Ratio (%)	11.9	12.3	13.2	14.1	15.1	15.3	16.9	18.2	20.0	21.3	24.1

Table 10.3 Status of major cashless payments in 2019

	Payment amounts		*Number of issues*
	2019	*Composition ratio (%)*	
Credit cards	¥64,454.4 billion	88.1	290 million
Debit cards	¥1,828.7 billion	2.5	N.A.
Electronic money	¥5,750.6 billion	7.8	423 million
QR code	¥1,120.5 billion	1.5	18 million (number of active users per month)

year. Credit card transactions account for about 90% of cashless payments (PJA, 2020a) and are the main driver of the cashless payment market.

The settlement amount of debit cards was ¥1,828.7 billion in FY 2019 (BOJ, 2021). Although its market size is still small compared to other payment methods, its settlement amount has been increasing rapidly in recent years, with year-on-year growth of approximately 18%–30% between 2016 and 2019.

In 2019, the number of cards issued by Japan's eight major e-money companies was 42,371 million and their settlement value was ¥5,750.6 billion (BOJ, 2021). In Japan, electronic money has been issued with contactless IC cards since November 2001, and its use has spread rapidly, with cards being issued at an accelerated pace in the transportation and distribution sectors.

In recent years, QR code payments have been growing rapidly in Japan. In 2018, ¥165 billion was spent, which increased 6.7 times to ¥1,120.5 billion in 2019 (PJA, 2020b). In 2019, major companies entered this market and competition has become fierce.

2.3 Promotion and challenges of cashless payments

The government has been promoting cashless payments, but it has not yet been promoted due to reasons such as good security as a social situation and low circulation of counterfeit bills. Therefore, the government is promoting point projects to encourage cashless payments, which has had some success.

The Japanese government is aiming to popularize cashless payments since they have various advantages in terms of preventing the spread of COVID-19 and strengthening national power. The trends are further discussed below.

In line with "Japan Revitalization Strategy: Revised in 2014", the government set the spread of cashless payment as a way to revitalize the financial and capital markets for the enhancement of fund settlement as well as the convenience and efficiency of foreign visitors to Japan during the Olympic and Paralympic Games, which were scheduled to be held in 2020 (PMJHC, 2014). Later, a study showed that the direct cost of cash payments from the private sector exceeded ¥1 trillion, and in April 2018, the Ministry of Economy, Trade and Industry (METI) announced "Cashless Vision", declaring that by June 2025, the ratio of cashless payments should be 40%. It will aim for the world's highest level of 80% in the future (METI, 2018). The process is currently ongoing.

In 2018, METI analyzed the reasons why cashless payments are difficult to spread in Japan.

The reasons why cashless payments are unlikely to spread in Japan are listed in Table 10.4 from four perspectives: (1) the social situation, (2) physical stores, (3) consumers, and (4) payment providers (METI, 2018). In terms of the social situation, it mentions the following four points: (a) "public safety" due to the rate of thefts being low, and the fact that cash is said to be returned, even if dropped; (b) "high level of trust in cash" due to clean bills and low circulation of counterfeit bills; (c) "Point of Sale (POS) (cash register) processing is fast and accurate" in stores, etc., where there are few complications with handling

Table 10.4 Factors preventing the spread of cashless payments in Japan

	Factors preventing the spread of cashless payments in Japan
1 Social situation	a Public Safety b High level of trust in cash c POS (cash register) processing is fast and accurate d Easy to obtain cash
2 Physical stores	a Cost burden at the time of introduction b High level of trust in cash c Time lag between payment and funding
3 Customer	a The existence of stores that do not accept cashless payments b Worry about cashless payments
4 Payment providers	Cost burden of maintaining the current payment system

cash; and (d) "easy to obtain cash" due to a large number of ATMs. The reasons regarding physical stores are: (a) the space cost of installing terminals at the time of introduction and the burden of installing internet lines; (b) the high cost (commissions) of operating and maintaining cashless payments compared to cash; and (c) the time lag in cash management, until funds are converted after payment. In addition, consumer factors include: (a) the existence of physical stores that do not support cashless payments, which makes consumers hesitant to shift to cashless payments, and (b) concerns about overspending which are associated with cashless payments. Last, payment providers have to bear a cost burden commensurate with maintaining the current payment system, and are in an environment in which they must be cautious about making new investments or lowering service fees.

The government implemented a "cashless point rebate project" from October 2019 to June 2020 as a measure to eliminate the factors on the side of physical stores that are difficult to spread and to promote the use by consumers. The results are described below. This measure has been evaluated as having had certain effects and is expected to serve as a reference for future measures.

METI and the Payments Japan Association implemented the "Cashless Point Rebate Project" over a period of nine months, with the aim of mitigating the potential impact after the consumption tax rate increase in October 2019 as well as improving the environment for small and medium-sized businesses to accept cashless payments. This project was designed to support physical stores by providing them with free payment terminals and lowering payment fees as well as to reward consumers with 2%–5% worth of points for using the terminals. METI provided approximately 420 billion yen for this project.

The focus on small and medium-sized businesses was to "broaden the base of cashless adoption", as shown in Figure 10.2. As of now, payment providers have focused on introducing cashless payments to shops with large sales volumes due to the volume of commission income, leaving small and medium-sized shops behind.

Approximately 1.15 million stores participated, and the total value of eligible settlements from the start date of March 16, 2020, reached ¥7.2 trillion (METI,

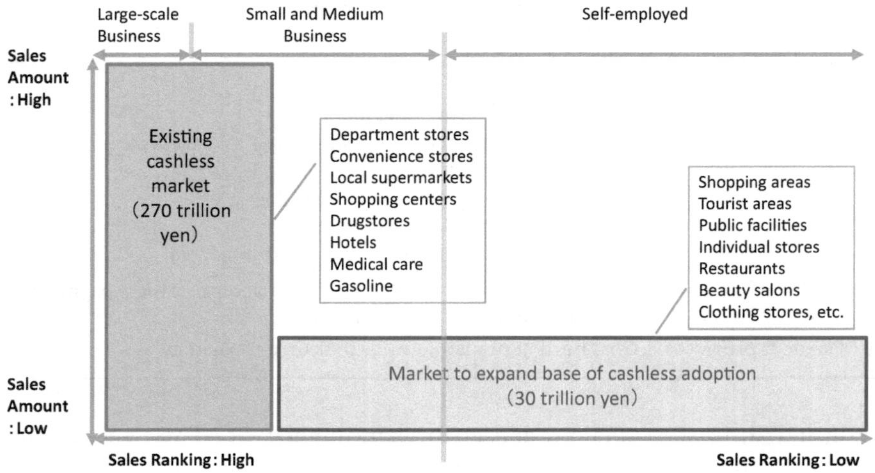

Figure 10.2 Business-to-consumer cashless market.
Source: PJA (2019).

2020). As for the number of participating stores, more than half of the two million small and medium-sized businesses participated.

In addition, surveys conducted before and after the start of this rebate project reported that its effects were as follows: Around 50% of consumers in their 20s–60s and 30% in their teens and 70s or older started or increased their cashless payment methods; the overall percentage of stores with cashless systems increased from about 27% to about 37%; and in town and village areas, in particular, there was a marked increase from about 23% to about 41%.

Regarding the stores that participated in the rebate project, about 46% reported that the project had an effect on sales, approximately 44% succeeded in attracting consumers, and as of October 2019, their percentage of cashless payments as a percentage of sales increased 1.19 times during September 2019 to July 2020, from an average of about 28% to about 33%. In addition, approximately 46% of stores that introduced or added cashless services as a result of the rebate project were effective in improving operational efficiency (PJA, 2020c).

As described above, this project has been evaluated as having achieved a certain level of success from the perspectives of both the users and stores.

3 Methodology

In this paper, we investigate the transaction process of the four payment methods shown in Table 10.1 in actual stores. The survey was conducted by observing payments in 20 target stores. The target stores are retailers and restaurants, and we observed cashless payment transactions. The specific processes of the payment operations were identified as "person-to-person" and "people and objects" contact. In particular, we checked for the presence of the issue of frequent person-to-person contact (visually confirmed).

4 Result

In this chapter, we visually checked the transaction process in actual shops for the four payment methods, identified the process of payment operation, and made explicit the contact between "person to person" and "people and objects".

From the perspective of avoiding contacts, in accordance with COVID-19 measures, the existence or nonexistence of contact with people or objects in the operation of cashless payment methods at a cash register in a physical store is illustrated in Table 10.5 by actual measurement survey. It shows that there is a high amount of contact for credit and debit cards. In this section, each payment method is described in terms of the existence or nonexistence of contact.

Table 10.5 also describes the existence or nonexistence of "person-to-person contact" and "contact between people and objects" during transactions for each payment method. The term "person-to-person contact" refers to the contact between a consumer and an employee when they hand over a device (card or smartphone) for payment. "Contact between people and objects" means (1) whether employees come into contact with consumers' devices and (2) whether consumers come into contact with payment terminals.

At a physical store, the main flow of cashless payment operations is as follows: at the cash register, consumers confirm the amount displayed, and if it is correct, they present their own cashless payment device. The store confirms (reads) the device with a payment terminal attached to its cash register and processes the sale. If using a credit or debit card, consumers enter their PIN to verify their identity before the sale is processed. The transaction method for each cashless payment is as follows. For electronic money, a card or smartphone is equipped with a contactless IC chip. At the time of payment, since consumers simply have to hold their cards over the store's payment terminal to complete their payment, there is no "person-to-person" or "people-and-objects" contact. There are two types of transaction methods for QR code payments: (1) the consumers launch an application on their smartphone, use their camera to scan a QR

Table 10.5 Payment methods and contact status

Contact status	*Person-to-person contact*	*Contact between people and objects*	
Payment	*Customer and employee contact*	*Employee and device contact*	*Contacting the customer's terminal*
Electronic money	Nonexistence	Nonexistence	Nonexistence
QR code	Nonexistence	Nonexistence	Nonexistence
Credit cards	Existence	Existence	Existence
Debit cards	Existence	Existence	Existence

code presented by the store, enter the payment amount themselves, and pay; and (2) the consumers pay by reading the barcode or QR code displayed on the smartphone application on their device using a barcode reader at the payment terminal. There is no contact between people or objects in either of these modes. The transaction flow of credit and debit cards is shown in Figure 10.3.

Both credit and debit cards have the same transaction flow, as shown in Figure 10.3, since in Japan, the majority of these cards are equipped with contact-type IC chips. A card equipped with a contact-type IC chip is inserted into a payment terminal, the terminal reads the credit card information written on the IC chip, and the sale is processed. Consumers hand their card to the store employee (① in the figure), the employee inserts the card into the terminal (② in the figure), and consumers confirm the payment amount and enter their PIN using the PIN pad (③ in the figure). When the payment is completed, the employee removes the card from the payment terminal (④ in the figure) and hands it to the consumer (⑤ in the figure). It has become increasingly common for consumers to insert their cards into the terminals (⑥–⑧ in the figure) by touching the payment terminal to insert their cards and entering their PINs, even without employee intervention.

As described above, credit cards and debit cards can be said to involve more contact between people and objects than electronic money and QR codes.

5 Discussion

As shown in Section 4, the challenge is that credit cards, which account for 90% of cashless payments, have the high level of "person-to-person" and "people and objects" contacts when using cards at physical stores. This section first clarifies the advantages of making credit cards contactless. Then, to promote the use of

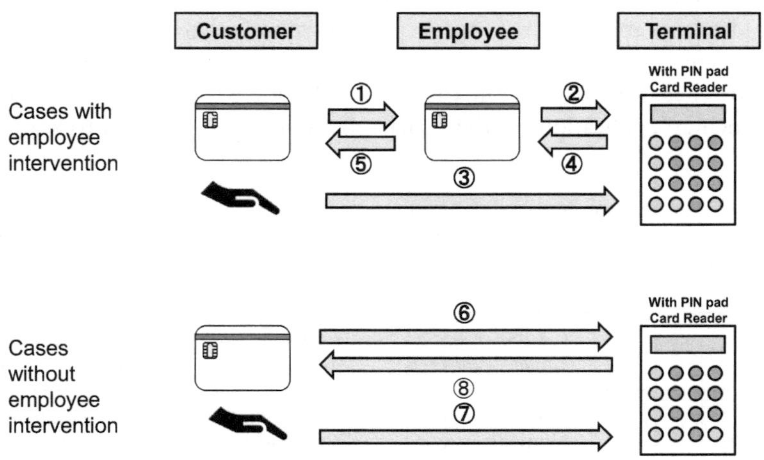

Figure 10.3 Credit and debit card transaction flow.

contactless credit cards to prevent COVID-19 infections, we will specify the challenges and make recommendations for solutions in comparison with past cases.

5.1 Advantages of making credit cards contactless

The system of contactless payments will increase safety for employees as well as consumers. Since it requires less time than conventional contact-based payments because of the elimination of the process of handing over the IC card, inserting the card into the terminal, and entering the PIN, it helps to reduce the wait in the checkout line, leading to greater efficiency in the store. While there are benefits for both users and stores, its hassle-free transaction of simply holding the card over the terminal is especially beneficial for elderly people who tend to take time at the cash register. Electronic money payments and QR codes are also highly safer because they are contactless transactions. However, QR code payments require launching an application on a smartphone, and since electronic money is prepaid, it must be charged in advance, i.e., prior to being used. Credit cards are easier to use than other cashless payments (especially for the elderly) because they do not require these steps.

5.2 Considerations for contactless credit card transactions

Credit card transactions account for about 90% of private final consumption expenditure (PJA, 2020a). By reducing contact between people and objects in credit card transactions, transactions at stores can be made more secure in the COVID-19 environment. This section will identify challenges in promoting contactless credit card transactions.

From previous research, the factors that led to the rapid spread of electronic money in Japan were analyzed (Takao, 2009). The results showed that it was important to overcome three challenges in disseminating information about its (1) convenience, (2) awareness, and (3) advantages over cash in the current pandemic situation. The three challenges identified during the experimental phase in the early 1990s were: the unpopularity of contact card transactions, lack of awareness, and insufficient advantages over cash. However, in 2001, transactions using contactless cards became remarkably more convenient. Their adoption by railway operators and major distribution companies increased awareness, and the fact that points are awarded for the use of electronic money, which provides an advantage over cash, led to their widespread use in the market.

Therefore, we propose to consider overcoming the challenges of the dissemination of e-money, described above, by applying the challenges of contactless credit cards to the situation. The contactless system will be much easier to use for both users and stores. In Japan, since contactless transactions are already more widespread in daily life than electronic money, it can be expected that there will be no confusion among users. The fact that credit cards can be used for contactless transactions will be recognized by users and stores as it becomes more widespread, but to raise awareness rapidly, payment providers will need to carry out promotions that encourage cardholders and stores to use credit cards. Contactless transactions, which take less time to complete than contact transactions, are advantageous in the current situation, since stores will be able to reduce the wait in the checkout line and increase the productivity of each transaction. In addition, with the spread of COVID-19, both users and stores benefit from the safety of less person-to-person and person-to-object contacts compared to contact transactions.

In fact, for contactless credit card transactions to become widespread, both credit cards and payment terminals must be contactless, and it is also necessary to devise ways to encourage their usage. In fact, some credit cards in Japan are now equipped with IC chips that can be used for both contact and contactless transactions, and terminals that can read contactless IC chips are beginning to be installed. However, the scope as well as the issuance of contactless credit cards is limited.

5.2.1 Switching to contactless credit cards

The use of contactless credit cards is more advanced overseas than in Japan. According to an announcement by Visa, use of contactless credit cards are already over 60% in the United Kingdom, the Netherlands, and Canada and over 90% in Australia, Singapore, Spain, Russia, and other countries (Visa, 2020). For making credit cards contactless, it is necessary to install a contactless IC chip in the card. In Japan, credit card issuers are gradually switching from contact-type credit cards to ones that are both contact and contactless, in accordance with the policies of various international brands (e.g., Visa, MasterCard, and JCB). For example, in the case of Visa, the number of contactless credit cards issued as of September 2020 was approximately 32.3 million (Visa, 2020). Since credit card issuers will follow the policies of these brands, the shift to contactless credit cards will gradually progress in Japan.

Existing members having contact only credit cards will be switched to cards with both contact and contactless capabilities when their cards are renewed, since credit cards have an expiration date. As of end-February 2021, the number of people infected with COVID-19 reached 431,740 in Japan. The proportion of COVID-19-infected individuals who become severely ill or die varies with age, and tends to be higher in the elderly and lower in the young. As compared to people in their 30s, the severity of the disease is 10 times higher among people in their 50s, 25 times higher among those in their 60s, and 47 times higher among those in their 70s (MHLW, 2021). According to the results of a survey conducted by Payments Japan Association, credit card use is more common among people in their 50s and 60s (PJA, 2020c), which coincides with the demographic group with the highest rate of severe illness and fatalities from the COVID-19 infection. For this group, a strategy is necessary to facilitate replacement of their cards on priority.

5.2.2 Contactless payment terminals

It is not easy to install contactless payment terminals at physical stores. Presently, a function needs to be installed in the terminals currently in use for contactless credit card payments to equip them to read the contactless IC chips, but due to its high costs, a simple, low-cost method has emerged. In addition, Japan's point rebate project, described in Section 3, has also produced results.

Although the early adopters of contactless payment terminals in physical stores were major national chain store operators, such as McDonald's, 7-Eleven, and Ito-Yokado, the spread of this technology is still limited. Even if only the equipment attached to cash registers are replaced, it would cost about ¥100,000 per payment terminal unit. Since replacing the terminals of the many merchants would be quite costly, it is necessary to have a driving force for such replacements.

However, the good news is that in September 2020 a simplified system was launched. This uses Apple iPads or iPhones, and at around ¥40,000 is cheaper than installing a dedicated terminal and could be a driving force.

Furthermore, Japan's point rebate project, which ended in June 2020, achieved solid results in the installation of merchant terminals. Therefore, a government-led exchange of payment terminals may be necessary.

5.2.3 Promoting the use of contactless transactions for credit cards

To promote the use of contactless transactions for credit cards, payment providers can adopt two measures: (1) widely publicize the safety and convenience of contactless transactions via the internet, social networking services, and TV; and (2) ask physical stores to encourage consumers to go contactless. When accepting payments in physical stores, employees should inform consumers that those with contactless cards can make contactless transactions and encourage them to adopt this practice. This experience would lead to subsequent use of the system.

5.3 Consideration of the spread of cashless payments

In addition to the shift to contactless credit cards, a higher percentage of overall cashless payments will lead to safer transactions. Regarding the government's move to advocate cashless payments, METI is continuing discussions with experts from industry associations, government, and academia on measures to further promote its introduction as well as its use by small and medium-sized businesses, after the "point rebate project". Among the issues raised are the costs of payment terminals at the time of implementation, merchant fees during operation, improvements in payment cycles, and the need to clearly explain the benefits of cashless payments to stores. For this reason, the METI plans to conduct an experiment in 2021 to quantitatively "visualize" the benefits of the introduction of a cashless system, such as increased productivity (e.g., reduced accounting operations, shorter waiting times in checkout lines, increased customer spending, etc.) and estimation of cash handling costs. In Japan, the merchant fee for small and medium-sized enterprises is 3.25%, and a reduction is being considered. Cashless payment infrastructures are made up of a variety of functions provided by multiple parties and the costs of these parties are combined to form the final merchant fee. Therefore, in order to consider lowering merchant fees, it is desirable to visualize the entire cost structure, including the costs of each function, and to examine the appropriateness of each cost (METI, 2021). In this way, discussions on industry-government-academia collaboration will deepen and the prevalence of cashless payments in stores will increase.

As for users, in a questionnaire administered after the point rebate project, the response to cashless payment by those in their 70s and older was slow (PJA, 2020c). The percentage of those in their 70s, who did not use cashless payments at all is 15.2%, which is more than 6% lower than the 9.1% in the 60s age group. Among those using cashless services, 36.8% of those in their 70s used it once a month or less, 9.7% lower than the 27.1% of those in their 60s. Among those in their 70s, since the total of those who did not use it at all and those who used it once a month or less exceeds 50%, it is unlikely that it has become a daily means of payment. Since Japan has an aging population, with average life expectancies for men and women being 81.41 and 87.45 years, respectively, it is essential for the elderly to own and use cashless payments to increase the percentage of cashless payments to 40% in the future. Contactless transactions, in which the device is simply held over the terminal, are not only secure, but also easy and fast. Since such transactions are easily accepted by this generation, it may be effective to collaborate with local governments and companies, where many elderly people live.

As mentioned in Section 5.2, promoting the use of contactless credit cards will increase convenience, and in addition, with the spread of COVID-19, its increased safety to users and physical stores will contribute to the spread of cashless payments.

6 Conclusion

In this paper, we first clarified the status of cashless payment penetration and efforts to promote it in Japan and the government's efforts after the COVID-19 pandemic. Next, whether or not contact is made for cashless payment transactions at physical stores was clarified and some considerations were proposed for safer transactions. The results reveal that credit cards need to be contactless. Although previous studies have shown concerns about "people and objects" in credit card payment operations, this study also checked whether there was contact between "people and objects" and "person to person" to examine safety. Since the installation of contactless terminals in physical stores is costly, government initiatives are important for promotion of a contactless system. The importance of promoting contactless credit cards to protect the elderly, who are more susceptible to COVID-19 infections, was also discussed. This recommendation suggests the safe spread of cashless payments to the industry in the future and provides consumers with measures for safe transactions. Further research toward the expansion of contactless transactions for cashless payments will continue.

References

Auer, R., Cornelli, G., & Frost, J. (2020). Covid-19, Cash, and the Future of Payments (No. 3). Bank for International Settlements.

BOJ (2021). Settlement Trends. *Bank of Japan (BOJ).* https://www.boj.or.jp/statistics/set/kess/release/2020/index.htm/ (accessed January 31, 2021).

Daqar, M. A., Constantinovits, M., Arqawi, S., & Daragmeh, A. (2021). The Role of Fintech in Predicting the Spread of COVID-19. *Banks and Bank Systems*, 16(1), 1.

Eger, L., Komárková, L., Egerová, D., & Mičík, M. (2021). The Effect of COVID-19 on Consumer Shopping Behaviour: Generational Cohort Perspective. *Journal of Retailing and Consumer Services*, 61, 102542.

Hartoneva, M. (2020). Contactless Payments with Inherence: Strong Customer Authentication and Biometrics. https://www.theseus.fi/bitstream/handle/10024/346627/Hartoneva%20Marko.pdf (accessed May 31, 2021).

JCCA (2020). Announcement of the Results of the Survey on the Number of Credit Cards Issued. *Japan Consumer Credit Association.* https://www.j-credit.or.jp/information/statistics/download/toukei_inumber_a.pdf (accessed May 31, 2021).

METI (2018). Cashless Vision 2018. *Minister of Economy, Trade and Industry.* https://www.meti.go.jp/press/2018/04/20180411001/20180411001-1.pdf (accessed May 31, 2021).

METI (2020). News Release: Recent Situation regarding the Cashless Point Rebate Project. *Ministry of Economy, Trade and Industry.* https://cashless.go.jp/assets/doc/200611_cashless_progress.pdf (accessed May 31, 2021).

METI (2021). Study Group for Improving the Environment to Promote the Further Spread of Cashless Payments to Small and Medium-Sized Stores, Interim Summary (Draft). *Ministry of Economy, Trade and Industry.* https://www.meti.go.jp/press/2020/01/20210126003/20210126003-5.pdf (accessed May 31, 2021).

MHLW (2021). 11 Points of Knowledge on the Current Status of COVID-19 Infections (as of February 2021). *Ministry of Health, Labour and Welfare.* https://www.mhlw.go.jp/content/000749530.pdf (accessed May 31, 2021).

PJA (2020a). Cashless Roadmap 2020. *Payments Japan Association.* https://www.paymentsjapan.or.jp/wordpress/wp-content/uploads/2020/06/roadmap2020.pdf (accessed May 31, 2021).

PJA (2020b). Survey on Code Payment Usage Trends. *Payments Japan Association.* https://www.paymentsjapan.or.jp/publications/research/pymt-trends/code-payment/code-pymt_20200622/ (accessed May 31, 2021).

PJA (2020c). Cashless Payment Survey Results. *Payments Japan Association.* https://cashless.go.jp/assets/doc/201211_questionnaire_report.pdf (accessed May 31, 2021).

PMJHC (2014). Japan Revitalization Strategy: Revised in 2014. *Prime Minister of Japan and His Cabinet.* https://www.kantei.go.jp/jp/singi/keizaisaisei/pdf/honbun2JP.pdf (accessed May 31, 2021).

Takao, M. (2009). The Growth Process of e-Money in Japan. Doctoral dissertation, The University of Tokyo.

Visa Inc. (2020). News Release Summary of 2020: Visa's Touch Payments to Expand Rapidly in Japan. https://www.visa.co.jp/about-visa/newsroom/press-releases/nr-jp-201217.html (accessed March 15, 2021).

Wisniewski, T. P., Polasik, M., Kotkowski, R., & Moro, A. (2021). Switching from Cash to Cashless Payments during the COVID-19 Pandemic and Beyond. Available at SSRN 3794790. https://papers.ssrn.com/sol3/papers.cfm?abstract_id=3794790 (accessed May 2, 2021).

11 COVID-19 pandemic impact on Japanese travel and tourism industry and new challenges in the "with COVID-19" and "after COVID-19" era

Emi Teshima

1 COVID-19 impact on Japanese travel and tourism industry

The Ministry of Land, Infrastructure, Transport and Tourism (MLIT) reported that the national Japanese government has positioned tourism as the key to regional revitalization and a pillar of Japan's growth strategy (MLIT, 2020a; p. 10). To increase the number of foreign tourists, in cooperation with the Japan National Tourism Organization and inbound stakeholders, the Japanese government has enhanced its customs, immigration, and quarantine system, its transportation networks at airports, railways, and ports, and its multilingual notations. In 2019, the number of foreign tourists visiting Japan reached a record high of 31.88 million (up 2.2% from the previous year), surpassing 30 million for the second consecutive year and reaching a record high for the seventh consecutive year (see Figure 11.1).

However, due to the rapid global spread of COVID-19 in 2020, many countries put immigration restrictions and overseas travel bans in place, which inevitably reduced global tourist numbers. According to MLIT (2020b; pp. 57–59),

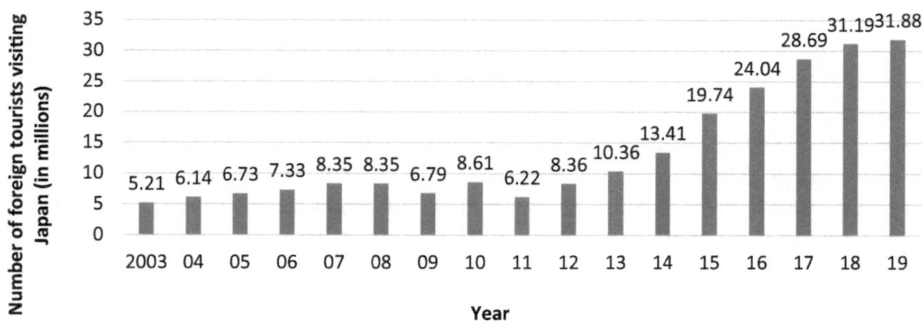

Figure 11.1 Changes in the number of foreign tourists visiting Japan.
Data Source. Ministry of Land, Infrastructure, Transport and Tourism (2020a).

DOI: 10.4324/9781003216049-13

Japan saw a 58.3% decrease in the number of foreign tourists in February 2020 compared to the same month in 2019, with only 1.085 million visitors; in March, numbers fell by 93.0% compared to 2019 to 194,000, and in April, decreased by 99.9% to 2,900 compared to 2019, which was the largest decrease since numbers started being collected in 1964. This massive decrease in foreign tourists obviously resulted in a commensurate 41.6% fall in tourist consumption compared to 2019 in the January-March period of 2020 to only JPY 672.7 billion. Domestic travel consumption also decreased by 53.1% compared to the same period in 2019 to JPY 786.4 billion in March, the largest decrease since the start of the current survey period in 2010. Domestic accommodation trends were also severely affected. The total number of overnight foreign guests in February decreased by 41.3% compared to 2019 to 4.85 million and decreased by 49.6% in March to 23.61 million. Of these, foreign tourists' nights decreased by 85.9% to 1.18 million nights and Japanese tourist nights decreased by 41.8% to 22.42 million nights, both of which were the largest decreases since statistics started being collected. Therefore, the tourism and tourism-related sectors are in a difficult situation because of this rapid decrease in foreign and domestic tourists.

As of April 2021, the number of foreign tourists to Japan has fallen to virtually zero, and there are no signs of recovery because of the continuing severe restrictions on movements across countries and regions. As there is no expectation of any regional revitalization in foreign tourism in the near future, domestic travel demand and the associated consumption needs to be stimulated; however, the domestic travel and tourism industry is also struggling. In July 2020, the government launched its "Go To Travel Campaign" (Go To Travel, n.d.) to encourage domestic travel, for which the government bears half the cost of the total domestic travel price (70% of the benefit is given as a discount on the travel price and 30% is given as a coupon that can be used only at the travel destination). The Japan Tourism Agency (2021) announced that the number of users (number of nights) from July to December 2020 was about 87.81 million, and the amount of support totaled around JPY 539.9 billion. However, the campaign was suspended due to the re-emergence of COVID-19, and as of April 2021, there was no prospect of resumption any time soon.

However, new travel styles and business models that do not fit conventional travel and tourism concepts have been emerging. In the next section, I introduce the new challenges for the Japanese travel and tourism industry which have been forced to shift to a paradigm due to the COVID-19 pandemic.

2 Online experience programs

The April-September 2020 financial results for Japan's largest travel industry company, JTB Corporation (2020a; 2020b; 2020c), showed an 81% year-on-year decrease in sales. Domestic travel sales, one of its two earnings pillars, fell 85% year-on-year, and overseas travel sales, the other pillar, fell 91% year-on-year. To revive their business, JTB decided on a drastic structural business reform that involved developing a "seamless integrated online and offline purchasing experience that offers a series of trips, including daily life and travel, that respond to each individual's needs". JTB has launched online experience programs, on which the customer can enjoy scenery using apps such as ZOOM, talk with local staff and shop staff, and enjoy shopping from home. In addition to the online experience programs for general customers, JTB is now also offering online educational travel, such as the "Virtual Study Trip 360", which is a new type of virtual reality-based travel, and its "online work experience Malaysia".

All Nippon Airways Co., Ltd. (ANA) (ANA, 2021a), Japan's largest airline company, announced that its consolidated financial results for the third quarter of the fiscal year ending March 2021 showed a 66.7% year-on-year decrease in sales, with international passenger revenue decreasing by 93.6% and domestic passenger revenue decreasing by 71.7%. To generate new demand, ANA has started an "ANA Travelers Online Tour", which offers a simulated online destination experience that includes contact with experts familiar with the area. There are several different online travel experience themes, such as "Japan", "Hawaii", "city walk", "world heritage", "nature", "gourmet", "history", and "art". New concept online experience programs have also become popular, such as the "Sneak in! ANA in-flight meal factory tour" (ANA, 2021b), in which the ANA chef appears live and customers can enjoy an in-flight meal that is sent to their home in advance, and a "Dream Tour to Space!" (ANA, 2021c), in which the online tourists are guided by space experts.

To support these new challenges, for example, the Tokyo Metropolitan Government (2020a; 2020b) started the subsidy program that subsidizes part of the cost to create the tours utilizing the new technologies such as Virtual Reality (VR) and Augmented Reality (AR) in June 2020 and the subsidy program to create the online tours in October 2020. According to "Future Outlook for AR/VR Related Markets 2020", announced by Fuji Chimera Research Institute, Inc. (2020), the global market for AR/VR display devices is predicted to grow 44.8 times from 2019 to JPY 16,171.1 billion in 2030. And the domestic market for business-to-consumer content is expected to grow 6.7 times from 2019 to JPY 516.5 billion in 2030. Therefore, there are great expectations for the development and popularization of online tours using AR/VR technology.

3 Micro tourism

3.1 Travel needs

A survey conducted by the JTB Tourism Research & Consulting Co. (2020) found that 40.9% of respondents said that they would like to go on a domestic trip when the COVID-19 restrictions from going out and traveling were lifted (followed by "eating out" 40.5%, "meet friends and acquaintances" 39.1%, "shopping at department stores and stores" 27.6%, and "meet family living away" 19.9%). Most respondents also stated that their domestic travel destination would be in the same region as their home. The Travel and Tourism Consumption Trend Survey conducted by the Japan Tourism Agency (n.d.) in 2018,

2019, and 2020 found that compared to the same period in the previous year, the percentage of overnight travel destinations within the same local block as the traveler's home rose significantly. Because of the risks of infection, these "micro tourism" experiences that involve short distances and short travel times could be one of the best solutions in this tough time (see Figure 11.2).

3.2 Accommodation campaign for local residents

Many local government discount campaigns have also been introduced to encourage travel within people's local areas. For example, Fukuoka Prefecture (2020) has started a campaign called "Rediscover the charm of Fukuoka", which offers accommodation, travel, and rental car subsidies up to JPY 5,000 per night per person in Fukuoka Prefecture and JPY 3,000 per person for day trips. Accommodation sites are also seeking new customers by initiating special plans that are limited to citizens and prefectural citizens. For example, the traditional Japanese hotel and restaurant Ohana in Yanagawa, Fukuoka Prefecture, offered special accommodation for Fukuoka and Yanagawa citizens from June 15 to August 31, 2020 (Ohana, 2020; n.d.). "Ohana" was originally a villa that was built in the corner of Yanagawa Castle in 1738 by Sadayoshi Tachibana, the fifth feudal lord of the Yanagawa domain. In the Meiji era, the Tachibana clan became a count, and in 1897, a western-style Tachibana clan house was built next to the traditional Japanese-style house. Because the former Kazoku (noble) people were in distress after the war, Ohana was relaunched as the "hotel and restaurant Ohana" in the former count's residence. Now Ohana is a popular cultural tourist attraction in Yanagawa that reveals daimyo (feudal lord) culture. However, for most Yanagawa and Fukuoka citizens, the venerable Japanese-style hotel and restaurant, whose vast site is designated as a national cultural property, is "too

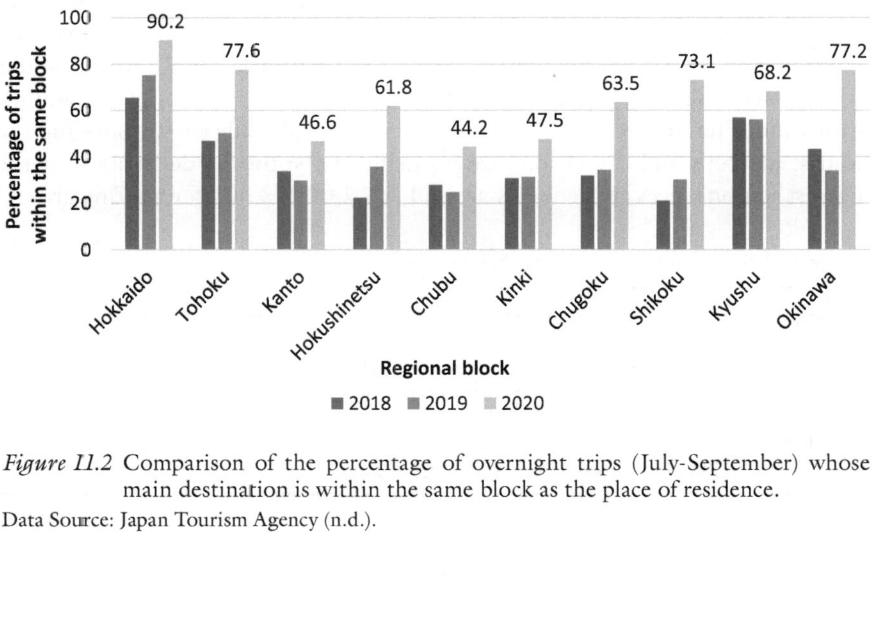

Figure 11.2 Comparison of the percentage of overnight trips (July-September) whose main destination is within the same block as the place of residence.

Data Source: Japan Tourism Agency (n.d.).

close to think about staying" or they "have wanted to stay, but it's too luxurious" and "have been to the restaurant but have never stayed at the hotel". Known for its history and beautiful, quaint streets, this small city had benefited greatly from the government's inbound policy. The Yanagawa City (2019) Tourism Dynamics Survey found that the number of foreign tourists increased from 21,506 in 2010 to 196,403 in 2019, a more than ninefold increase, with the number of guests more than doubling from 42,239 to 100,584. For a small city with a population of only around 60,000, the economic impact of the foreign tourists was significant. However, as the number of foreign tourists has dropped sharply because of COVID-19, they are seeking to attract locals and neighboring residents, but have been struggling to develop new customers. However, Ohana's limited campaign aimed at Fukuoka and Yanagawa citizens resulted in increased reservations from local citizens, which has greatly contributed to the occupancy rate and new local fans.

3.3 Even weeds can be a tourist resource

"Dai-Nagoya tours", Great Nagoya Tours, has been actively developing tourism products based on their new business model of moving people and money within a two-hour drive from Nagoya, Aichi Prefecture. "Dai-Nagoya Tours" is operated by the Dai-Nagoya Tours Executive Committee (based in Nagoya, Aichi Prefecture), and offers an experience program tour based on the keywords "experience", "learning", and "walking", the six main features of which are as shown in Table 11.1.

For example, some of the experience programs developed for April 2021 are: "Enjoy spring at Nagoya's traditional restaurant Kawabun Tour"; "learning Kawabun-history and culture from the landlady of Kawabun"; "Nagoya's Traditional 90 cm long! radish pickle-making experience"; "Finding the roots of the modern castle tour"; "Ten most popular animals at the Higashiyama Zoo and a Botanical Gardens Tour with former Zoo directors"; and "Kuzuri woolen industry techniques to support the world's top brand fashion". All programs have professional tour guides who provide in-depth but easy-to-understand information. The time required for each tour is generally only a few hours and the tourist meetups and dispersions are normally at the tourist destination or the nearest stations. Fees are generally around JPY 2,000–3,000 for walking around

Table 11.1 Six main features of Dai-Nagoya Tours

1	Welcome and participate alone, where people meet at the destination and then explore alone
2	Small groups tours, with a capacity of around 20 people
3	Destinations within two hours by car centered on Nagoya
4	Reasonable fees from only JPY 2,000
5	unique, professional tour guides
6	short trip experiences from one hour to one day

Source: Author; based on an interview survey.

the town (including materials and insurance fees) and more than JPY 10,000 for tours that include food and drink, with the average fee being from JPY 3,000 to JPY 4,000. These fees include a secretariat fee (JPY 1,500 per person) for the guide and the materials costs. For example, a JPY 3,000 program includes JPY 1,500 for the guide and JPY 1,500 for Dai-Nagoya Tours. As the tour participants gather and disperse at the tour destination, arranging transportation such as large buses is not necessary, which means that most of the fees go to Dai-Nagoya Tours. Most tour guides are employed by the respective companies and organizations and most tour operations are supported by volunteers, which allow Dai-Nagoya Tours to keep their operating costs low. The tour advertising and application to participate are on the official Dai-Nagoya Tour website.

In September 2020, when COVID-19 was widespread, a unique experience program was launched called "Weed Observation Tour – What can we see from the world of weeds? Discovering nature in the middle of the city", which was focused on the weeds that grow naturally on the city roadside. In this tour, the participants met at Fushimi Station on the Nagoya Municipal Subway and dispersed at Sakae Station, the proximate station. The tour involved walking and closely observing the plants and weeds along the streets. Participants were given a handmade weed information guidebook and loupes (return required) at the beginning and then walked slowly with the tour guide, who pointed out the small and pretty flowers blooming on the roadside, the strength of the weeds growing in the cracks in the asphalt, and the butterflies and small insects. During a break, participants were given a drink from the leaves of the *Houttuynia cordata*, which grows naturally even in the middle of the city. While enjoying the experience of drinking "weed juice (for those who do not know the Houttuynia cordata)", the participants were impressed with the wisdom of our predecessors in determining what was good for the body from these apparent weeds. This program provided information about the adventures of alien species carried by wind and birds, the effects of climate change, the role of the open space between buildings, and the relationships between the types of roadside trees and city planning. Because of the professional tour guide, the other participants with the same interests, and the quietude of the Fushimi Station area on Sunday, which is usually crowded on weekdays with office workers, the participants felt free to enjoy this "unusual experience", which at times involves crouching on the asphalt to look more closely at the weeds with their loupes. Because of the success of the first Weed Observation Tour in September 2020 and its apparent popularity, it has been decided to hold this event four times a year in spring, summer, autumn, and winter.

As shown in Table 11.2, the main feature of the Dai-Nagoya Tours is that 80% of participants are residents of Nagoya City or Aichi Prefecture, that is, the local people are showing a willingness to pay to visit local companies, stores, and facilities to receive in-depth information and have unique experiences. For example, the most attractive part of the "Weed Observation Tour" was the ability to have an "extraordinary everyday life experience" by observing weeds that grow naturally on the streets in one of the best business and commercial areas in Nagoya. The professional plant expert guide gave participants the names of and recounted stories about the common plants that people do not usually care about and informed them about the seasonal and social environment changes. This two-hour short program taught the local people how to enjoy walking around their own town. While tourism has generally been focused on attracting people from outside the local region, Dai-Nagoya Tours' concept to attract local people to rediscover the charm of their local area demonstrates the significant potential in developing local tourism (see Table 11.2).

3.4 A world that seems to know but does not know

This local tourism tendency was also developed in Tokyo. A weekly magazine published by Asahi Newspaper Company, *AERA*, (2021), reported on the release of "Tokyo 2021–22" (Diamond, Inc., 2020), which was the first domestic version of the 40-year overseas travel guidebook "Chikyu no Arukikata" ("How to walk around the earth") in September 2020 (AERA, 2021; pp. 66–67). It had a circulation of over 80,000. The article claimed that 60% of the readers lived in Tokyo and 90% in metropolitan areas such as Kanagawa, Chiba, and Saitama. Instead of introducing the latest, most popular tourist spots, the guidebook introduced Tokyo from specific unique perspectives, such as "Learn Oedo culture, challenge traditional crafts", "Tokyo's strongest power spot", "Stores and tastes loved by literary masters", and "7 free observation spots". There is so much information and so many discoveries in the guidebook that even people who have lived in Tokyo for a long time feel surprised and proud.

Some airlines have been developing new services to stimulate demand for micro tourism. For example, one regional airline based in Shizuoka, Shizuoka Prefecture, Fuji Dream Airlines (n.d.), has launched low-altitude sightseeing flight tours from Shizuoka Airport to Shizuoka Airport that fly over Mt. Fuji, the Japanese Alps, and Shimizu Port, and have also developed new types of field trips for local people and local schools at the airport that include commentaries from mechanics. Therefore, Fuji Dream Airlines is working hard to secure new sources of revenue by placing the airplane itself as the centerpiece of its tourism.

Table 11.2 Breakdown of tour participants in Dai-Nagoya Tours

Gender ratio	Male: 40%; Female: 60%
Age group	Under 20s: 3%; 20s: 12%; 30s: 26%; 40s: 26%; 50s: 19%; 60s and above: 14%
Repeat rate (participate more than once)	60%
Single participation rate	60%
Participant's place of residence	Nagoya City: 60%; Aichi Prefecture (other than Nagoya City): 20%; Gifu Prefecture: 10%; Mie Prefecture: 5%; Other: 5%
Average capacity sufficiency rate	Capacity varies, depending on the program; 20 people on average
Implementation rate	A little less than 95% (minimum five people)

Source: Author; based on an interview survey.

4 Regional industrial tourism initiatives

Several companies have launched industry tourism systems in cooperation with other companies in the same industry and other industries in the region to attract customers. For example, in Kitakyushu, Fukuoka Prefecture, which is also known as the "town of manufacturing that supported the modernization of Japan", the Kitakyushu City Industrial Tourism Center has been playing a central role in gathering information on the companies and facilities scattered throughout the city, disseminating information to the general public and specific groups, and arranging industrial tours based on four pillars: "factory night view"; "environmental tourism"; "factory tour/museum"; and "industrial heritage" (Kitakyushu Sangyo Kanko, n.d.).

In Sanjo and Tsubame, Niigata Prefecture, where there are many metal processing factories that have outstanding technology, factories have been opening to local people for several days in October every year since 2013. During the "Tsubame Sanjo Kouba no Saiten Factory Festival" (Kouba no Saiten, n.d.) period, anyone can visit the manufacturing sites, talk with the craftsmen, and buy the products direct from the factory. During this "factory festival", many people from all over Japan and even from abroad visit these small, quiet towns, with some people even wanting to work in the factories as a result. In October 2020, when it was difficult to hold face-to-face events, the factories distributed videos and set up live streams to show off their precise manufacturing to the world.

In Kuwana, Mie Prefecture, a Kuwana City Industrial Tourism (n.d.) Town Development Council was established. A list of manufacturing, finance, education, food, commercial facilities, and local government places that can be inspected has been developed and model half-day and one-day tours proposed for the region. By touring the various companies and government agencies in Kuwana, visitors can better understand how local companies work hard to grow together with the region and that the longer they stay in the city, the greater the regional economic contribution.

In this way, industrial tourism, which is focused on the characteristics of each region, has the potential to attract customers even in areas where it has been difficult to attract customers with conventional tourist offerings.

5 Super solo socialization and the changing travel and tourism needs

"Super solo socialization" had gradually been influencing the travel and tourism industry in Japan even before the COVID-19 pandemic. According to National Institute of Population and Social Security Research (NIPSSR), by 2040, almost half of Japanese population (20s and over) will be "single" due to the increase in the number of both unmarried and non-married, divorces, and elderly singles due to the loss of their spouses (NIPSSR, n.d.), which means a commensurate increase in "super solo socialization" (Arakawa, 2017) in Japan. A survey by the

Ministry of Health, Labor and Welfare (2019) found that as of 2018, 27.7% of all Japanese households (including under 20s) were single-person households, and that the rate was increasing every year, and that so-called "standard households" with married couples and unmarried children only made up 29.1% of households, which was decreasing every year (see Figure 11.3).

The increase in double-income households, the number of people who continue to work after retirement, and the busyness of children due to competitive entrance requirements for prestigious kindergartens and elementary schools are also factors leading to "temporarily-solo" people, which does not appear in statistics. With changes in household structures and lifestyles, leisure time activities have been changing from enjoying activities together with spouses and children to activities based on individual personal interests. Because of the continuing risk of COVID-19, the demand for solo travel experiences is expected to increase. In fact, according to the survey, 60% of the participants on the Dai-Nagoya Tours come alone, and in a survey by Dai-Nagoya Tours (Note, 2021), 60% answered that "it was easier for them to participate alone".

It should be noted here that the increase in the number of single households and the increase in "solo time", regardless of the presence or absence of a family, does not necessarily mean that more people live a "do not rely on anyone, do not want to be tied up, or want to spend time on my own" type of life. Everyone has feelings of connection, empathy, and addiction; however, now that it is easy to keep in contact with others through communication devices such as smartphones and it is easy to search for information anytime and anywhere, it has become easier to find like-minded people to connect loosely with outside the framework of the family.

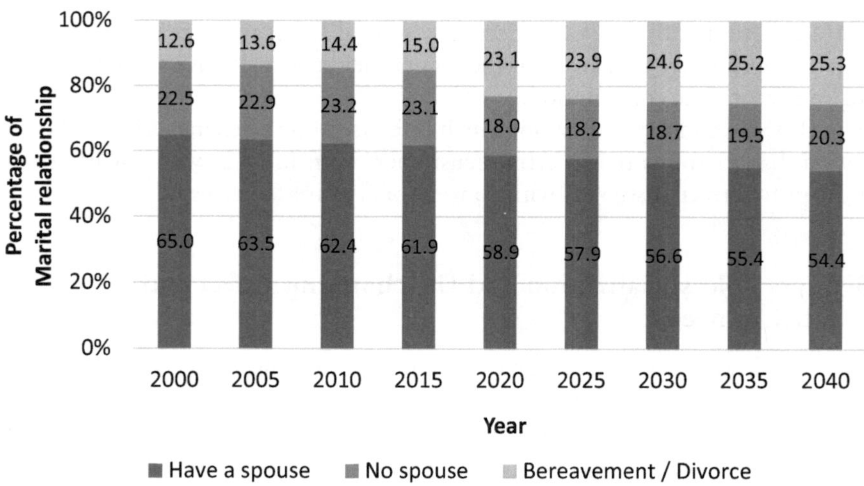

Figure 11.3 Population trends and future estimates by spouse.
Data Source: National Institute of Population and Social Security Research (n.d.).

6 Travel and tourism in the era of "with COVID-19" and "after COVID-19"

6.1 Five keywords to boost the travel industry

While COVID-19 has exposed the Japanese travel and tourism industry's reliance on the foreign tourist market, it has also given rise to the opportunity to reaffirm the importance of stimulating domestic travel, rediscovering local tourism resources, and developing tourism content that responds to changes in population structure and consumer needs. The travel and tourism market potential in Japan in the future can be summarized in five keywords: "online experience programs", "micro tourism", "local initiatives", "civic pride", and "super solo socialization".

6.2 Online experience programs

The "online experience program" market is expected to continue expanding to some extent. Not only in the "with COVID-19 era" but even after COVID-19 has diminished, it is attractive to enjoy the feeling of traveling with realistic images and real-time, two-way communication for many people, and especially for those who cannot afford the time, money, or physical strength to visit the place in reality. The ability to easily connect with sites such as YouTube allows people to enjoy various videos for free anytime, anywhere; therefore, further ingenuity is needed to make consumers want to participate for a fee. Even now, there is a plan for special products from a region to be delivered to a person's home in advance, so that all participants can enjoy an online tour while eating and drinking the same thing. I have high expectations that we can also experience the extraordinary feeling and taste the air that we feel in a real trip through online experience programs in the near future. The new possibilities of being able to go to places through online experience programs that are not normally accessible, such as space travel, in-flight meal factories, and airplane hangars, have already been proven possible in various industries and regions as possible future income sources. In the future, we need to find effective ways to guide these online customers to offline (real travel) activities, promote local community interactions, and increase consumption. I also hope that the use of VR/AR technology accelerated by COVID-19 will be utilized in creating the society where people living in remote areas, children, the elderly, and people with disabilities can also enjoy travel and entertainment more easily.

6.3 Micro tourism

"Micro tourism" has been shown to be useful for regional revitalization. As we face difficulties in going out, there is currently a great demand for safe sightseeing nearby. However, "micro tourism" power is weak at the moment as each group and local government is disseminating its information separately. Therefore, it is necessary to develop systems that allow us to search micro tourism plans from all over the country. The keys to revitalizing the micro tourism market are "information that induces tourism" and "creating a mechanism that allows easy participation", so that people with an interest in a specific theme or region can visit various parts of the country to deepen one theme or see one region from a different perspective to further deepen their understanding of the region.

6.4 Local initiative, civic pride

The idea of the "local initiative" and "civic pride" are also indispensable in creating new travel and tourism trends. By actively involving local people in the development of tourism content and reviewing local areas together with the local people, we can rediscover the charm and potential in an area that had not been previously noticed and cultivate civic pride in the region. By developing civic pride in the region in which we live, we can proudly and warmly welcome people from outside. Until the day when COVID-19 is no longer a global threat and people from outside the region and overseas can return, we need to develop leaders who can work together with local residents to rediscover local communities and create tourism systems that contribute to the local economy.

6.5 Super solo socialization

"Super solo socialization" is becoming a reality, which means that family and group trips where everyone indulges in gourmet food, scenery, shopping, and activities by adjusting their own needs to others will gradually shrink in the future. While being single or living alone may seem sad and lonely, the increase in the number of people who can freely use their time and money for themselves is a plus for the travel and tourism industry. Therefore, it is important to develop tourist activities that provide a place, method, and atmosphere that anyone can participate in without hesitation and can "connect loosely" to share the joy and satisfaction of their common interest.

6.6 Conclusion

COVID-19 has hit the travel and tourism industry hard in Japan, with the conventional business model inoperable at the moment. However, just as weeds sprout from the cracks in the paved road and small and pretty flowers bloom, there have been brave challenges by the industry to make the best use of its resources and stand up to the adversity. Even in our current self-restrained life, we consumers continue to look for new pleasures and have a desire to support companies and communities that take on these brave challenges. I hope that the travel and tourism industry will see this difficult situation as an opportunity for a paradigm shift to develop new measures to grow together with the region. I also expect that in addition to subsidizing travel costs such as the Go To Travel Campaign (Go To Travel, n.d.), the government can assist in developing a system that embraces new travel and tourism styles, such as online experience programs, micro tourism, and industrial tourism, and allows anyone to search for information in one place. In the end, I send my heartfelt ale to all challengers who struggle to open up a new tourism market by sometimes crawling on the side of the road looking for local attractions and sometimes boldly jumping into the cutting-edge technology field.

7 Acknowledgements

This research was realized with the great cooperation of all concerned parties. I thank my editors for giving me the opportunity to research and write on what is going on in the travel and tourism industry in Japan. Through the research, I had been greatly encouraged by the people trying to overcome the difficult situation caused by COVID-19. I especially thank Dai-Nagoya Tours for their cooperation in the repeated interview surveys, valuable data, and inspiring me a lot with their fun tours. I also thank Ohana for their warm hospitality. Staying at a cultural property really was a valuable experience. From the bottom of my heart, I sincerely hope that COVID-19 will converge someday soon in the future and we will be able to enjoy traveling around the world again.

References

AERA (2021). AERA (February 22 issue). Asahi Shimbun Publications Inc.

ANA (2021a). Official Press Release (January 29). All Nippon Airways Co., Ltd. https://www.anahd.co.jp/group/pr/202101/20210129.html (accessed April 22, 2021).

ANA (2021b). Official Press Release (February 26). All Nippon Airways Co., Ltd. https://www.anahd.co.jp/group/pr/202102/20210226.html (accessed April 22, 2021).

ANA (2021c). Official Press Release (March 2). All Nippon Airways Co., Ltd. https://www.anahd.co.jp/group/pr/202103/20210302.html (accessed April 22, 2021).

Arakawa, Kazuhisa (2017). Cho solo shakai. PHP Publishing.

Diamond Inc. (2020). Chikyu no Arukikata. Tokyo 2021–22.

Fuji Chimera Research Institute, Inc. (2020). Official Press Release (August 21). https://www.fcr.co.jp/pr/20088.htm (accessed May 17, 2021).

Fuji Dream Airlines (no date). Official Website. New Travel Style. https://www.fujidream.co.jp/newstyle/ (accessed April 22, 2021).

Fukuoka Prefecture (2020). Official News Release (June 26). https://www.pref.fukuoka.lg.jp/uploaded/attachment/115874.pdf (accessed April 22, 2021).

Go To Travel. (no date). Go To Travel Campaign. Official Website https://goto.jata-net.or.jp (accessed April 22, 2021).

Japan Tourism Agency (2021). Official News Release (February 10). https://www.mlit.go.jp/kankocho/news06_000499.html (accessed April 22, 2021).

Japan Tourism Agency (no date). Travel and Tourism Consumption Trend Survey (July-September 2018, 2019, 2020). https://www.mlit.go.jp/kankocho/siryou/toukei/shouhidoukou.html (accessed April 22, 2021).

JTB Corporation (2020a). Official News Release (August 6). https://press.jtbcorp.jp/jp/2020/08/vr-360.html (accessed April 22, 2021).

JTB Corporation (2020b). Official News Release (September 1). https://press.jtbcorp.jp/jp/2020/09/jtb-14.html (accessed April 22, 2021).

JTB Corporation (2020c). Official News Release (November 20). https://press.jtbcorp.jp/jp/2020/11/jtb-202049.html (accessed April 22, 2021).

JTB Tourism Research & Consulting Co. (2020). Official Press Release (May 28). https://www.tourism.jp/tourism-database/survey/2020/05/covid19-tourism/ (accessed April 22, 2021).

Kitakyushu Sangyo Kanko (no date). Official Website http://sangyokanko.com/ (accessed April 22, 2021).

Kouba no Saiten (no date). Official Website. https://kouba-fes.jp/#a08 (accessed April 22, 2021).

Kuwana City Industrial Tourism (no date). Official Website. https://www.avex-factory-tour.com/kuwana/kuwana.html (accessed April 22, 2021).

Ministry of Health, Labor and Welfare (2019). Welfare Statistics Handbook. https://www.mhlw.go.jp/toukei/youran/index-kousei.html (accessed April 22, 2021).

MLIT (2020a). White Paper on Tourism. Ministry of Land, Infrastructure, Transport and Tourism. https://www.mlit.go.jp/statistics/content/001348581.pdf (accessed April 22, 2021).

MLIT (2020b). White Paper on Tourism. Ministry of Land, Infrastructure, Transport and Tourism. https://www.mlit.go.jp/statistics/content/001348582.pdf (accessed April 22, 2021).

NIPSSR (no date). Population by spouse. National Institute of Population and Social Security Research. http://www.ipss.go.jp/syoushika/tohkei/Popular/Popular2021.asp?chap=0 (accessed April 22, 2021).

Note (2021). Dai-Nagoya Tours Survey (March 12). https://note.com/dainagoyatours/n/nc6649b1d7e57 (accessed April 22, 2021).

Ohana (no date). About. http://www.ohana.co.jp/about/index.html (accessed April 22, 2021).

Ohana (2020). Official News Release (July 6). http://www.ohana.co.jp/topics/topics424.html (accessed April 22, 2021).

Tokyo Metropolitan Government (2020a). Official News Release (June 30). https://www.metro.tokyo.lg.jp/tosei/hodohappyo/press/2020/06/30/09.html (accessed May 17, 2021).

Tokyo Metropolitan Government (2020b). Official News Release (October 8). https://www.metro.tokyo.lg.jp/tosei/hodohappyo/press/2020/10/08/26.html (accessed May 17, 2021).

Yanagawa City (2019). Tourism Dynamics Trend Survey. https://www.city.yanagawa.fukuoka.jp/library/download/02kanko/doutaityousa/201901-12.pdf; 15p. (accessed April 22, 2021).

12 System development and new human resource development in the Japanese IT industry

Tetsuro Saisho

1 Introduction

In recent years, while the Japanese IT industry has seen the spread of advanced technologies, the shortage of IT human resources (including system engineers) in system development has become critical. Such shortage is notable not only in regional cities but also in the Tokyo metropolitan area.

Going forward, the Japanese IT industry is expected to continue to see a significant shortage of IT human resources. In an effort to address this shortage, system development companies are hiring new graduates, making mid-career hires, and actively recruiting women.

Under these circumstances, Miyazaki City, a regional city and the prefectural capital of Miyazaki Prefecture, is creating a new business case called the Miyazaki-Bangladesh model, based on international industry-government-academia collaboration, to address the shortage of IT human resources in the region.

A business case is a logical systematization of what kind of business will generate profits, where to set the target group of the business, and what kind of products and services will be provided to the market. In this paper, based on the author's empirical research (Saisho, 2019), we consider the current situation and issues regarding the construction of a new business case for IT human resource management, which is being promoted through international industry-government-academia collaboration between Miyazaki City, Miyazaki Prefecture (in regional Japan), and Bangladesh, the least developed country (LDC).

Specifically, the current situation will be clarified by focusing on interviews targeting those involved in the Miyazaki-Bangladesh model. We will then consider issues of this model in relation to the spread of the new coronavirus (COVID-19).

2 Japan's IT industry and IT human resource shortage

Today, the Japanese IT industry is under pressure to control supply and demand of IT human resources in system development, due to the spread and sophistication of advanced IT technologies such as DX, AI, RPA, IoT, VR/AR, 5G, cloud computing, security, and Blockchain. In particular, the information security field is gaining importance in modern information society (Tsujii, 2012).

DOI: 10.4324/9781003216049-14

In addition, there is a great demand for information systemization in Japanese society due to the deterioration of extant information systems, the increasing complexity of business processing stemming from corporate mergers, the expansion of system maintenance and operations, and the spread of remote work as a result of the COVID-19 pandemic.

Finally, in the Japanese IT industry, there is a marked shortage of IT human resources on the back of the aging IT human resources who can engage in information systemization, worsening working conditions, and difficulties both in passing on IT technology and in diversification of IT technology skills to be acquired in response to the emergence of newer, more advanced IT technology.

The supply-demand gap first emerged in 2018, and the shortage in IT human resources is expected to increase from the current 164,000 to 787,000 by 2030 (MIRI, 2019).

The ratio of job offers to applicants by occupation (excluding part-time workers) in January 2020 was 2.30 for information processing and communication engineers in professional and technical occupations, significantly higher than for all occupations (1.40), and the IT human resource field continues to have many job openings (MHLW, 2020).

The working-age population (i.e., the population at the center of production activities, between the ages of 15 and 65) in Japan peaked in 1997, and has continued to decline—more significantly so than other developed countries (DBC, 2017).

The shortage of domestic IT human resources is becoming even more serious due to the general labor shortage caused by the declining birthrate. Thus, it is expected that the ratio of job offers to applicants for IT human resources in Japan will remain high and that the shortage of domestic IT human resources will not be resolved easily.

Furthermore, it is currently difficult for the Japanese IT industry to recruit enough young people to take on system development work. In fact, to address the shortage of IT human resources, a new international division of labor system and business model is being constructed to actively recruit overseas IT human resources.

In Asian LDCs, the labor cost of IT human resources is significantly lower than that of IT nations such as India and China, and there are many fluent English speakers; hence, Asian LDCs are attracting attention from the United States and developed countries in Europe as IT outsourcing hubs.

3 The Miyazaki-Bangladesh model and IT human resource management

3.1 Bangladesh economy and IT industry

The official name of Bangladesh is the People's Republic of Bangladesh. Its total area is 147,570 km^2, capital is Dhaka, population is 167.56 million (2019–2020), official language is Bengali, and main religion is Islam (MFA, 2020).

The three Asian countries of Bangladesh, Laos, and Myanmar will maintain their new status of "transitioning to a developing country" till 2026, if they meet targets in 2021, and are expected to see further growth in their domestic economies due to their graduation from LDC status. Bangladesh aims to spearhead its domestic economic expansion through growth in its software development and Business Process Outsourcing (Komori, 2017).

In recent years, the Bangladesh government has established the Digital Bangladesh policy aimed at making the domestic IT industry the second pillar of its economy, following the garment and apparel industry.

The Digital Bangladesh initiative was announced by the Awami League (i.e., one of Bangladesh's two major political parties) in 2008 as part of its general election campaign set forth in "Vision 2021," which aims for Bangladesh to become a middle-income country by the 50th anniversary of its independence (Nanbara, 2018).

As a side note, the economic and industrial policies of Asia have hitherto promoted heavy and chemical industries centered on manufacturing, and this has caused significant environmental destruction.

Bangladesh's GDP (%) has been stable, with steady economic growth of 6% or more per year for 2014–2020, and the increase in the nation's nominal GDP per capita is projected to be close to USD 2,000 for 2020 (Furuya et al., 2020; IMF, 2020). In addition, the real GDP per capita (based on Bangladesh Taka), which is obtained by subtracting the effect of price fluctuations from the nominal GDP, has continued to grow at a high rate (IMF, 2020).

Overall, Bangladesh's per capita GDP, average age, and Internet penetration rate are at the same levels as those of India and Myanmar (FRI, 2018).

In Bangladesh, IT education is comparable to that of India, and university exchanges (study abroad) between India and Bangladesh are also actively conducted. For this reason, the skills of IT human resources in Bangladesh are evaluated highly. Bangladesh is also focused on English education, and many people are fluent in English, so its IT human resources are attracting attention from all over the world.

However, in Bangladesh, it is difficult to find employment for IT personnel with university degrees because the domestic IT industry is not yet large or developed. Therefore, many Bangladeshi IT personnel become migrant workers to support their household budgets from overseas.

Meanwhile, Japanese IT companies have set up local subsidiaries in Bangladesh and are hiring excellent Bangladeshi system engineers from top-class technical universities in Bangladesh. It is worth noting that in offshore development, Bangladeshi system engineers have the same level of IT skills as in neighboring India.

3.2 What is the Miyazaki-Bangladesh model?

Miyazaki Prefecture's income ranking in Japan is sluggishly low, while its population is forecast to significantly decrease, and both are not expected to increase in the near future.

At the same time, there is a chronic shortage of IT human resources in the Japanese IT industry.

Thus, Miyazaki City, the prefectural capital of Miyazaki Prefecture, is developing a new business case called the Miyazaki-Bangladesh model through international industry-government-academia collaboration, whereby the shortage of IT human resources in the region is addressed by utilizing IT human resources from Bangladesh.

Meanwhile, in major cities in emerging countries, active software development is taking place with a large concentration of programmers (i.e., IT human resources) (Ito, 2020).

The business case involves neither "offshore development," where information system development is outsourced to overseas companies or corporations, nor "nearshore development," where such development is outsourced to companies and business establishments in regional cities in Japan. In offshore development and nearshore development, software development is outsourced for the main purpose of cost reduction (MISA, 2015).

The model matches the abundant IT human resources in Bangladesh with IT companies in Miyazaki Prefecture to promote information system development work in the prefecture. IT companies not only in Miyazaki Prefecture but across Japan actively welcome Bangladeshis who want to work in Japan, thereby boosting employment of Bangladeshis.

Thus, the model creates a win-win relationship that addresses the problems of both Japan and Bangladesh by hiring Bangladeshi people to solve the shortage of IT human resources in Miyazaki and other prefectures. In other words, the Miyazaki-Bangladesh model is founded on a win-win relationship between Japan, which has a serious labor shortage, and Bangladesh, which has abundant human resources, thereby controlling the supply and demand of IT human resources between Japan and Bangladesh.

The concept of the Miyazaki-Bangladesh model originated in 2014, when several IT companies based in Miyazaki City participated in a survey for project creation in Bangladesh by Japan International Cooperation Agency (JICA), an agency of the government sector. Under the Digital Bangladesh policy, a technical cooperation project coined the "Capacity Building on ITEE Management Project" was promoted with the aim of introducing to Bangladesh the Japanese Information-Technology Engineers Examination (ITEE) for IT human resource development (JBO, 2012).

In response, the "Capacity Building on ITEE Management Project" is promoting the introduction of a national examination and qualification system for the IT industry in Bangladesh led by the ITEE agency (JBO, 2012), and training programs and improvements of operational capabilities are being offered as well. In Bangladesh, systematic technical education and vocational training in the IT industry have not yet been developed, nor have technical standards been established. In addition, Bangladesh lacks an accurate measure for the quality of IT human resources, such as IT-related exams and qualifications, and also lacks indicators around which system engineers can design their career paths.

In response, the "Capacity Building on ITEE Management Project" is promoting the introduction of a national examination and qualification system for the IT industry in Bangladesh led by the ITEE agency (JBO, 2012).

After 2014, the IT company based in Miyazaki City that participated in the JICA project survey hired two IT personnel from Bangladesh.

In recruiting IT human resources in Bangladesh, international industry-government-academia collaboration took place, leveraging on the demands and strengths of the respective parties, i.e., the difficulty faced in hiring IT personnel locally on the part of IT companies, the desire to attract IT companies to the region on the part of Miyazaki City, and the offering of Japanese language education for international students on the part of Miyazaki University.

The operating capital for implementing the model is provided by JICA on the Bangladeshi side, and the total project cost is approximately JPY 530 million, assuming a four-year duration from August 2017 to July 2021. On the Miyazaki side, companies that participate in the Japanese Language & IT Internship Program (JIP) bear the costs (JBO, 2017).

Meanwhile, Bangladeshi students participating in the JIP program bear no costs.

3.3 The Miyazaki-Bangladesh model and IT human resource management

The Miyazaki-Bangladesh model envisages a new form of human resource management in the IT field through international industry-government-academia collaboration between the Miyazaki side—consisting of IT companies (i.e., industry) that plan to accept and hire internships, Miyazaki City (i.e., government) which provides subsidies to local companies hiring internships, and Miyazaki University (i.e., academia) which providers Japanese language education and internships—and the Bangladesh side—consisting of Ministry of Posts, Telecommunications and Information Technology (MoPTIT) (i.e., government which concludes agreement, JICA (i.e., government) which bears the costs, Bangladesh Computer Council (BCC) (i.e., government) which is responsible for project management, IT companies (i.e., industry) that provide IT training facilities and systems, Miyazaki University (i.e., academia) which dispatches Japanese teachers, and Dhaka University (i.e., academia) which offers university facilities (Figure 12.1; MU, 2019).

In the Miyazaki-Bangladesh model, incentives for each party include regional revitalization and securing sources for tax revenue on the part of Miyazaki City, providing specialized education on the part of Miyazaki University, solving the shortage of IT human resources on the part of IT companies, and creating official development assistance (ODA) achievement on the part of JICA.

In this international industry-government-academia collaboration, JICA (i.e., Japanese government sector) bears the costs of project implementation which are led by the Faculty of Engineering and Technology, Dhaka University (i.e., academia sector) located in Dhaka, the capital of Bangladesh.

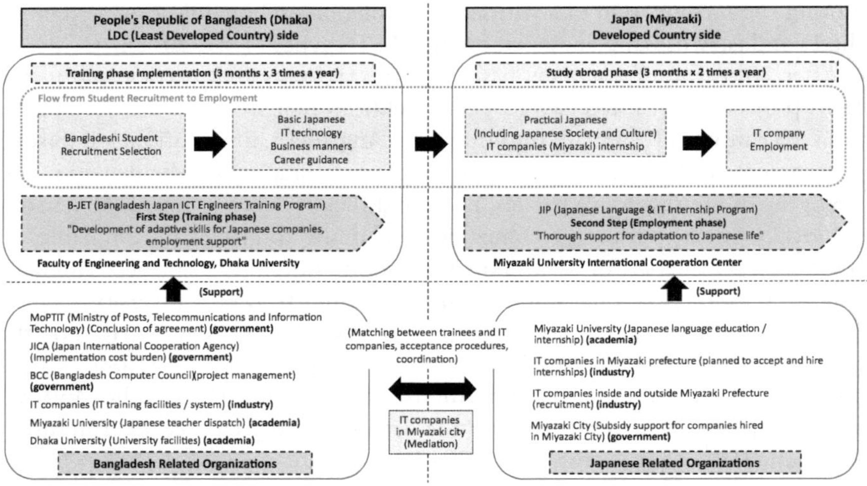

Figure 12.1 Scheme of Miyazaki-Bangladesh model.
Source: Based on MU (2019).

Currently, the Miyazaki-Bangladesh model is operated by JICA funding as a JICA project. However, each company respectively bears the costs of internships. In the future, if this model case proves to be sustainable and successful, and if IT companies can subsequently hire such interns as IT personnel, such IT companies are expected to be funded with subsidies.

The MoPTIT in the Bangladeshi government sector concludes the project agreement and the BCC in the Bangladeshi government sector is in charge of local project promotion and management. In addition, Miyazaki University in the Japanese academic sector is in charge of Japanese language education for Bangladeshis. Finally, several Japanese IT companies are participating in this model as outsourcers on behalf of JICA.

In November 2017, JICA, representing Japan, and BCC, representing Bangladesh, forged an international industry-government-academia collaboration to launch the Bangladesh-Japan ICT Engineers Training (B-JET) Program (JICA, 2018), which is a training course for IT human resources in Bangladesh aiming for employment in Japanese IT companies. Miyazaki University has been entrusted with offering Japanese language education programs and developing teaching materials catered to IT engineers in Bangladesh. The university is also developing Japanese language learning materials for Bangladeshis working at an IT company in Miyazaki Prefecture.

Additionally, Miyazaki University has dispatched three Japanese teachers to Bangladesh as part of the B-JET Program and IT specialists from IT companies in Miyazaki City have been hired as local lecturers in Dhaka (MU, 2019). The B-JET Program is a training course for IT human resources in Bangladesh aiming for employment in Japanese IT companies after the agreement was concluded between JICA and MoPTIT.

This program is part of an ODA technical assistance project implemented by JICA in Bangladesh, and in November 2017, JICA and BCC jointly commenced the training phase, which consists of three terms per year, with each term lasting three months and accepting 20–40 students.

The total duration of the B-JET Program is three years, and a total of 320 Bangladeshis will be trained by the end. The three-month training in Dhaka provides an educational curriculum that focuses on the skills necessary to obtain a job at a Japanese IT company, represented by basic Japanese, IT technology, and Japanese business manners.

The B-JET Program education is provided to Bangladeshi students free of charge (JBO, 2020). The program accepted 20 applicants (out of 1,825 total applicants, i.e., 1 out of 91.25) for the first semester in 2017 and 40 (out of 4,707 total applicants, i.e., 1 out of 117.85) for the second semester in 2018. Currently, the B-JET Program is training 40 applicants (out of 3,419 total applicants, i.e., 1 out of 85.48) for the eighth semester in 2020 and is implementing Japanese language education (JBO, 2020).

Up to the eighth semester, the program has had a total of 26,989 applicants, with 280 accepted, for an average acceptance rate of approximately 1.0%, and is a very popular educational program in Bangladesh. A total of 320 trainees are scheduled to graduate from the program counting from the first semester in 2017 to the ninth semester in 2020. As of April 2019, 21 B-JET graduates lived in Miyazaki City.

Many of the trainees in this program are graduates of universities that are among the top 10% in Bangladesh (e.g., University of Dhaka, Rajshahi University of Engineering and Technology, Khulna University of Engineering and Technology, Dhaka University of Engineering and Technology, Chittagong University of Engineering and Technology, and Bangladesh University of Engineering and Technology). They are either new graduates of IT-related faculties or young engineers in their 20s and 30s who have had several years of practical experience in IT companies.

3.4 The Miyazaki-Bangladesh model as a new business case

As part of the B-JET Program, after each semester, an IT company based in Miyazaki City serves as an intermediary and conducts matching, acceptance, procedures, and adjustments between Japanese IT companies and Bangladeshi international students who want to work for a Japanese company.

On the Japan side, Miyazaki University welcomes international students from Bangladesh as part of the JIP. This program provides study-abroad Japanese language education for those who wish to study in Japan and internships at IT companies in Miyazaki Prefecture which last several months (i.e., three months, twice a year; Figure 12.1).

The Bangladeshi students learn business etiquette, relevant know-how, communication, and other contents through internships at IT companies in Miyazaki

Prefecture. In addition, the students may be officially hired by IT companies in Miyazaki City after their internship, and in this case, Miyazaki City provides a subsidy to the hiring companies.

B-JET Program achievements are as follows: Miyazaki University started the training phases of the B-JET Program in April 2018, October 2018, and April 2019; and Miyazaki City IT companies conducted recruitment in July 2018, January 2019, and July 2019, with four companies hiring six people each, four companies hiring seven each, and one company hiring two (MCTC, 2019).

If an IT company in Miyazaki City hires a Bangladeshi IT engineer (i.e., B-JET graduate) using a recruitment agency, part of the recruitment fee—more specifically, "referral fee × 1/2 (up to 500,000 yen/person)"—is provided as a subsidy by the city (if requirements are met) (MCTC, 2019).

In Miyazaki City, subsidies are provided for research that are determined to contribute to solving regional issues in "Miyazaki City or surrounding areas." In FY2017, Miyazaki University received a JPY 1.8 million grant from Miyazaki City for academic research that contributes to the region, termed "research on Japanese language/career education for advanced foreign human resources employment and internationalization of regional industrial human resources."

The grant stipulated that Miyazaki University shall establish a program for employment and retention of advanced IT foreign human resources (i.e., Bangladeshi IT engineers), internationalization of regional industrial human resources, and accumulation of advanced IT human resources.

Supported by this grant, Miyazaki University has developed a short-term training program (i.e., JIP) that combines Bangladeshi study abroad in Japan and a Japanese internship. In addition, 16 of the 20 first-year students who completed the B-JET program have been studying abroad at Miyazaki University for short periods since April 2018.

Through the JIP, they have studied such topics as Japanese and culture, society and business manners, and have participated in internships at IT companies in Miyazaki City. After the program ends, the Bangladeshi students are expected to find employment in Japanese companies (JBO, 2020).

So far, all 20 of the first-year international students accepted at Miyazaki University have found employment at IT companies in Japan, among which 16 have been employed in Miyazaki Prefecture. This has greatly contributed to securing personnel in response to the shortage of IT human resources (MU, 2019).

4 Challenges for the Miyazaki-Bangladesh model

4.1 Current state of the Miyazaki-Bangladesh model and the effects of COVID-19

By accepting IT human resources from Bangladesh, Miyazaki Prefecture can augment and diversify its IT human resources.

The initiatives undertaken by Bangladesh and Miyazaki City will offer implications for increasing the number of young people in regional cities in Japan.

The Miyazaki-Bangladesh model aims for a win-win relationship in terms of supply and demand of IT human resources between Japan, a developed country, and Bangladesh, a developing country.

Since early 2020, COVID-19 has spread throughout the world, and many companies are suffering adverse effects such as contraction and even closure, with IT companies being no exception (Matsuura, 2020).

In the Japanese IT industry in 2020, not only IT companies but also the IT market size will be greatly affected by the COVID-19 pandemic. The size of the Japanese IT market (as of the end of September 2020) was JPY 17,116.2 billion, down 6.3% from the previous year due to the influence of COVID-19 (IDC, Japan, 2021).

The Japanese IT market has seen an expansion in specific fields such as telework, satellite offices, and games, but the market size is shrinking in many other fields affected by the disappearance of demand deriving from inbound tourism, the request by governments to refrain from going out, and a decrease in exports.

Meanwhile, according to the "Corporate IT Trend Survey 2021" (FY2020 survey) conducted by Users Association of Information Systems (JUAS) from September to October 2020, the IT budget of Japanese companies in FY2021 is expected to increase (JUAS, 2021). JUAS' "Corporate IT Trend Survey" has been investigating corporate IT investment and trends in IT strategy since FY2016.

As mentioned above, in Japan, the IT market size in 2020 is shrinking due to the influence of COVID-19. However, the IT budget of Japanese companies in 2021 is expected to increase in two fields: IT for products/services and IT for processes. IT for products/services consists of creating new added value by connecting all products and services to the Internet. IT for processes consists of reforming business processes, which are a series of activities common to all organizations, using IT in order to achieve a specific purpose.

In Japanese companies, more than half of total IT budgets is expected to increase year-on-year in both IT for products/services and IT for processes. In addition, more than 70% of the total is expected to increase even in the medium to long term (i.e., 3–5 years). Furthermore, the IT budget of Japanese companies is expected to increase significantly by "50% or more" in about 10% of the companies.

In 2020, under the influence of COVID-19, IT investment by Japanese companies will slow down, and the IT labor market will also become less tight. However, from 2021, Japanese companies are expected to actively invest in IT. At the same time, the man-hours (i.e., development scale) for information system development are expected to increase, and the IT labor market is expected to tighten as well.

So far, the Japanese IT industry has built business cases such as the Miyazaki-Bangladesh model for the purpose of establishing new human resource management in the field of information system development. The business case of the Miyazaki-Bangladesh model was developed in an effort to enhance IT human resources management based on a "win-win relationship" between Miyazaki

City and Bangladesh. Currently, the Miyazaki-Bangladesh model is being used to make up for the shortage of IT talent in the regional city of Miyazaki and to create jobs for the Bangladeshis.

In 2020, Japan will undoubtedly be affected by COVID-19 and thus the shortage of IT human resources will be alleviated. However, we must not perceive the issue of the shortage of IT human resources based on short-term fluctuations, such as the temporary contraction of the IT market.

Human resource management in the IT field needs to be deployed based on a long-term perspective that is not bound by immediate fluctuations in demand. For the Miyazaki-Bangladesh model, it is necessary to pursue a sustainable business model.

4.2 Evaluation of the Miyazaki-Bangladesh model

The Miyazaki-Bangladesh business model cannot necessarily be applied successfully to all LDCs. The success factor of this business case is the special circumstances of Bangladesh. There are three factors that make Bangladesh special: (1) English education, (2) IT education, and (3) immature industry:

1 Regarding English education in Bangladesh, wealthy people are learning English from the age of six. In addition, some paid private high schools offer all classes in English to improve students' English proficiency. In Bangladesh, those who are highly educated are excellent and fluent in English and perform actively in foreign-affiliated companies. Ultimately, economic and social opportunities in Bangladesh depend on knowledge of English (Hossain, 2018).
2 Regarding IT education in Bangladesh, there are five major national technical universities in the country, tuition is free, and accommodation facilities are provided to students. The acceptance rate of IT-related faculties of national universities is about 2%, and the ability of IT human resources in Bangladesh is comparable to that of India. In addition, there are many IT human resources in Bangladesh who are active overseas. Bangladeshis have the same IT and English skills as Indians, but their wages are less than half that of Indians (Okabe, 2013).
3 Regarding the Bangladesh industry, the manufacturing industry, which is a labor-intensive industry represented by garment, is drawing attention. Bangladesh's industrial structure breakdown based on GDP (FY2020) is 51.30% for the service industry, followed by 35.36% for the manufacturing industry, and 13.35% for the agriculture, forestry and fisheries industry. Most of the service industry, excluding banking, education, and wholesale, is part of the informal sector (MFA, 2020).

Bangladesh's domestic industry has long been dependent on the garment industry, but finally industries such as bicycles, home appliances, and shipbuilding are growing (Yamagata, 2014). On the other hand, as of 2020, the IT industry as a service industry is not growing.

In the meantime, Bangladeshis have been migrating abroad for work for about half a century, so they are highly adaptable and responsive to foreign cultures. The motivation of such migrant workers derives from economic factors such as high employment potential, expected income, high savings, and assistance to family and relatives (BRI, 1993).

Bangladeshis are easily able to constitute a part of and operate in the Miyazaki-Bangladesh model because of their highly migrant nature and adaptability to foreign cultures. In Bangladesh, this new business case has been successful due to the combination of social, economic, and industrial backgrounds not found in other LDCs.

It is worth noting that many Japanese companies in labor-intensive industries have entered LDC markets such as Cambodia and Laos, but few IT companies have entered the service industry. Recently, IT industries such as DX have been developing in LDCs, but since there are few Japanese IT companies expanding into LDCs, support for new business cases cannot be expected. In addition, a very high portion of Cambodians and Laotians living in Japan live in Kanagawa Prefecture, and since Cambodian and Laotian communities have not yet been formed in regional cities, support from such communities will not be available in regional areas.

Collaboration between Japan and the IT field of LDCs makes it easy to establish a business model for software development. This is because the establishment of new business cases for Japan and LDCs require the establishment of companies or other organizations, which involves little capital investment with only minimum infrastructure investment and operating costs.

In the future, further shortage of IT human resources related to software development in Japan will make it easier to establish a new business case. Therefore, by understanding the relationship between Japan and LDCs, and the domestic circumstances and issues of LDCs, and by utilizing the social system based on such circumstances and issues, the possibility of establishing a new business case and of making sustainable efforts will increase.

4.3 Challenges for the Miyazaki-Bangladesh model

Currently, the Miyazaki-Bangladesh model is developing steadily, but the following issues should be noted.

First, the resources (i.e., funds) in the model are mainly public funds centered on ODA project resources provided by JICA, an independent administrative agency which plays a leading role in implementing the project.

Miyazaki University (i.e., a national university corporation), Miyazaki City (i.e., a local government), as well as JICA utilize Japanese public funds (i.e., Japanese taxes). After July 2021, however, when the latest period for the JICA budget ends, the model will no longer be able to rely on public funds, and sustainable activities that introduce private funds will be required.

Second, the model cannot be expected to significantly reduce system development costs. In offshore development of information systems, large reductions can be expected through the utilization of overseas resources. Also, in nearshore development of information systems, business based on tacit knowledge (i.e., Japanese-style business) can be carried out through utilizing Japanese resources. Tacit knowledge management is management based on knowledge that cannot easily be verbalized, including experience and intuition.

However, hiring talented overseas IT personnel to make up for the shortage of IT human resources in Japan basically requires the same labor costs as those for Japanese workers. In other words, the model cannot be expected to have a large cost reduction effect. Therefore, IT companies are required to take on businesses that are suitable for utilizing overseas IT human resources (i.e., tasks that are unsuitable for Japanese workers).

Third is the understanding of religion and culture in the working environment of Japanese companies. The main religions in Japan are Shinto, Buddhism, and to a minor extent Christianity, whereas the main religion in Bangladesh is Islam. In each religious view, there are fundamental and cultural differences regarding concepts such as nature/God/humanity, reason/order, and life/fertility.

For example, a devout Muslim must worship five times a day. Therefore, each company is required to secure a place of worship. In addition, there are special considerations to be made in daily IT work, such as creating a contingency plan for cases of system failure or scheduling worship time during working hours.

Fourth is the response to the impact of COVID-19 on IT companies. The Miyazaki-Bangladesh model has also been affected by COVID-19.

Currently, plans beyond the end of 2020 are undecided, informal job offers by Japanese IT companies that were made before the COVID-19 pandemic may be canceled, and a system is required that enables remote (i.e., online) internships and pre-visit training.

Although corporate performance is declining even in IT companies, companies must resume recruiting activities by making the best possible response to the COVID-19 pandemic.

In Japan, when a crisis such as the COVID-19 pandemic occurs, IT personnel from LDCs may not be able to enter Japan; yet, a feature of the information system development business is that one should be able to work from any place as long as there is an Internet environment. Going forward, it will be necessary to utilize such work styles as remote work and telework to enable securing IT human resources from LDCs even in the case of a crisis.

5 Conclusion

The Miyazaki-Bangladesh model is an international industry-government-academia collaboration based on a win-win relationship between Miyazaki and Bangladesh with respect to IT human resources.

The model is attracting attention in the IT industry as a new business model for human resource management in information system development in response to the shortage of IT human resources in Japan.

The initiative is, in part, an effort to secure IT human resources in the regional city of Miyazaki; however, the efforts of Miyazaki City provide implications as a valuable new business case for securing human resources which may be applied to other regional cities in Japan as well.

Furthermore, the model can be applied not only to the IT industry but also to other industries, and not only to Bangladesh but also to other countries and regions. However, there remain technical, social, financial, and cost issues, as mentioned above.

Moving forward, such issues need to be resolved for the sustainable development and widespread application of the Miyazaki-Bangladesh model.

6 Acknowledgment

This work was supported by JSPS KAKENHI Grant-in-Aid for Scientific Research (B) Number 19H01532.

References

BRI (1993). *Fact-finding Survey of Bangladesh Workers Working in Japan*. Bangladesh Institute for Development Problems Research Institute (in Japanese).

DBC (2017). *The Action Plan for the Realization of Work Style Reform (Provisional)* (in Japanese). Decided by the Council for the Realization of Work Style Reform. http://www.kantei.go.jp/jp/singi/hatarakikata/pdf/The_Action_Plan_for_the_Realization_of_Work_Style_Reform.pdf (accessed April 6, 2021).

FRI (2018). 2nd Bangladesh IT Market and Business Opportunities. *Attractiveness of Bangladesh Market* (in Japanese). Fujitsu Research Institute. https://www.fujitsu.com/jp/group/fri/knowledge/opinion/consul/2018/2018-12-2.html (accessed April 6, 2021).

Furuya, R., Ando, Y., & Yamada, K. (2020). Ask a Private Think Tank about the Future of the Booming Bangladesh Economy. *Region/Analysis Report* (in Japanese). https://www.jetro.go.jp/biz/areareports/2020/b516ca0e833f1892.html (accessed April 6, 2021).

Hossain, T. (2018). The Historical-structural Approach to Language Policy: It's Application in the Context of Bangladesh (English Language Education). *International Christian University Publications*. 2008-03, 235–250.

IDC Japan (2021). Announcement of the Impact of COVID-19 on IT Expenditure by Domestic Region and Future Forecast. *Press Release* (in Japanese). https://www.idc.com/getdoc.jsp?containerId=prJPJ47295221 (accessed April 6, 2021).

IMF (2020). *World Economic Outlook Database April 2020*. International Monetary Fund. https://www.imf.org/external/pubs/ft/weo/2020/01/weodata/index.aspx (accessed April 6, 2021).

Ito, A. (2020). *Digitalizing Emerging Countries-Overcoming Developed Countries, The Arrival of Surveillance Society-*. Chuokoron (in Japanese).

JBO (2012). *ITEE Management Capacity Improvement Project Detailed Plan Formulation Survey Report* (in Japanese). JICA Bangladesh Office. https://openjicareport.jica.go.jp/pdf/12082434.pdf (accessed April 6, 2021).

JBO (2017). *Business Preliminary Evaluation Table* (in Japanese). JICA Bangladesh Office. https://www2.jica.go.jp/ja/evaluation/pdf/2017_1600344_1_s.pdf (accessed April 6, 2021).

JBO (2020). *B-JET Bangladesh IT Engineer Training Program for the Japanese Market* (in Japanese). JICA Bangladesh Office. https://www.jica.go.jp/bangladesh/bangland/b-jet.html (accessed April 6, 2021).

JICA (2018). *Bangladesh-Japan ICT Engineers' Training Program* (in Japanese). Japan International Cooperation Agency. https://www.jica.go.jp/bangladesh/bangland/b-jet.html (accessed April 6, 2021).

JUAS (2021). Corporate IT Trend Survey 2021. Japan Users Association of Information Systems. *Press Release* (in Japanese). https://juas.or.jp/cms/media/2021/01/it21_digital.pdf (accessed April 6, 2021).

Komori, M. (2017). A Study of Japanese Firms' Clustering and Innovation Creation in Bangladesh. Asia University. *Management Review*, 52(2), 19–33 (in Japanese).

Matsuura, T. (2020). The IT Industry may Suddenly Brake with the New Corona, and the Project may be Canceled for a Long Time. *Nikkei XTECH* (in Japanese). https://xtech.nikkei.com/atcl/nxt/column/18/00989/111100039/ (accessed April 6, 2021).

MCTC (2019). Bangladesh IT Engineer Employment Promotion Project. *Industry/Business Operator* (in Japanese). Miyazaki City Tourism and Commerce Department. https://www.city.miyazaki.miyazaki.jp/business/location/kougyou-link/1516.html (accessed April 6, 2021).

MFA (2020). Bangladesh Basic Data. *People's Republic of Bangladesh* (in Japanese). Ministry of Foreign Affairs of Japan. https://www.mofa.go.jp/mofaj/area/bangladesh/data.html (accessed April 6, 2021).

MHLW (2020). General Employment Placement Status by Occupation [Real Number] (Regular(Excluded Part)). *General Employment Placement Status (January 2nd year of Reiwa)* (in Japanese). Ministry of Health, Labor and Welfare. https://www.mhlw.go.jp/content/11602000/G38-202001.pdf (accessed April 6, 2021).

MIRI (2019). *FY2018 Infrastructure Development for Data-Driven Society in Japan-Survey on IT Human Resources Supply and Demand-Survey Report* (in Japanese). Mizuho Information & Research Institute. https://www.meti.go.jp/policy/it_policy/jinzai/houkokusyo.pdf

MISA (2015). Aiming for Near Shore Development Advanced Area. *JISA quarterly:bulletin*, 118, 133–138 (in Japanese). Miyagi Information Service Industry Association.

MU (2019). Implementation of an Internal Debriefing Session by Local Japanese Teachers of the 'Miyazaki-Bangladesh Model'. *International Exchange/Study Abroad* (in Japanese). Miyazaki University. https://www.miyazaki-u.ac.jp/newsrelease/international-info/post-308.html (accessed April 6, 2021).

Nanbara, S. (2018). What Is the Impact on the 'Thailand+One' Garment Industry after Graduating from LDC? - Businesses Pay Attention to the Tariff Incentive System to be Utilized-. *Regional/Analysis Report.* (in Japanese) https://www.jetro.go.jp/biz/areareports/2018/e895c60096291408.html (accessed April 6, 2021).

Okabe, H. (2013). Impact of Unknown Emerging IT Forces: IT Human Resources in Bangladesh 'Strong in Mathematical Thinking'. *Nikkei XTECH.* (in Japanese) https://xtech.nikkei.com/it/article/COLUMN/20130510/476053/ (accessed April 6, 2021).

Saisho, T. (2019). A Study on Offshore Development in System Development in Japan -Case Study of the Miyazaki-Bangladesh Model-. *Information Management, 79th National Convention Proceedings [Autumn Issue].* 151–154 (in Japanese).

Tsujii, S. (2012). *Information Society, Security, and Ethics.* Corona (in Japanese).

Yamagata, T. (2014). Industrialization in Bangladesh: East Asian Pattern of Development Proceeding to the Second Phase. *Global Communication Studies*, 1, 19–41 (in Japanese).

13 Issues in research universities to realize large-scale joint research

Akihiko Nagai

1 Introduction

Starting in 2004, each year the Japanese government has strategically reduced the budget for operating expenses of national universities by 1%. Correlating with the government's policy, national universities have ambitiously made an effort to gain more funds externally, through public research funds, patent revenues, and joint research with companies. As a result, these national universities focus more on industry-academia collaboration, since the research conducted at the universities enlarges social contribution. Furthermore, some of the country's major research universities, such as Hokkaido University, Tohoku University, the University of Tokyo, the University of Tsukuba, Tokyo Institute of Technology, Nagoya University, Kyoto University, Osaka University, Kyushu University, Keio University, and Waseda University, are pursuing larger longer-term contracts engaging in joint research projects over multiple years. These efforts have led to obtaining more beneficial results but require more time and money to be spent on industry-academia collaboration. To accomplish that, these universities employ more people specialized in these types of inquiries aimed at attracting potential collaborator companies by using the research findings and technological developments that are produced by university researchers (Edamura, 2020). In addition, companies expect ever more valuable results to be obtained from the collaborative research conducted over expanded timelines. However, universities cannot provide great added value to companies simply by employing additional personnel. A strong relationship of trust in which universities and companies work together to create added value is needed. Therefore, a new framework for industry-academia collaboration to build value-creating relationships in collaboration with businesses is needed.

2 The role of industry-academia collaboration in Japanese national universities

The 86 national universities in Japan have a defined role stated in Article 7 of the Fundamental Law of Education (revised in December 2006) that universities, as academic centers, are to cultivate advanced knowledge and professional abilities

DOI: 10.4324/9781003216049-15

and deeply explore the truth in order to create new knowledge. National universities are also mandated to contribute to the development of society by providing these results to society at large.

Industry-academia collaborations accelerated when the National University Corporation Act of 2004 altered the legal status of national universities from government-owned institutions to independent administrative agencies. National universities became national university corporations. Meanwhile, the operating expenses at national universities were reduced by 1% every year. Prior to this, the purpose of joint research between a university and industry, which employed many people and provided a great deal of innovation to companies, was seen as "social contribution." Currently, the acceleration of joint industry-academia research is to offset the reduction of the operating expenses received from the government. As a result of these conditions, the government announced the "Japan Revitalization Strategy 2016" (Japanese Government, 2016). Before this, industry-academia collaborations were limited both in number and in budget. This growth strategy aims at fostering organization-to-organization-based industry-academia collaboration, involving both the top universities and the top companies that can generate large revenue. Inter-organization collaboration also attempts to correct for the fact that, like in the United States, it is no longer possible to have a central research institute and the country must rely on universities, but universities alone are not able to meet the demand.

There is also an aspect of governmental guidance policies created to solve problems such as the limits of corporate self-reliance. The "Japan Revitalization Strategy 2016" points out that joint research funds from companies to the Japanese universities were far lower than those of overseas universities, especially American universities.

According to "Academic-Industry Collaboration Implementation Status at Universities in 2018" published by the Ministry of Education, Culture, Sports, Science and Technology (MEXT, 2020), companies provided approximately USD 99.7 million to academic institutions in Japan, of which USD 63.3 million was directed toward joint research. This is a fraction of the amount provided to research institutions in other countries. During that same year, the "Survey on Management and Systems of Industry-Academia Collaboration at Overseas Universities" conducted by Mitsubishi Research Institute, Inc. (2018) indicated that one university in the United States of America, the University of California, San Diego, had received external funding of USD 943.5 million, of which USD 840.7 million were taken from companies, approximately 850% higher than the entirety of Japan. The funds invested by companies into universities include scholarships, donations (except for Kyoto University), but most of them are joint research funds. In addition, another university in the United States of America, the Massachusetts Institute of Technology (MIT) had external funding of USD 669.4 million, of which USD 119.4 million were taken from companies. Compare this to Kyoto University, which received the highest external funding of any university in Japan during that same period at USD 61.7 million. Interestingly, the disparity of private funding is not that different when compared to other high-ranking universities overseas. For example, the California Institute of Technology had external funding of USD 281.4 million, of which USD 12.9 million were taken from companies, and the Swiss Federal Institute of Technology had external funding of USD 1,276 million, of which USD 57.4 million were coming from companies. The amount of external funding these universities received was smaller than that of Kyoto University (see Table 13.1).

Government research funding for universities in major countries is compared differently. According to a survey by the Ministry of Economy, Trade and Industry (METI, 2019), in Japan, the ratio of government expenditures on research and development (R&D) in 2017 averaged 25.81% in the Organisation for Economic Co-operation and Development nations, but was 15% in Japan, which is the lowest among the major countries. Certainly, the policy that "private investment [joint research] from companies to universities must triple by 2025 compared to 2014" is an important indicator of the importance of this funding. If R&D expenses from companies do not increase, it will be difficult for Japanese universities to compete with universities around the world. It is, however, difficult to achieve the government's goal with the current industry-academia collaboration method. In order to compete with universities around the world, collaborative groups of university researchers and research groups within companies need to be established rather than maintaining the traditional model in which individual researchers from universities and companies collaborate. This implies that companies would provide large research funding to universities, which in turn would lead to the achievement of the goals established by the government.

Hence, universities need to consider the new framework for industry-academia collaboration rather than investing their time in employing more coordinators in the pursuit of industry-academia collaboration. The joint research between the top private companies and university research groups (research centers, etc.), as indicated in "Japan Revitalization Strategy 2016" (Japanese Government, 2016), is thought to be one of the most effective methods.

Table 13.1 Status of acceptance of external funds in overseas universities (2018)

University	*Country*	*External funding (in million USD)*	*Funds raised from companies (in million USD)*
Massachusetts Institute of Technology	USA	669.4	119.4
University of California, San Diego	USA	943.5	840.7
California Institute of Technology	USA	281.4	12.9
Cambridge University	UK	627.7	31.4
Oxford University	UK	715.7	88.5
Swiss Federal Institute of Technology (ETH)	SWISS	1,276.8	57.4
Kyoto University	JAPAN	391.6	61.7

Source: Mitsubishi Research Institute, Inc. (2018) and Kyoto University (2020).

Traditionally, in Japan, instead of post-doctoral fellows or technicians, undergraduate and graduate students often play a central role in joint research in most university laboratories, which are usually smaller projects that do not involve large grants. This tradition is good in some ways, but universities should increase their capability. In terms of inter-organization joint research, the influx of large amounts of research funding into a university allows the academic research group in its research facility to closely interact with the company's research department. Since in companies the research themes change, often becoming more challenging and developing a different scope or moving from a short-term to a long-term project, company researchers might prefer to move to the university, often by becoming university researchers. However, in order for this ideal type of joint research to be accepted properly, it is necessary for both organizations to share the value of "implementing the research results of universities in society."

3 Industry-academia collaboration creates relational rent

Joint research conducted between organizations is interpreted in terms of the theory of relational view. In the theory of relational view, organizations are not considered as single entities but as a group of organizations, and investment for new value, exchange of knowledge, and complementation of resources occur between these organizations. This theory further suggests that these activities create value that is both rare and difficult to imitate. When an organization does not have the necessary resources, they will try to find them through its network (Nagai et al., 2012). Active exchange and sharing of knowledge between organizations develops inter-organizational learning, resulting in the creation of new values and synergies (Le Pennec & Raufflet, 2018). However, important knowledge and information within the organization is highly specialized, and knowledge transfer requires great expense (Szulanski, 1996). Hippel suggested that this phenomenon is "Sticky Information" (von Hippel, 1998). Also, a lot of confidential information cannot be disclosed outside of the organization and any information that can be released is very fragmented (Hayek, 1945). It is, therefore, extremely difficult to create inter-organizational learning (von Hippel, 1998). Most organizations will not invest in inter-organizational learning even if it is known that sharing and utilizing knowledge will create new value for themselves. In addition, to realize the benefits of active exchange and sharing of knowledge that develops into inter-organizational learning, various organizations need to form a strong relationship of trust between organizations (Swärd, 2016). According to Sako (1992), the trust relationships built between organizations are classified into three categories: contractual relationship of trust, competence relationship of trust, and strong relationship of trust. Of these three trust relationships, contractual relationship of trust is a trust relationship in which limited knowledge and information is shared. Through contractual relationship of trust, competence relationship of trust is built between organizations that recognize each other's competencies. Then, trust evolves into strong relationship of trust where the one party believes that the other will not betray them. Hence, contractual relationship of trust helps the organizations produce results based on contractual promises, while competence relationship of trust produces results based on each organizations competence. Strong relationship of trust takes a long time to form through both contractual relationship of trust and competence relationship of trust and produces results that exceed expectations. The reason why investments should be made in situations where strong relationship of trust exist are that they will ultimately be able to lead to inter-organizational learning and produce results that exceed expectations (Ring, 1997).

According to Dyer and Singh (1998), the performance that produces the most results between organizations is closely related to ties. To measure performance, it is necessary to consider inter-organizational cooperation as a partnership. Especially among organizations with strong inter-organizational ties, organic collaboration becomes active through investment in new value, knowledge sharing, and the supplementation of resources. It then creates new value that is difficult for other organizations to imitate. This "value created by the contribution of collaboration between specific organizations that cannot be obtained by a single organization" is "relational rent" (Dyer & Hatch, 2006) and is a determinant of value in the relationships between organizations. First, knowledge sharing between organizations is "specialized knowledge transfer, and rejoin, and mutual utilization that enables creation." Investment in knowledge sharing between organizations increases the competency of each organization to absorb specialized knowledge from the outside, thereby facilitating mutual use of knowledge. Next, complementary resource utilization is the activity of retrieving missing resources from other organizations with which one collaborates. It is possible to create value by acquiring essential resources from collaborating organizations. The higher the utilization of complementary resources, which are created through the collaboration, the greater the value of the collaboration, rarity of the information, and difficulty for competitor imitation when the resources are combined, which result in the creation of relational rent.

Inter-organizational relationships that produce relational rents have four components: (1) mutual utilization of assets between organizations, (2) rarity of collaborating organizations, (3) inseparability (synergies) between organizations, and (4) strong relationship of trust. First, mutual utilization of assets between organizations creates a competitive advantage through mutual utilization of assets across organizational boundaries. Second, the rarity of collaborative organizations means that they have the capability to create value and resources that can be expected to have synergistic effects, and this rarity is the factor that facilitates collaboration. Third, indivisibility (synergy) between organizations is to combine resources between collaborating organizations and to exert their competence through that collaboration. The indivisibility in an inter-organizational collaboration can create unique and indivisible (closely connected and inseparable) resources that could not possibly be produced without this collaboration. The resources created by inter-organizational collaboration co-evolve over time, making it even more difficult for other organizations to imitate. Co-evolution is a concept found in biology, but it is one that has been used in economics in recent years as a phenomenon in which a change in one organization triggers a change in another related organization. The fourth component, strong relationship of trust, indicates that taking steps toward building a strong relationship of trust between collaborating organizations has a significant impact on relational rent. Organizations need to build strong relationship of trust in order to increase relational rent.

4 Universities should increase large joint research collaborations

Japanese universities aimed to conduct joint research with as many companies as possible. In other words, universities focus on increasing the number of collaborative research projects. Consistent with this, universities increased the number of people with the titles of "coordinators or technology-transfer managers" (Nagai & Uchida, 2019). Their roles are to facilitate industry-academia collaboration, that is, to visualize the research findings and technological developments of university researchers and to provide such information to companies. In the past, national universities traditionally attempted to conduct as many joint research projects as possible in order to maximize their research results to provide a more impactful contribution to society and to supplement governmental operating funds, as mentioned earlier. However, even if universities visualize their research findings and technological developments and provide that information to companies, it is difficult to spontaneously induce innovation. Obviously greater innovation requires greater time and larger investments. Therefore, to accelerate innovation for this purpose, a new framework should be established for industry-academia collaboration. Then the universities should inform companies of how this framework provides significant new value for companies. In addition, the government hopes industry-academia collaboration will become "organization" vs. "organization" projects with large investments rather than continuing to be "individual" vs. "individual" initiatives with paltry investments. Using the "organizations" vs. "organizations" collaborative research framework, the government is keen to promote innovative outputs rather than just to get research funding for universities. The government believes that one of the major purposes of industry-academia collaboration is the increase in innovation. However, in order for collaborative research to create innovation, shift to a strong relationship of trust that is built on the belief that each other's organizations will not be betrayed by each other is needed.

This chapter focuses on trust relationships and will describe how strong relationship of trust leads to better outcomes and a higher likelihood that additional joint research will be initiated by partner companies and suggests a new framework in industry-academia collaboration and/or joint research. The collaborative research conducted builds on a relationship that fulfills active exchange and sharing of knowledge in a trustworthy manner. In the end, these organizations become confident that they will produce results beyond their initial predictions. That is, building of strong relationship of trust with a company leads to better quality, large-scale joint research.

The balance between the academic contribution of a university and the potential commercial interests of a company in collaborative research is determined by understanding the values of the other party. To build strong relationship of trust is able to achieve the discussion in the interests of the partner.

4.1 Organizational collaborative team of "university" and "company"

To establish joint research initiatives through collaboration between a university and a company, the company should grasp that new value can be produced by the new framework. Next, in order for companies to invest a lot of time and a large amount of funds into any industry-academia-based collaboration, the company should understand the following. First, mutual utilization of assets that transcends the boundaries between academia and industry builds a competitive advantage (i.e., mutual utilization of assets) (Nakada, Terano & Nagai, 2019). Second, the university has the capability to create value and resources from basic research that can be expected to have synergistic effects (i.e., rarity of collaborative organizations). Third, by combining the resources of a university and the company, it is then possible to create additional resources through this inter-organizational collaboration (i.e., synergy). By the common recognition that inter-organizational collaborations have these advantages, the trusted relationship will be deepened and the benefits of the joint research endeavor will be spontaneously enlarged. The resources created by the collaboration will co-evolve over time, making them even more difficult for other companies to imitate. Interestingly, additional co-evolution of resources as more time passes during the collaboration will result in restrictions on the utilization of the shared resources by either organization individually.

4.2 Build "strong relationship of trust" for inter-organizational relationship

To increase relational rent, it is necessary to build stronger relationships of mutual trust. The strong relationship of trust means the organizations have formed a relationship of trust that goes one step further than simply trusting each other, which has a great influence on relational rent. Industry-academia collaboration and/or joint research begins under a contract to share limited knowledge and information. At this time, the joint research contract is signed. Clause for non-disclosure provides a strong basis for confidentiality and trust between the contracting parties. This implies that contractual relationship of trust has been built.

Once the collaboration starts, then it deepens to a competence relationship of trust that recognizes each other's capabilities during the collaboration. After that, through long-term partnership, they will shift to the strong relationship of trust that have been formed since they believe that they will not betray one another (see Table 13.2). The collaborative research conducted while strong relationship of trust exist build on a relationship that fulfills active exchange and sharing of knowledge. In the end, these organizations become confident that they will produce results beyond their initial predictions.

5 Examples from university of Tsukuba

In this section, examples of efforts at the University of Tsukuba in Japan are introduced. The funding of joint research projects with companies has grown significantly at this university. For example, there were projects valued at JPY 474 million (equivalent to USD 4.39 million) in FY 2014, but this increased to JPY 1,686 million (equivalent to USD 15.6 million) in FY 2019 (see Table 13.3) (Nagai & Uchida, 2020). The research funds in FY 2019 were three times greater compared to those in FY 2014. In addition, looking at the breakdown, the number of large-scale joint research projects that are valued at JPY 10 million or more have increased about 10 times to JPY 1,183 million (70.1% of the total). The reason why this university has successfully increased the number of large-scale joint research projects will be explained in terms of two perspectives as follows:

- Organizational collaboration team between universities and companies.
- Build "strong relationship of trust" between inter-organization parties.

Table 13.2 How trust patterns shift among organizational collaboration teams during projects

Contractual relationship of trust	*Competence relationship of trust*	*Strong ties relationship of trust*
An organizational collaboration team produces the research results promised in the joint research contract.	The organizational collaboration team produces the expected research results by respecting the research capabilities of the university.	The organizational collaboration team produces unique and valuable research results through synergies.

Table 13.3 Changes in the amount of investment in joint research projects at the University of Tsukuba

FY	*Under JPY 10 million*	*Over JPY 10 million*	*Ratio %*	*Total JPY million*
2014	355	129	27.2	474
2015	432	608	58.4	1,040
2016	443	577	56.5	1,020
2017	504	568	52.9	1,072
2018	539	1,221	71.1	1,716
2019	503	1,183	70.1	1,686

Source: MEXT (2014–2019).

5.1 Organizational collaboration team between universities and companies

At the University of Tsukuba, one of the efforts aimed at increasing the number of large-scale joint research projects is to execute a new strategy called "the special joint research project." This project is a system in which a company researcher joins the university as a faculty member, so that both the university researcher and the company researcher work together equally on research to solve common problems. Hence, a major feature of the project is that research can be carried out under one roof, leading to closer interaction and better communication between these researchers. In this system, the University of Tsukuba can fulfill the diverse demands of society and secure long-term collaborative research that is carried out on its campus. The most important thing is that strong relationship of trust is built by conducting joint research under one roof.

Simultaneously, the University of Tsukuba can achieve its goals that are an enhancement of both research output and social contribution. This system, therefore, allows both of the researchers to produce a greater output compared to that obtained from conventional joint research structures. The features of the special joint research project are as follows:

- A researcher of the University of Tsukuba and a company researcher conduct joint research at a research facility (under one roof) on the campus.
- The University of Tsukuba employs the company researcher as a faculty member using funds from the company.
- As such, the company researcher, as a faculty member, can also receive any benefits given to faculty (education) at the University of Tsukuba.

For the company to agree to a large-scale, joint research project, ideas like this new framework are needed to show that any joint research project has the potential to create new value for the company. For example, as a benefit, the company can acquire the following value by investing in the special joint research project:

- Mutual utilization of assets that transcends the traditional boundaries between the university and the company develops a competitive advantage (mutual utilization of assets between the organizations).
- Research results obtained from the project create value through synergistic effects (rareness of collaborative organizations).
- Collaboration between the university and the company produce unique and valuable resources that can be earned only through this inter-organizational collaboration (synergistic effect between organizations).

However, if conventional small-scale collaboration is carried out without a decent plan, it does not, of course, mean an organizational collaborative relationship will be properly formed or that the joint research will make more progress than expected. In the end, stepping up to the next stage such as a special joint research project will not be considered at all. Since special joint research projects require a vast time and large financial investments, the university must convince the company that a large-scale investment is necessary to further accelerate the joint research project to obtain even greater results.

Analyzing how joint research projects at the University of Tsukuba are conducted, we can find the following three starting points. First, the most common starting point for collaborative research is that the university is approached by a company that is interested in a particular research paper or a patent document created at the university that was presented at an academic conference. The next most common starting point is that joint research projects begin with a company paying attention to some research presented at an event by the university's industry-academia collaboration department. However, the purpose of these joint research projects does not seem to one that expects future innovation. These companies tend to expect a solution for an immediate issue, and they don't expect the joint research venture to produce a high-end output. Unlike these examples above, there is a type of joint research project that starts with a vague question from a company such as "Is there any interesting research happening?" or "We are looking for interesting research in a specific field." Collaborative research starting from this point could build a research team with researchers from various fields at the university as well as company researchers. The University of Tsukuba conducts hearings on each of these vague inquiries and proposes a research plan that could produce results. Some of these cases lead to joint research projects. So, this third starting point creates more innovation than expected.

5.2 *Build "strong relationship of trust" for inter-organization relationship*

5.2.1 *Illustration: research to find the function of natural resin subfossils*

The author shows a case of collaborative involvement at the University of Tsukuba. Company A's business is the sale of high-end cosmetics that have a whitening effect. This cosmetic utilizes a natural subfossil resin, commonly known as amber. The main component of this subfossil is a high molecular weight isoprenoid as well as many other compounds. Isoprenoids are polymers produced by chemical changes such as oxidation, evaporation, or polymerization under high temperature and high pressure in the process, in which the terpene (hydrocarbon having isoprene as a constituent unit) contained in sap becomes a natural resin or its fossil. Company A's laboratory tried to find new applications for bioactive compounds contained in the subfossil and it considered several ways to identify such components. In 2015, Company A consulted a researcher at the University of Tsukuba about whether it was possible to scientifically determine the functions of these compounds. This university researcher is an expert in bioassays (analysis of biological responses) using worms (scientific nomenclature: *Caenorhabditis elegans* or *C. elegans*) as a model organism and has a lot of knowledge about the functional verification of how biochemical substances affect living things. In 2016, Company A started a collaborative research project with this researcher in an attempt to find new applications for natural resin subfossils. A coordinator in University of Tsukuba held regular monthly meetings with the university researchers and Company A's researchers to discuss research progress and to plan for their next experiments. These monthly progress meetings played an important role in deepening mutual trust and in taking the project to higher levels. The collaborative project discovered that some chemical compounds in the natural subfossil resin could potentially be useful for bone care, muscle gain, and fat decomposition. To obtain solid scientific evidence that these compounds have such functions, it was necessary to experiment using these compounds on cultured cells and mice. However, the university researcher was aware that these experiments require a large budget and many personnel. To solve this problem, a coordinator at the University of Tsukuba proposed creating a special joint research project as the appropriate strategy for the next step. Company A could then relocate its research facility onto the University of Tsukuba's campus and have the company's researchers become faculty members as well. Company A, which already built a strong relationship of trust with the University of Tsukuba, readily accepted this proposal and started this special joint research project in April 2017. Its research theme is "functional search and component identification of natural subfossil resins." This special joint research project was formed because of the strong relationship of trust. Now it is smoothly producing new exciting results and new intellectual property, and this collaboration will continue beyond April 2021.

The joint research project with Company A started with a small budget as a feasibility study (FS). Yet it produced great research output, resulting in building strong relationship of trust. The reason why Company A decided to pursue the special joint research project was the expectation that the natural subfossil resin contained beneficial ingredients. On the other hand, it seemed that building strong relationship of trust through "collaboration" in joint research was also one of the major factors. The most important thing is how to build a strong relationship of trust in joint research. Collaborative research does not always produce the expected results. If no one makes the extra effort, the strong relationship of trust that creates synergies will not be formed in the research team, resulting in unsuccessful collaboration. In the above example, the joint research started as a FS which explored the possibility that new applications for compounds in natural subfossil resins, using model organisms and cultured cells, could be discovered. Therefore, university researchers fulfilled the contractual role (search for new functions) assigned to the joint research project (building contractual relationship of trust). During that time, the coordinator in the University of Tsukuba held monthly research meetings with university researchers and Company A representatives to exchange information and discuss results. By discussing the next steps, they deepened the relationship of trust that respects each other's competency in the search for beneficial components contained in the subfossils. This trust produced research results that exceed expectations (building competence relationship of trust). Because the team was able to produce results that exceed expectations, the trust relationship had created "cooperation that goes one step further". In other words, Company A decided that this collaboration could synergistically produce unique and vital research results (expectations for the building of strong relationship of trust). Framework on the University of Tsukuba is a mechanism for building a strong relationship of trust through joint research and can consider contributing academically to different universities and creates research results for companies.

6 Industry-academia collaboration under the COVID-19 pandemic

The COVID-19 pandemic of 2019 has significantly changed not only the social environment but also joint research initiatives with private companies. Universities need to carry out joint research during the pandemic. The COVID-19 pandemic caused companies to reconsider the importance of returns versus investments. Some companies are evaluating the value gained from joint research projects with academia and are stopping particular projects that are seen as less important. Concurrently, others are increasing their investments in joint research initiatives that they consider important. That is, companies are selecting and concentrating their investments in collaborative research projects with universities that they foresee fulfilling a pressing need, creating abundant opportunities to universities. However, universities want joint research that can be expected to create innovation, not joint research that solves the urgent problem of companies. Universities are able to obtain sizeable research investments from joint research projects of creating innovation if they have already built strong relationship of trust with companies.

Due to the impact of the COVID-19 epidemic, opportunity for face-to-face meetings with company representatives dramatically decreased in 2020 and online meetings using Zoom or other video conferencing software became more popular. Until now, when a university consulted with a company, a company researcher visited the university to examine the laboratory and have a meeting with a university researcher. However, due to the COVID-19 pandemic, it became difficult for people to move around and important to avoid face-to-face meetings as much as possible. For this reason, online tools that allow people to have a meeting without visiting are widely accepted. These online telework tools enable people to work from home and the company researcher is able to remotely communicate with the university researcher. Researchers can use online tools to hold a meeting at any time, so they can exchange information and have in-depth discussions, except for "the last one mile" (important) meeting. Until now, in general, companies located far away from a university could use the telephone, email, or Slack to communicate with a university. However, the spread of online video conferencing tools has made it easier to hold a meeting where multiple parties get together frequently, and it becomes possible to build strong relationship of trust through live discussion.

Again, the most important thing is how to build a strong relationship of trust in joint research. The most important communication in joint research is limited under COVID-19 pandemic. In the new framework of industry-academia collaboration proposed in this chapter, a strong relationship of trust is built by conducting research under one roof by researchers of university and company. Communication that tends to be interrupted under COVID-19 pandemic can be deepened by using online tools. Also, it is possible to carry out a minimum experiment. However, online meetings require in-depth discussions with each other. The strong relationships of trust built by joint research under one roof realizes in-depth discussions during online meetings.

7 Conclusions

Joint research is one method of industry-academia collaborations and is comprised of an organizational collaboration team that serves a university and a company. However, for joint research to progress properly, it is necessary for the organizational collaboration team to create new value. Large-scale, joint research projects involving a lot of time and large financial investment from a company needs to have an organizational collaboration team that can mutually utilize the assets of the university and the company. As such, the organizational collaboration team creates unique and valuable resources that can be created only through this inter-organizational collaboration. The strong relationship of trust built by the organizational collaboration team will become stronger and joint research projects will increase, producing even greater results. The resources created by joint research initiatives will co-evolve over time, making them even more difficult for other companies to imitate. Interestingly, additional co-evolution of resources as more time passes during the collaboration will result in restrictions on the utilization of the shared resources by either organization individually.

Also, the most important thing is how to build a strong relationship of trust in joint research. The organizational collaboration team needs to build strong relationship of trust to increase the relational rent through joint research. The team has a great influence on relational rent by building a relationship of trust (strong relationship of trust) that goes one step further. However, strong relationship of trust takes a long time to form and consequently produce results that exceed expectations. First, joint research is initiated based on contractual relationship of trust, in which limited knowledge and information are shared, it will become a joint research project based on competence relationship of trust that show respect for each other's capability. Over time, the university and the company will believe that they will not betray one another, and they will shift to joint research with strong relationship of trust. Collaborative research conducted while strong relationship of trust exist help with an exchange of knowledge that creates the best conditions for inter-organizational learning, and it is thought that it can produce results far beyond initial expectations.

8 Acknowledgment

I would like to thank Dr. Yutaka Nibu and Ms. Marianna Nibu for critically reading the manuscript.

References

Dyer, J. H., & Hatch, N. W. (2006). Relation-specific capabilities and barriers to knowledge transfers: Creating advantage through network relationships. *Strategic Management Journal*. Vol. 27, No. 8, pp. 701–719.

Dyer, J. H., & Singh, H. (1998). The relational view: Cooperative strategy and sources of interorganizational competitive advantage. *Academy of Management Review*. Vol. 23, No. 4, pp. 660–679.

Edamura, K. (2020). Empirical analysis of industry-university collaboration and research productivity. *Japan Society for Intellectual Production*. (in Japanese). Vol. 35, No. 3, pp. 316–328.

Hayek, F. A. (1945). The use of knowledge in society. *The American Economic Review*. Vol. 35, No. 4, pp. 519–530. https://www.jstor.org/stable/1809376 (accessed April 15, 2021).

Japanese Government (2016). Japan revitalization strategy 2016, Cabinet decision in June 2016. (In Japanese). https://www.kantei.go.jp/jp/singi/keizaisaisei/pdf/zentaihombun_160602_en.pdf. (accessed April 15, 2021).

Kyoto University (2020). Acceptance of external funds (FY2019). (In Japanese).

Le Pennec, M., & Raufflet, E. (2018). Value creation in inter-organizational collaboration: An empirical study. *Journal of Business Ethics*. Vol. 148, No. 4, pp. 817–834.

METI (2019). Trends in R & D activities related to Japan's industrial technology. *Ministry of Economy, Trade and Industry*. (In Japanese). https://www.meti.go.jp/policy/economy/gijutsu_kakushin/tech_research/aohon2019.pdf. (accessed April 15, 2021).

MEXT (2014–19). Result of industry-academia-government collaboration. *Ministry of Education, Culture, Sports, Science and Technology*. (in Japanese). https://www.mext.go.jp/a_menu/shinkou/sangaku/sangakub.htm. (accessed April 15, 2021).

MEXT (2020). Status and issues of progress of industry-academia collaboration in Japan. (in Japanese). *Ministry of Education, Culture, Sports, Science and Technology*. (In Japanese). https://www.mext.go.jp/b_menu/shingi/gijyutu/gijyutu2/090/shiryo/__icsFiles/afieldfile/2017/10/13/1397197_6_1.pdf. (accessed April 15, 2021).

Mitsubishi Research Institute Inc. (2018). Survey on management and systems of industry-academia collaboration at overseas universities (Report). (in Japanese). https://www.mext.go.jp/a_menu/shinkou/sangaku/1409478.htm. (accessed April 15, 2021).

Nagai, A., Nakagawa, H., Ito, T., & Tanabe, K. (2012). Effectiveness of cooperation with semiconductor trading companies in entering the market with LSIs for specific markets of Japanese fabless semiconductor high-tech startups. *The Journal of Science Policy and Research Management*. (in Japanese). Vol. 27, No. 1–2, pp. 39–56.

Nagai, A., & Uchida, F. (2019). A study on method which exposes potential technology seeds -a case of university of Tsukuba. *Japan Society for Intellectual Production*. (in Japanese). Vol. 15, No. 2, pp. 112–118.

Nagai, A., & Uchida, F. (2020). A study on larger joint research with companies, In the Proceedings of 19th annual meeting, Japan Society for Intellectual Production. (in Japanese). pp. 63–64.

Nakada, Y., Terano, M., & Nagai, Y. (2019). Function and role of URA in collaborative research based on collaboration among local organizations. *Japan Society for Intellectual Production.* (in Japanese). Vol. 15, No. 2, pp. 112–118.

Ring, P. S. (1997). Processes facilitating reliance on trust in inter-organizational networks. *The Formation of Inter-organizational Networks.* pp. 113–145. https://www.clusterobservatory.in/articles/Article%20No.%20133.pdf. (accessed April 15, 2021).

Sako, M. (1992). Price, quality, and trust: inter-firm relations in Britain and Japan. (No. 18). pp. 36–41. Cambridge University Press Cambridge, UK.

Swärd, A. (2016). Trust, reciprocity, and actions: the development of trust in temporary inter-organizational relations. *Organization Studies.* Vol. 37, No. 12, pp. 1841–1860.

Szulanski, G. (1996). Exploring internal stickiness: impediments to the transfer of best practice within the firm. *Strategic Management Journal.* Vol. 17 (Special Issue). pp. 27–43.

Von Hippel, E. (1998). Economics of product development by users: the impact of "sticky" local information. *Management Science.* Vol. 44, No. 5, pp. 629–644.

Index

Note: **Bold** page numbers refer to tables and *italic* page numbers refer to figures.